IMAGES
of America

Bristol Business and Industry

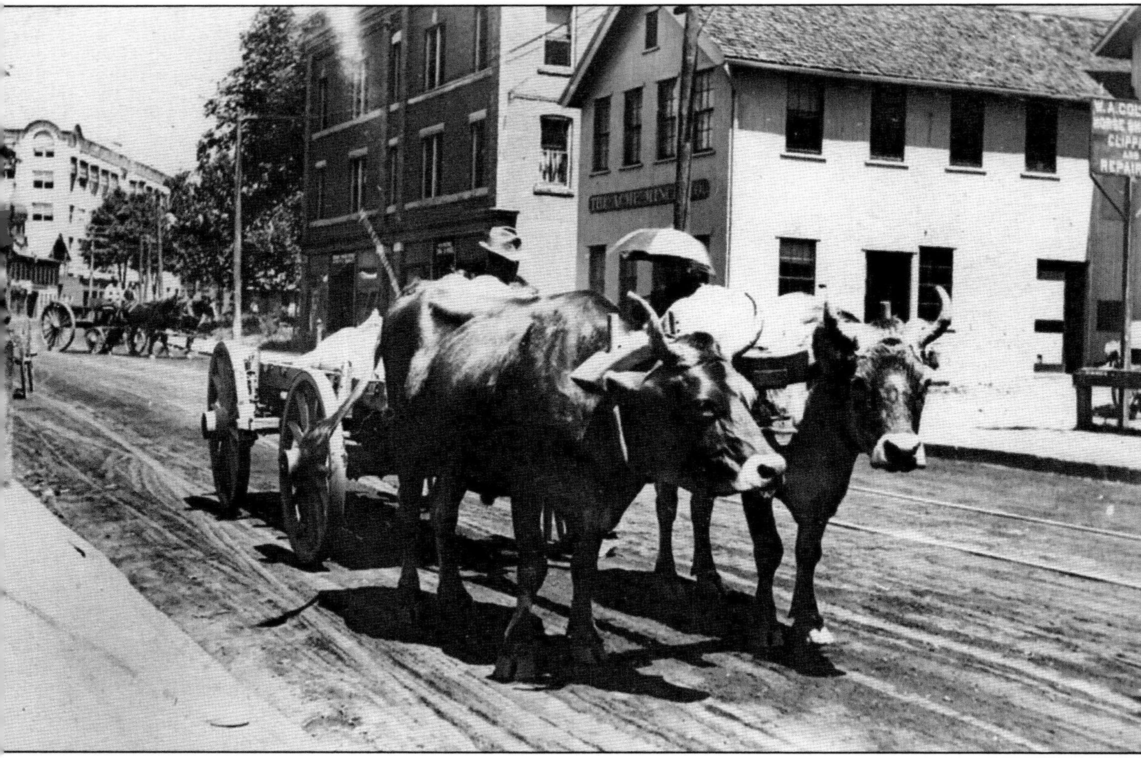

This 1910 picture shows oxen pulling a wagon on North Main Street. On the right, the center building was the Acme Mince Company located at 130 North Main Street. They manufactured pie filling and were dealers in extracts. Willard Collins's blacksmith shop was next door to Acme. In the far left, New Departure's building can be seen. (Courtesy of Charlie Nyberg.)

ON THE COVER: This 1920s view looking down Main Street shows on the left the Bristol National Bank, Mitchell's men's clothing store, Woodruff's Bakery, Bristol Savings Bank, and the Masonic building where Muzzy's Store was located. (Courtesy of Bristol Public Library.)

IMAGES
of America

BRISTOL BUSINESS AND INDUSTRY

Lynda J. Russell

ARCADIA
PUBLISHING

ISBN 978-0-7385-7337-3

Published by Arcadia Publishing
Charleston SC, Chicago IL, Portsmouth NH, San Francisco CA

Printed in the United States of America

Library of Congress Control Number: 2010921145

For all general information contact Arcadia Publishing at:
Telephone 843-853-2070
Fax 843-853-0044
E-mail sales@arcadiapublishing.com
For customer service and orders:
Toll-Free 1-888-313-2665

Visit us on the Internet at www.arcadiapublishing.com

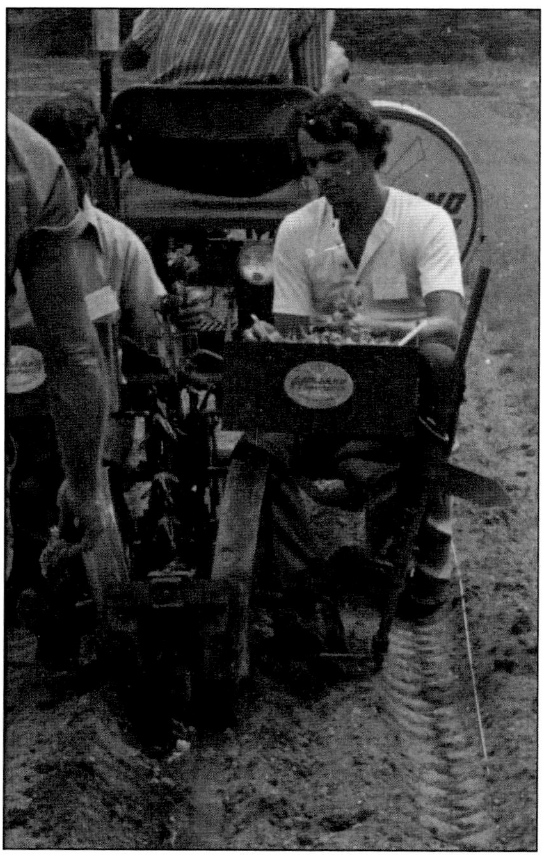

This book is dedicated to Jerry Heresko, who owned Bristol Mums, Inc. Through his friendship, his business, and his love for history, he inspired me to write all of my books, including this one. In this 1970s picture, Jerry is planting the fields when the business was owned by Bristol Nurseries. (Courtesy of Jerry Heresko family.)

Contents

Acknowledgments

I would like to thank the Bristol Public Library and the Historical Documents Preservation grants from the Connecticut State Library to the city of Bristol's town clerks' office.

I would also like to thank Jay Manewitz, Linda DiMatteo, Tom Dickau, Gary Potter, Jerry Heresko, Therese Pac, Don Muller, Chris Bailey, Louise DeMars, all of the business owners that I interviewed, and a very special note of thanks to my husband, Chet, for his help again for this project.

The American Clock and Watch Museum will receive all royalties from this book. Unless otherwise noted, all images appear courtesy of the Bristol Public Library.

INTRODUCTION

The villages of New Cambridge and West Britain (Burlington) were originally part of the town of Farmington. Joseph Byington of New Cambridge and Simeon Hart of West Britain were chosen to be the representatives of the two villages and sent a petition to the state general assembly requesting their separation from Farmington in May 1785. The petition was granted in June 1785 as a new town called Bristol. On June 13, 1785, Bristol held its first town meeting. By 1795, the former village of West Britain separated from Bristol to later become the town of Burlington.

Bristol's first settlers were farmers that settled along the Pequabuck River, using the water power to establish the grist and saw mills. The tinware manufacturers made the utensils, plates, and cups and relied on the peddlers with their wagons to sell their products along with other merchandise. One of the first clockmakers, Gideon Roberts, was making wooden clocks in 1790. As the demand grew for clocks increased, Gideon started selling his clocks to early merchants Thomas Barnes Jr. and George Mitchell. Besides clocks, Barnes and Mitchell used the Yankee peddlers to sell tinware, cloth, and general goods. By the 1820s, Bristol had become the leader in clock manufacturing, led by George Mitchell, who helped established clockmakers come to Bristol. In 1837, a group of clockmakers started the Bristol Manufacturing Company making knitted woolen cloth. In 1850, clockmakers from both Bristol and Waterbury started Bristol Brass Company. The established E. L. Dunbar spring factory became partners with Wallace Barnes, first making springs and then hoopskirts in 1858. In 1859, Elias Ingraham and his son, Edward, formed E. Ingraham Company. In 1868, John Humphrey Sessions established his trunk hardware business on North Main Street. In 1870, Bristol Savings Bank opened with Henry A. Seymour as president. The *Bristol Press* began publishing in 1871 as a weekly paper with Rev. Charles H. Riggs as its editor. The Bristol National Bank was established as a commercial bank by prominent businessmen. In 1888, Albert and Edward Rockwell came to Bristol and began manufacturing under their company name, New Departure Bell. In 1894, Sessions Foundry moved their manufacturing company to Farmington Avenue. In 1889, a group of businessmen established the Bristol Board of Trade, which became the Bristol Chamber of Commerce in 1915.

As immigrants arrived in Bristol in the early 1900s, many became employees in the factories. Some of the factory owners established housing for the workers. Some of these immigrants wanted more than just working in a factory. With hard work and determination, they started up small businesses. When World War II started, all of the manufacturers, including Bristol Brass Company, New Departure Manufacturers, E. Ingraham Company, and Associated Spring, were manufacturing for the government. After World War II, some businesses slowed down and others did not survive. In 1958, the Redevelopment Agency started when Mayor James P. Casey was in office. A flooding problem downtown, commercial and retail stores vacancy, and lack of parking were just a few concerns. It would take until 1960 to come to a plan that would involve 67.7 acres of land and the demolition of 176 buildings, including 85 commercial buildings. The redevelopment plan tore down buildings along North Main, Main, Laurel, and School Streets,

Riverside Avenue, and along the Memorial Boulevard. New roads replaced old ones, and the city needed to correct the overflowing of the North Creek that at certain times of the year would cause flooding. In 1960 on Farmington Avenue, the first group of retail stores was being built by Carpenter Construction called the Bristol Shopping Plaza. In 1961, Superior Electric moved from Laurel Street to their new factory on Middle Street. The Bristol Centre Mall opened in 1969 on North Main Street. On land ready for developing, Associated Spring built their factory on Memorial Boulevard in 1970, and in 1979, Barnes Group built their international headquarters on Main Street. In 1979, ESPN, Inc., founded by Bill Rasmussen, constructed a building and put up satellites on Middle Street; the business would become internationally known.

As Bristol approaches its 225th anniversary, there is opportunity for new growth with the completion of U.S. Route 72 and plans to revitalize a new downtown.

One

The Clockmakers

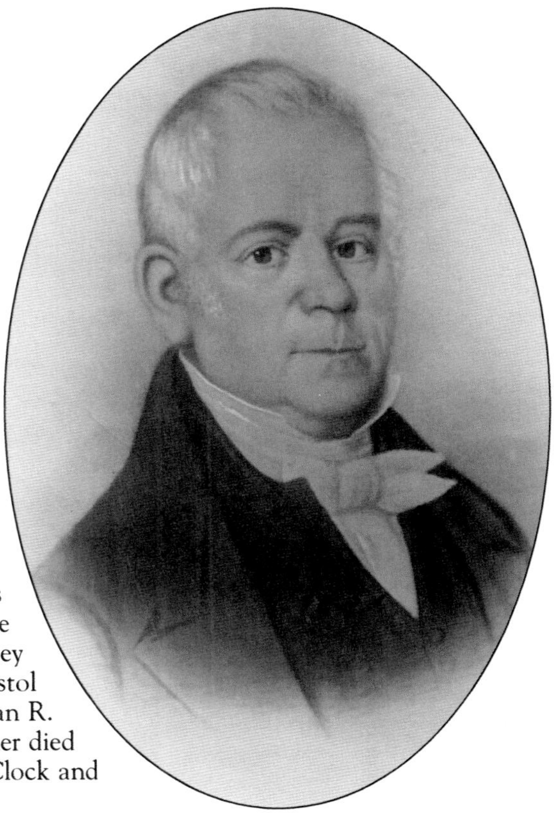

George Mitchell was born in Bristol in 1774. In 1796, George and Thomas Barnes Jr. opened a general store on South Street. They supplied the peddlers' products made in Bristol, including tinware, clocks, and woven goods. Mitchell ended his business with Barnes and opened his own store. As the demand grew for clocks, he helped Chauncey Jerome and Elias Ingraham come to Bristol to make clocks. Mitchell's oldest son, Julian R. Mitchell, continued the store after his father died on July 29, 1892. (Courtesy of American Clock and Watch Museum.)

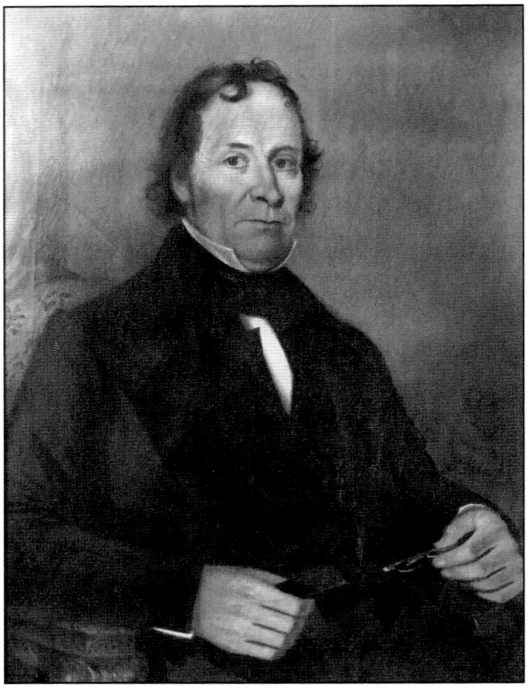

Ephraim Downs was born in Wilbraham, Massachusetts, on December 20, 1787. He came to Bristol with his wife, Chloe Painter Downs. Downs purchased a gristmill, pond, and home from George Mitchell and started manufacturing wooden clocks. Ephraim was elected town selectman and later represented Bristol in the Connecticut legislature. Ephraim died in 1860 and is buried in the "Old South" burial ground near Downs Street. (Courtesy of American Clock and Watch Museum.)

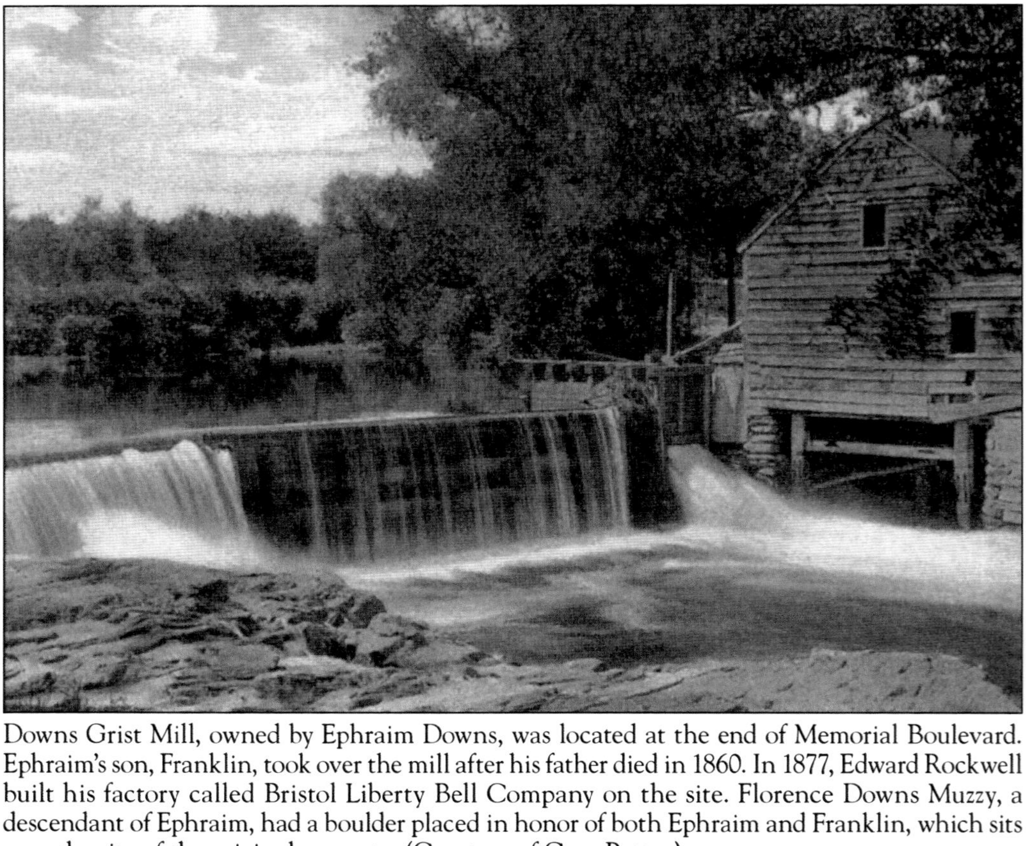

Downs Grist Mill, owned by Ephraim Downs, was located at the end of Memorial Boulevard. Ephraim's son, Franklin, took over the mill after his father died in 1860. In 1877, Edward Rockwell built his factory called Bristol Liberty Bell Company on the site. Florence Downs Muzzy, a descendant of Ephraim, had a boulder placed in honor of both Ephraim and Franklin, which sits near the site of the original property. (Courtesy of Gary Potter.)

Irenus Atkins was born in Southington on November 15, 1792. He married Eunice Beckwith on September 14, 1814. In the early 1820s, he opened a clock shop with his brother, Rollin, in the old Baptist church near Divinity Street. In 1830, the church building was moved to the corner of Divinity and Park Streets. Irenus and his brother formed a clock company called I. and R. Atkins and Company. By 1832, the brothers changed to manufacturing saws. They continued until 1846 when the saw business was sold. Irenus went back to making clocks for 30 years with various partners. The Atkins Clock Company ended as a business in 1879. Irenus died on April 19, 1882. (Courtesy of American Clock and Watch Museum.)

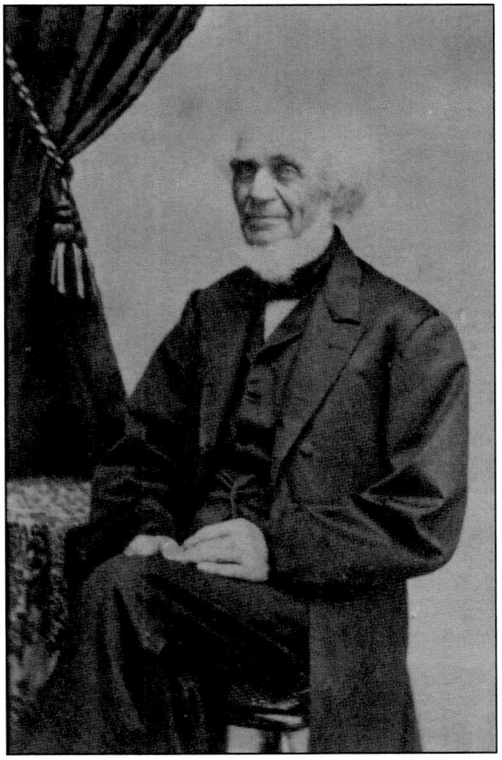

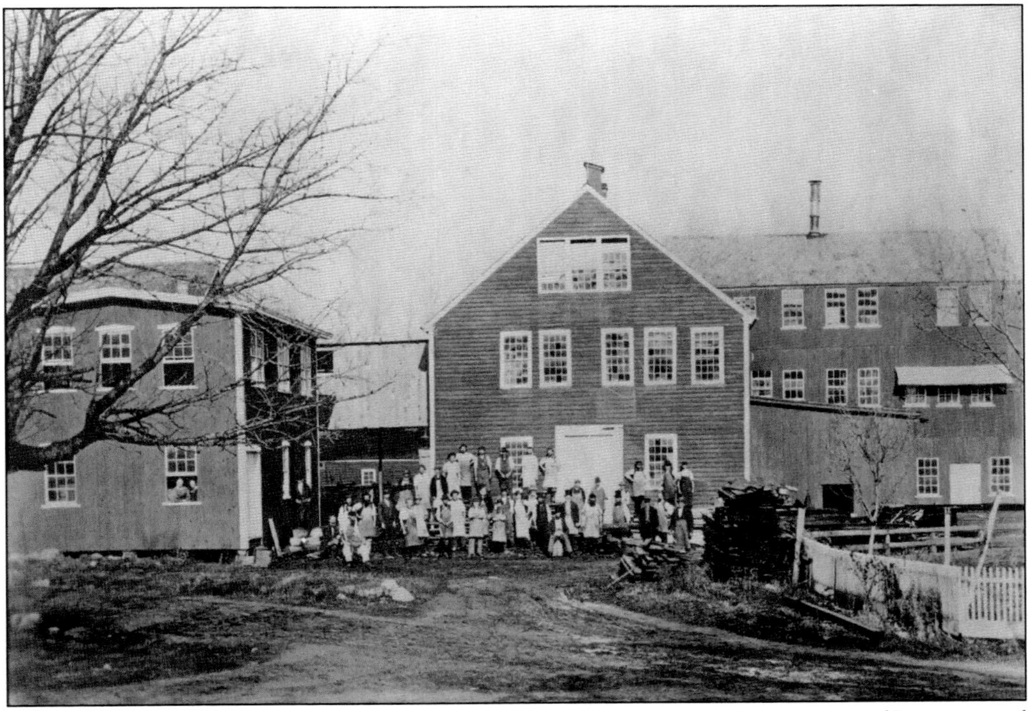

This is a picture of the Atkins Clock Company when it was located on the corner of Divinity and Park Streets. In 1879, the building was sold to Barnes Brothers Clock Shop. In 1894, the building was destroyed by a fire. (Courtesy of American Clock and Watch Museum.)

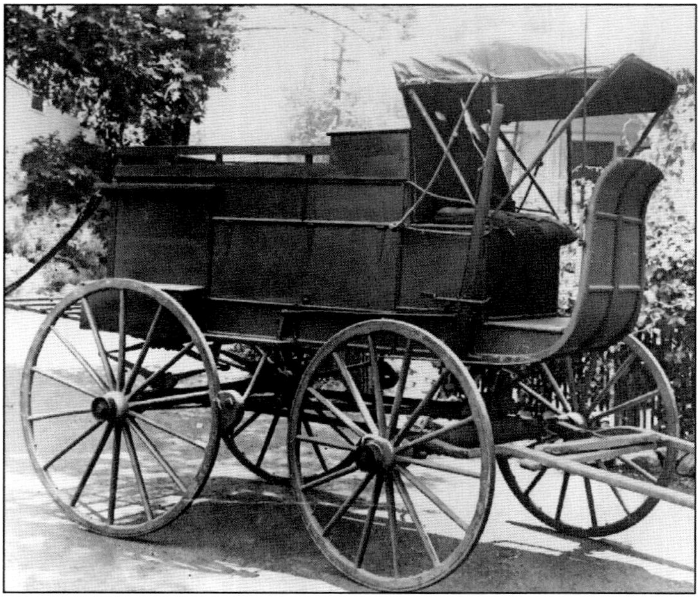

When the Yankee peddlers first started selling their wares, they traveled by foot with their packs on their backs. Then they traveled by horseback. In the early 1800s, the roads improved enough to use wagons and carts. The peddler designed his wagon to carry many types of merchandise. When the clocks became popular, a wagon was designed to carry them. This Yankee clock wagon was used till the 1830s. (Courtesy of American Clock and Watch Museum.)

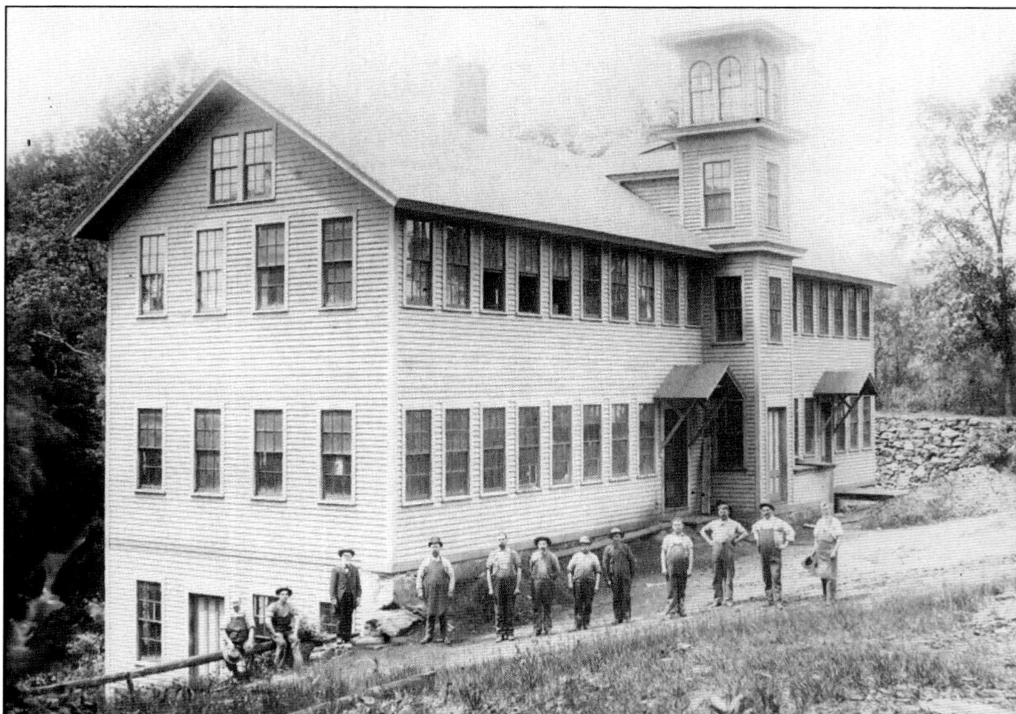

In 1828, in an old gristmill, George W. Bartholomew and his cousin, Eli Bartholomew, started making clocks. The mill was located on Maple Avenue in the section of Bristol known as Edgewood. George continued making clocks until 1844 when the building was destroyed by fire. George's son, Harry S. Bartholomew, built a new factory in the same location. The business was now manufacturing augur bits and braces. In 1902, Harry's son, Joseph P., sold the business to the Stanley Rule and Level Company of New Britain. The factory was destroyed by fire in April 1918. (Courtesy of American Clock and Watch Museum.)

In 1844, clockmakers John Birge and Thomas Franklin Fuller formed a partnership. The business was located on Riverside Avenue and East Street. When Fuller died in 1848, a new company was formed called Birge, Peck, and Company. When their business ended in 1859, Solomon C. Spring purchased the building and continued making clocks under the business S. C. Spring and Company. In 1868, Spring formed a partnership with Elisha Welch forming a new company Welch, Spring, and Company. Eventually Spring's equipment was moved to Forestville. This photograph was taken of Solomon in the 1860s. He died in 1906. (Courtesy of American Clock and Watch Museum.)

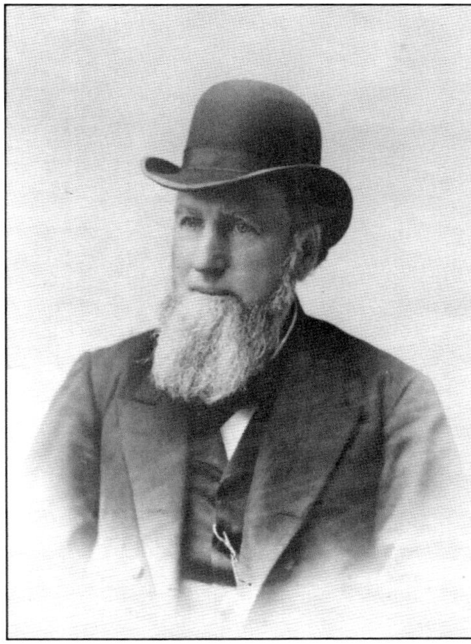

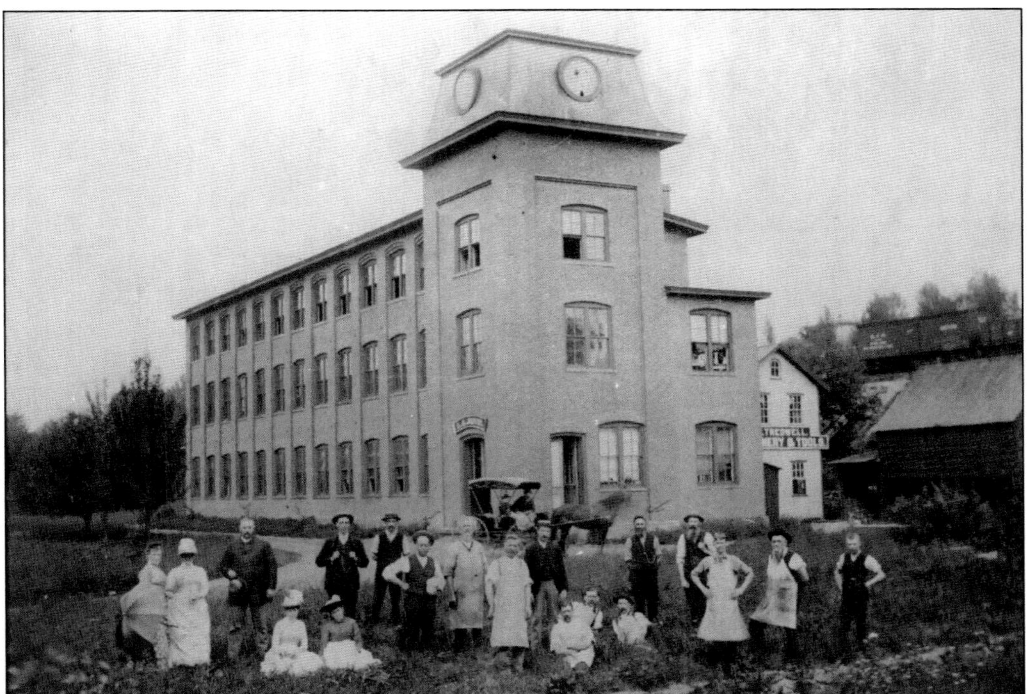

Wilfred Hopkins Nettleton was born in Waterbury in 1825. He came to Bristol in 1837. In 1850, he built this factory located on North Main Street. His factory made clock movements for the clockmakers and manufactured parts for sewing machines. In 1880, George Jones purchased the building and continued making clock parts, adding hardware gas meters and burglar alarms. The Ingraham Company was the next business in the factory. When New Departure Company moved out of Hiram C. Thompson's factory they used this building where they had more space and better equipment. (Courtesy of American Clock and Watch Museum.)

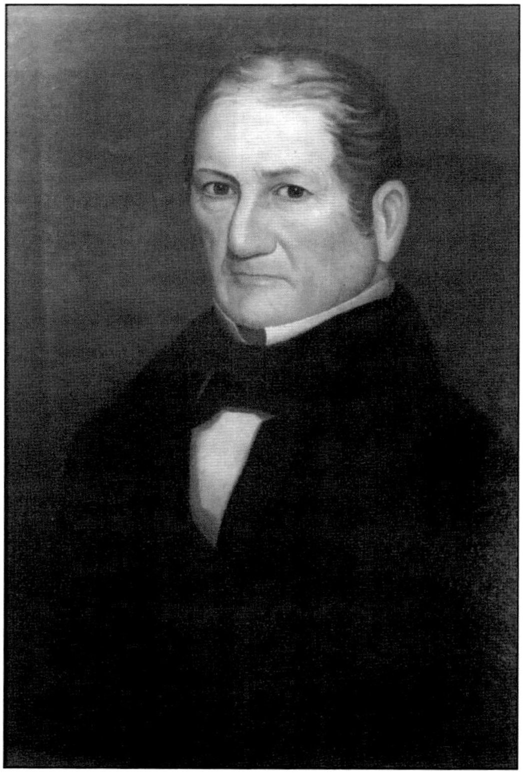

Thomas Barnes Jr. was born in Bristol in 1773. In 1796, Thomas partnered with George Mitchell, owning a general store on South Street. When they ended their business together, Barnes operated a button factory until 1818, when he became partners with clockmaker Joseph Ives and Lott Newell manufacturing Ives clocks. In 1819, Barnes started Thomas Barnes Jr. and Company, making clocks until 1823. Barnes formed another partnership in 1838 with Elijah Darrow under the name Barnes, Darrow, and Company. Barnes died on May 23, 1855. (Courtesy of American Clock and Watch Museum.)

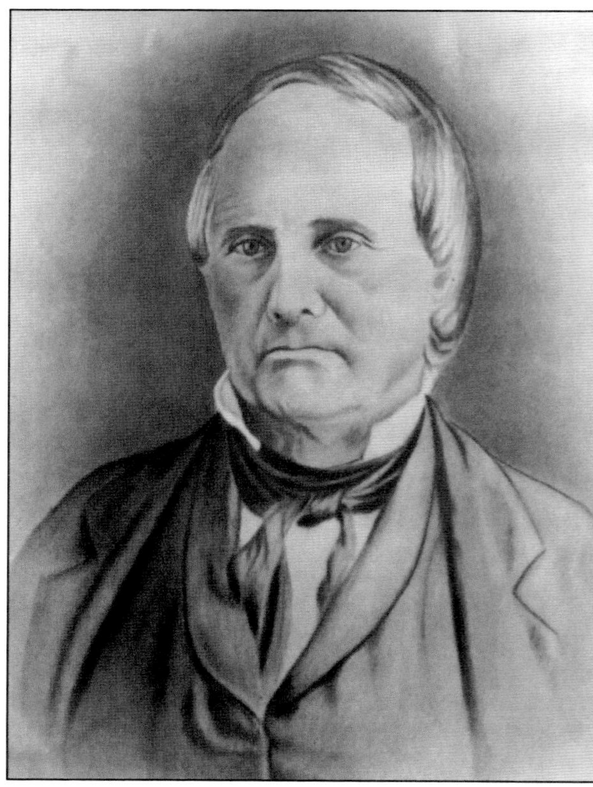

Elisha Manross was born in Bristol on May 11, 1792. He worked for Chauncey Boardman making wooden clocks. In 1840, Manross formed a partnership with Albert Wilcox called Manross and Wilcox. In 1845, now known as Manross and Pritchard, Manross bought out his partners, built a factory, and manufactured eight-day brass clocks. He was one of the businessmen from Bristol who formed the Bristol Brass Company. Manross died on September 27, 1856, at the age of 64. (Courtesy of American Clock and Watch Museum.)

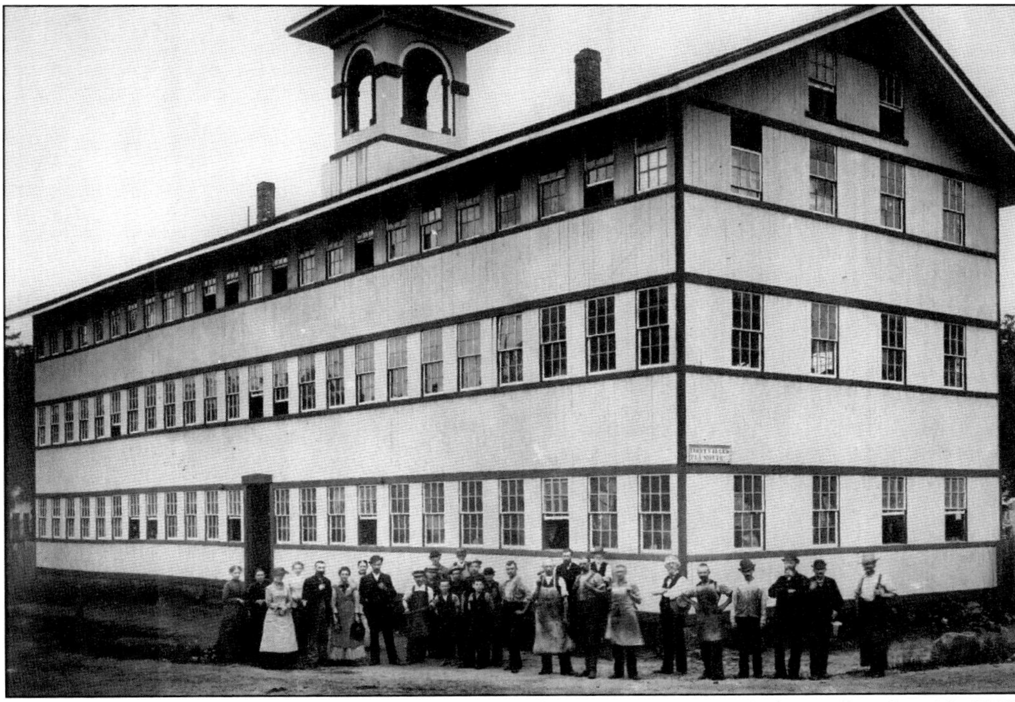

Samuel Emerson Root was born in Broadalbin, Fulton County, New York, on October 12, 1820. He was the nephew of Chauncey Ives of Bristol. Samuel came to Bristol at an early age. Joel H. Root, Samuel's brother, was already manufacturing clock trimmings in Bristol. Samuel built his factory in 1853 located on the corner of Main and School Streets. His son-in-law Edward E. Newell was the super at the factory. When Samuel died on April 7, 1896, Edward took over the business. (Courtesy of American Clock and Watch Museum.)

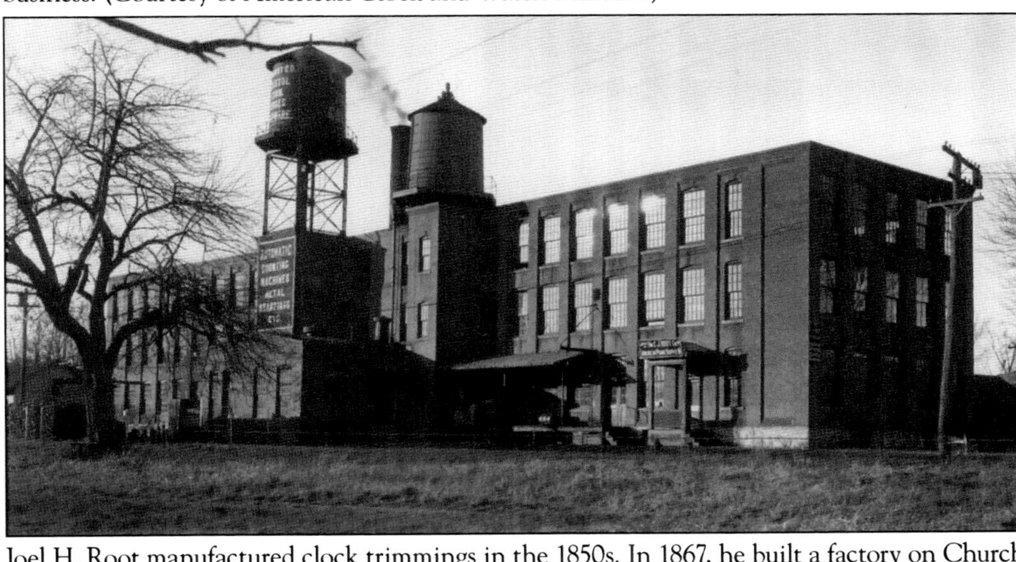

Joel H. Root manufactured clock trimmings in the 1850s. In 1867, he built a factory on Church Street. In 1885, his son, Charles, took over the business. Charles invented the automatic counter called the "Bristol Counter." When Charles died in 1907, the business was bought by John T. Chidsey and became C. J. Root Company. In 1928, C. J. Root Company merged with the Veeder Company of Hartford and became Veeder-Root, Inc.

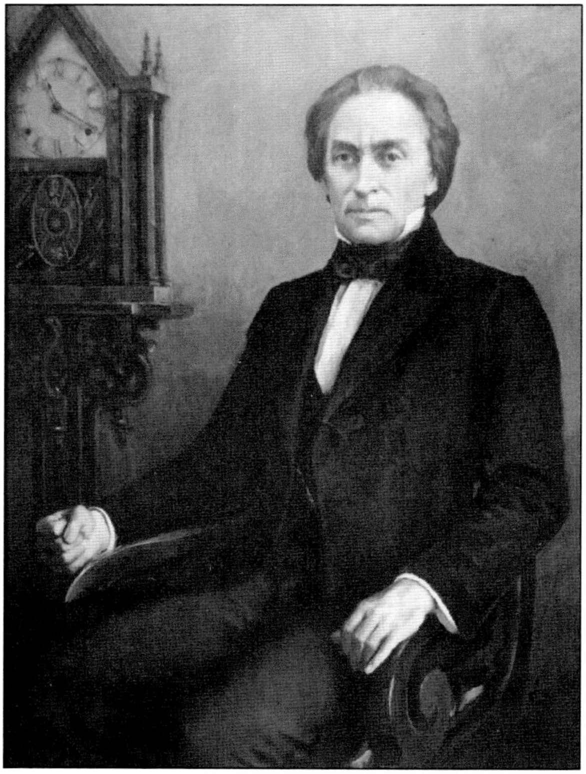

Elias Ingraham was born in Marlborough on November 1, 1805. In 1824, he came to Bristol to work for George Mitchell. In 1843, Elisha C. Brewster and Ingraham formed a partnership called Brewster and Ingraham. When Brewster ended his partnership with Ingraham in 1848, Elias and his brother, Andrew, formed the business E. and A. Ingraham Company. In 1859, Elias and his son, Edward, formed the E. Ingraham Company. By 1881, the company was on North Main Street. Elias died in August 1885. (Courtesy of American Clock and Watch Museum.)

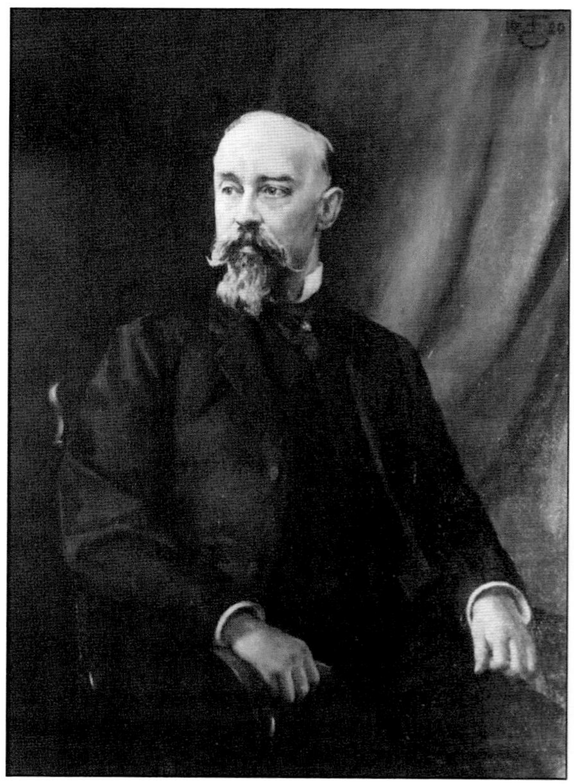

Edward Ingraham, the only child of Elias, became president of the E. Ingraham Company when his father died in 1885. Edward and his wife, Jane Beach Ingraham, had three sons: Walter A., Irving E., and William S., who became officers of the company. When Edward died in August 1892, his son, Walter, became president, and William became treasurer and general manager of the company. (Courtesy of American Clock and Watch Museum.)

Walter A. Ingraham, son of Edward and Jane Beach Ingraham, worked with his two brothers, William and Irving, at the E. Ingraham Company started by their grandfather, Elias. When his father, Edward, died in 1892, Walter became president of the company. Walter also served on the board of directors for both the Bristol Savings Bank and the Bristol National Bank. (Courtesy of American Clock and Watch Museum.)

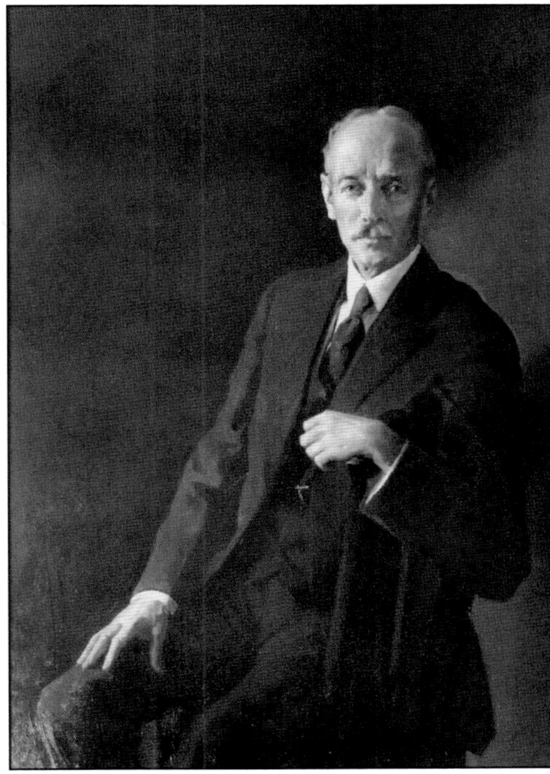

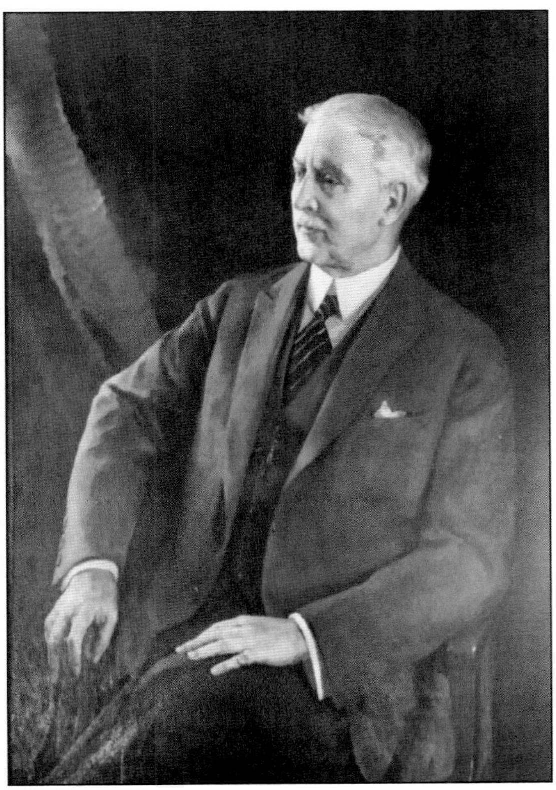

William S. Ingraham became treasurer and general manager of the E. Ingraham Company in 1892. William also served on the board of directors when the new bank called North Side Bank and Trust opened in 1929. (Courtesy of American Clock and Watch Museum.)

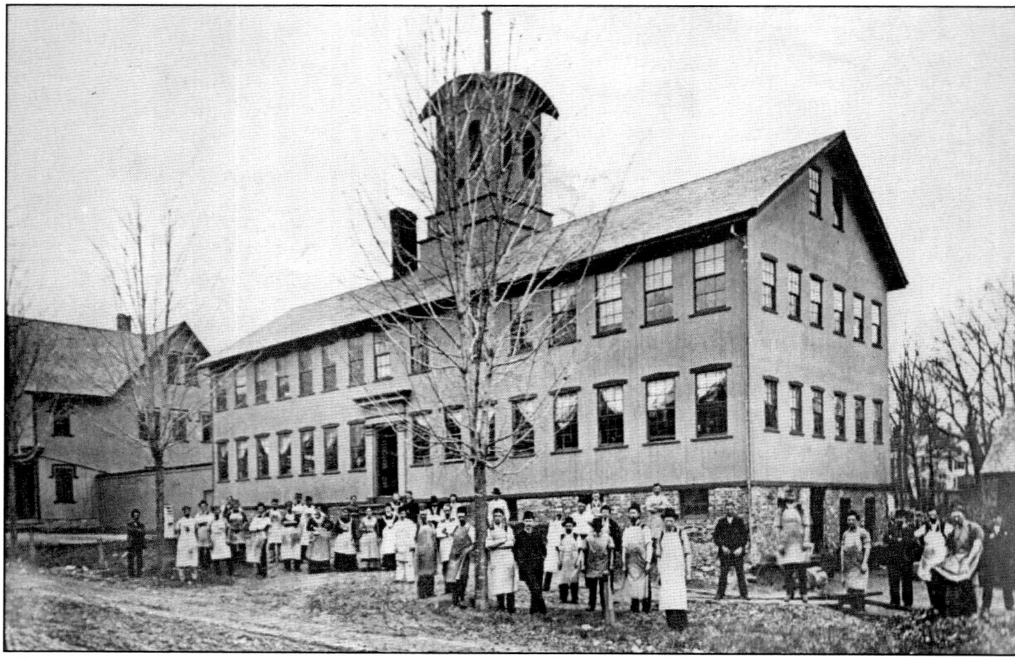

The E. Ingraham Company Movement Shop was located on North Main Street. The house on the left was the main office from 1902 to 1903. In this picture are the employees and William S. Ingraham standing behind the tree wearing a derby hat and a dark suit. (Courtesy of American Clock and Watch Museum.)

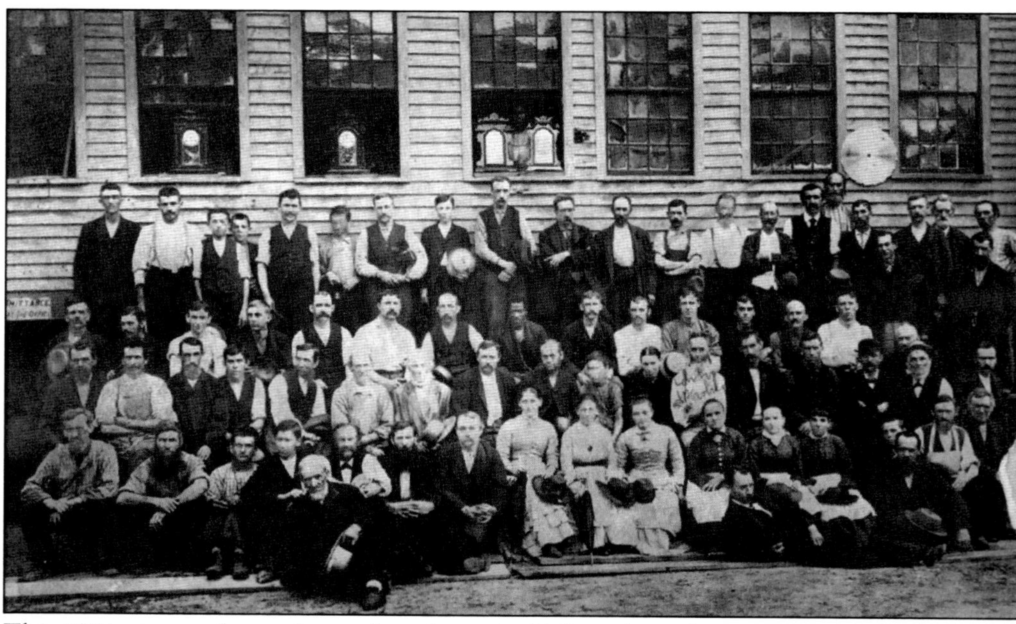

This 1884 picture shows the workers from the E. Ingraham Company Case Shop that was located on Pond Street (North Main Street). In the windows are four Ingraham clocks. When Ingraham moved out of this building to their new location on North Main Street, the Turner Heater Company purchased it in 1890. This building was destroyed by fire in 1904. (Courtesy of American Clock and Watch Museum.)

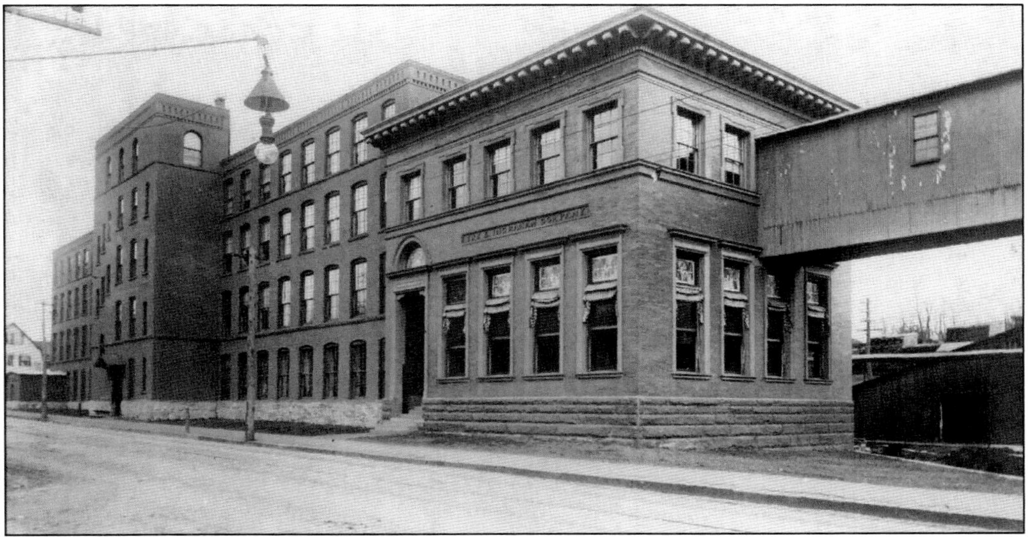

When Edward Ingraham and his three sons, Walter, Irving, and William, reconstructed E. Ingraham Company in 1884, their sales continued to increase by improving machinery. They replaced the wooden buildings with brick ones. In this picture on the left was the movement shop with the general manager's office. The building was constructed between 1902 and 1904 and was located on North Main Street. (Courtesy of Gary Potter.)

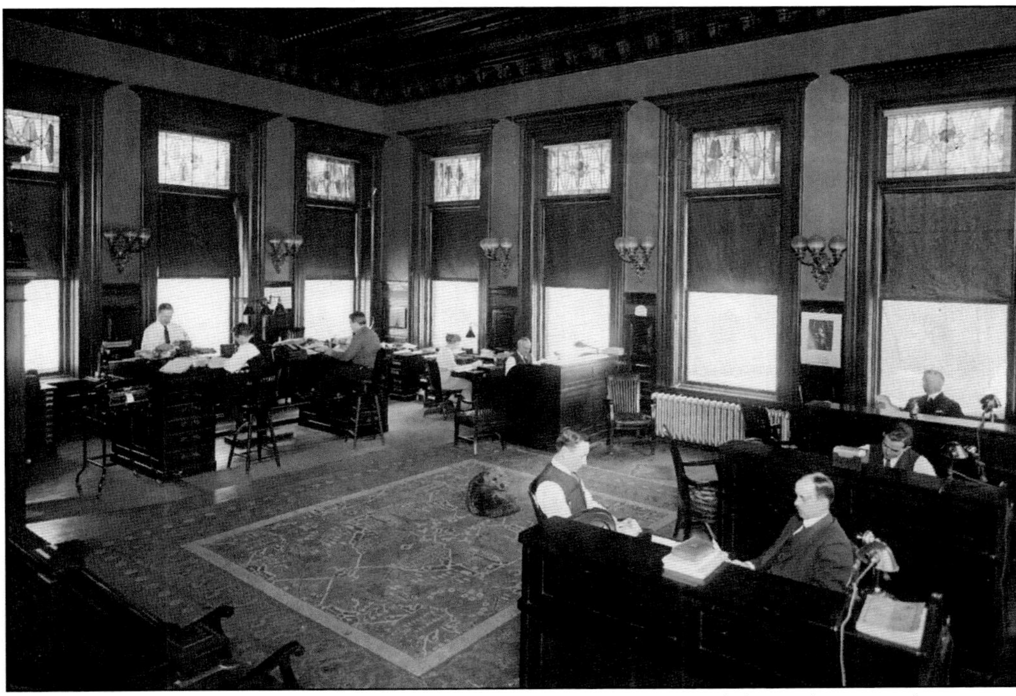

This picture of the interior office was taken on February 16, 1914, and shows the general managers of E. Ingraham Company. From left to right on the left side of the photograph are William P. Aynds, Dudley S. Ingraham, Roydon Barton, Mildred Hart, and Alfred Roe. On the back wall at right, framed by the window, is William S. Ingraham, general manager. In front of William is his brother, Irving E. Ingraham, and Will Large is taking diction for Elmer E. Stockton. Rajah, the dog, is owned by William. (Courtesy of American Clock and Watch Museum.)

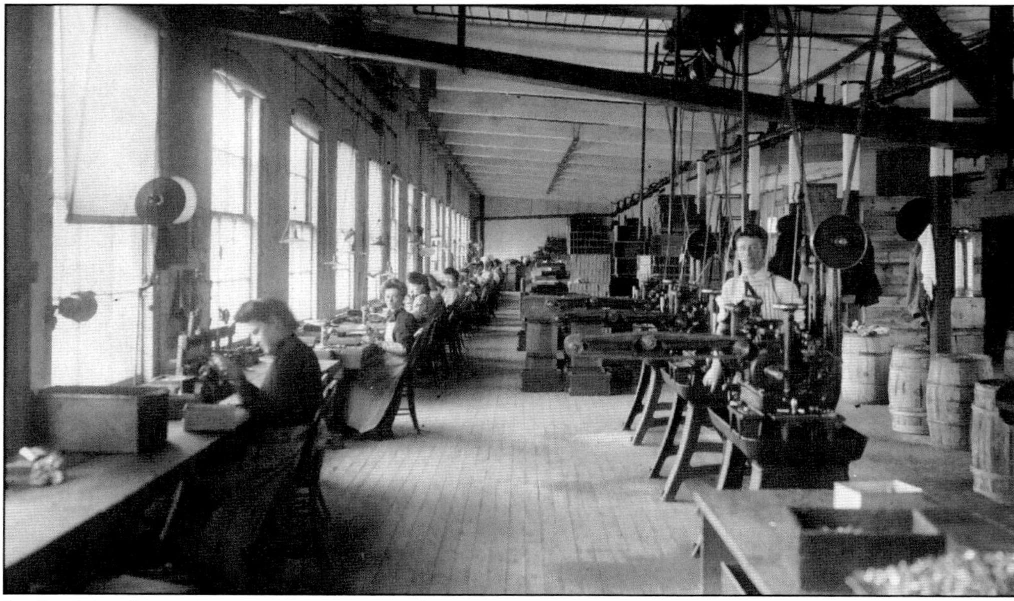

In this March 1906 picture are a group of women working in the E. Ingraham Company Movement Shop. The women did a lot of the intricate work on the clocks. Note the women are sitting next to the large windows getting natural light to do their job. (Courtesy of American Clock and Watch Museum.)

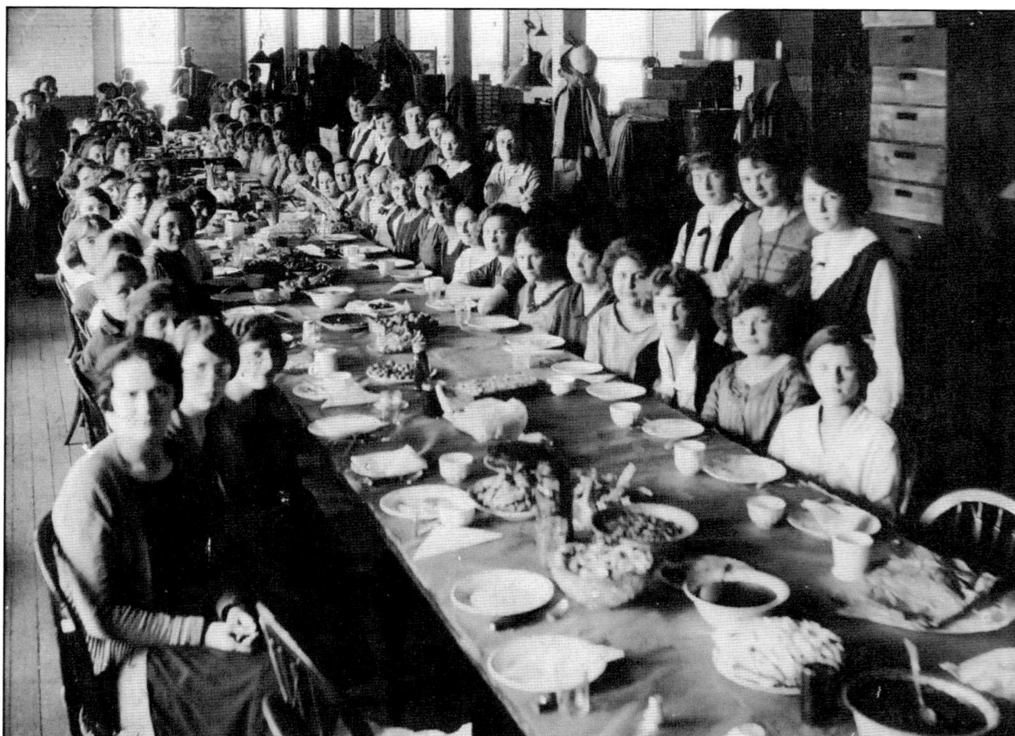

A group of the E. Ingraham Company employees are sitting in the movement shop during their Christmas party in 1927. The wooden boxes on the right were used for finished clock movements. (Courtesy of American Clock and Watch Museum.)

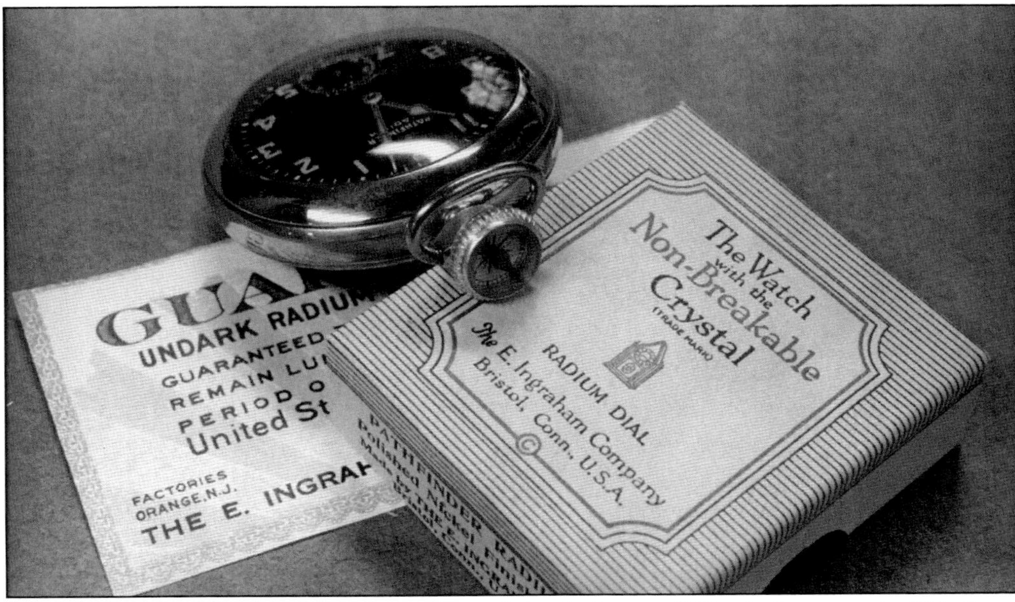

The popular "Dollar Watch" was originally made by the Ingersoll Watch Company in 1881. It was a pocket watch made less expensive so workers could afford to buy them. In 1913, E. Ingraham purchased machinery, equipment, and inventory from Bannatyne Watch Company of Waterbury so they could manufacture the popular "Dollar Watch." This pocket watch was manufactured in May 1933. (Courtesy of American Clock and Watch Museum.)

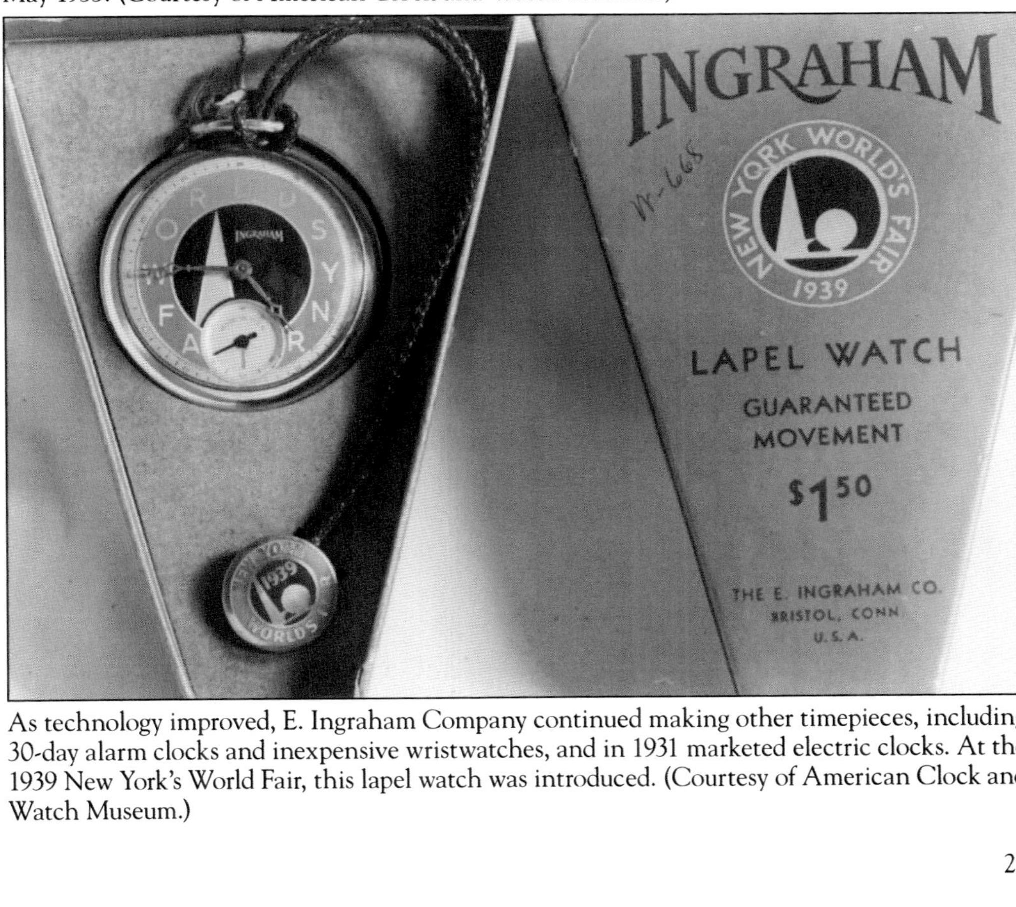

As technology improved, E. Ingraham Company continued making other timepieces, including 30-day alarm clocks and inexpensive wristwatches, and in 1931 marketed electric clocks. At the 1939 New York's World Fair, this lapel watch was introduced. (Courtesy of American Clock and Watch Museum.)

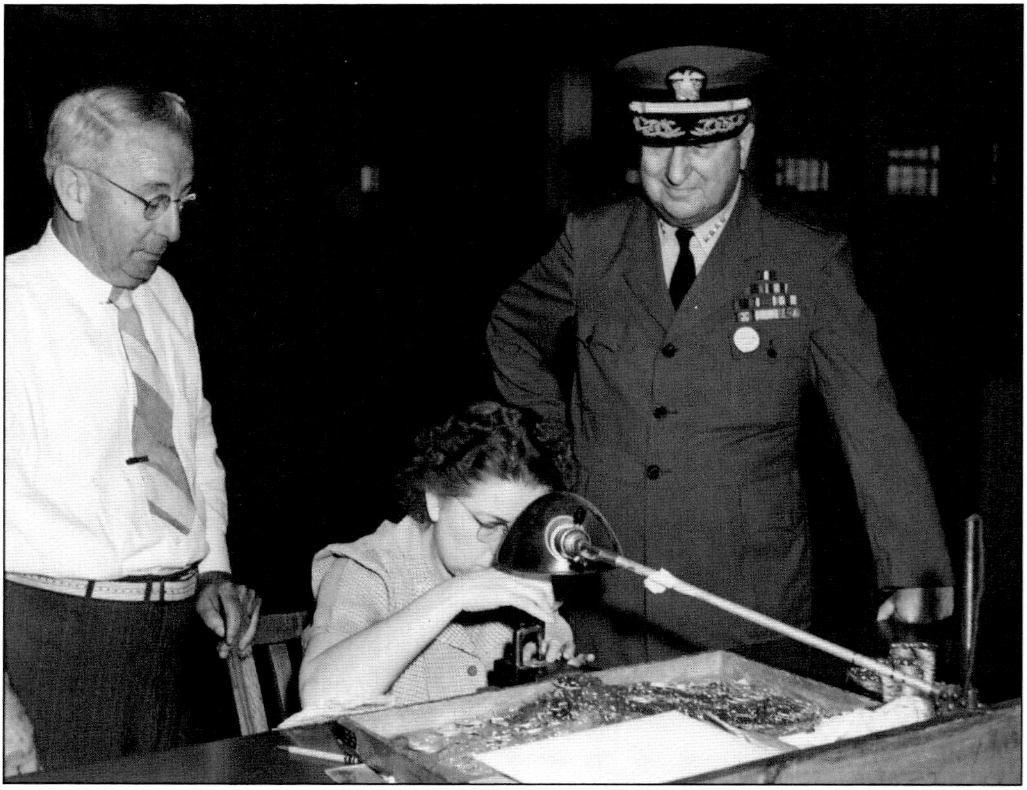

In 1942, the War Production Board ordered E. Ingraham Company to cease the manufacturing of clocks and watches. By that August, they were making mechanical time-fuse parts for army and navy antiaircraft and artillery. Taken on June 16, 1944, this photograph shows Elof Carlson (left), superintendent for E. Ingraham Company and an employee burring fuse plates for the artillery shell-timing device with Adm. Edward Clifford Kalbfus from the navy looking on. (Courtesy of American Clock and Watch Museum.)

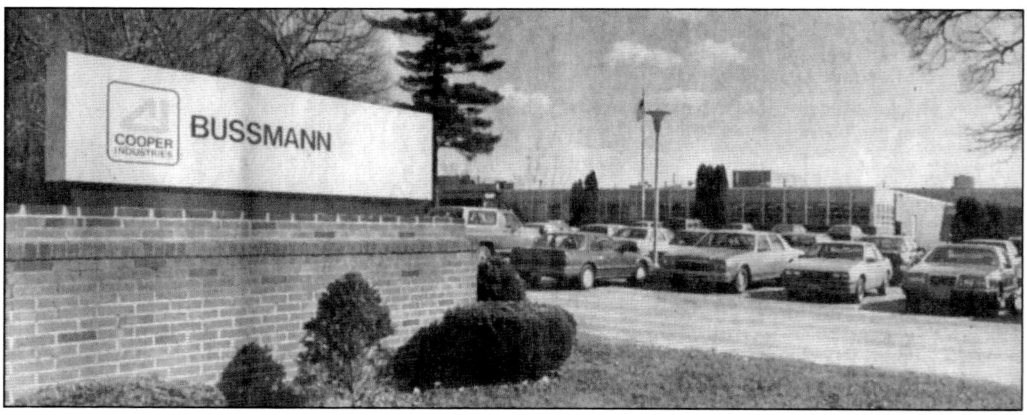

In 1946, the E. Ingraham Company started manufacturing clocks and watches again. In 1958, the company name was changed to Ingraham Company. With help from the city of Bristol, Ingraham Company moved to Bristol's Redstone Hill Industrial Park at 210 Redstone Hill Road, leaving the North Main Street location that was later torn down with redevelopment. In 1967, Ingraham was bought by McGraw-Edison and renamed Bussmann Division. Today the building is owned by Rowley Spring and Stamping Corporation. (Courtesy of the *Bristol Press*.)

Two

EARLY INDUSTRIES

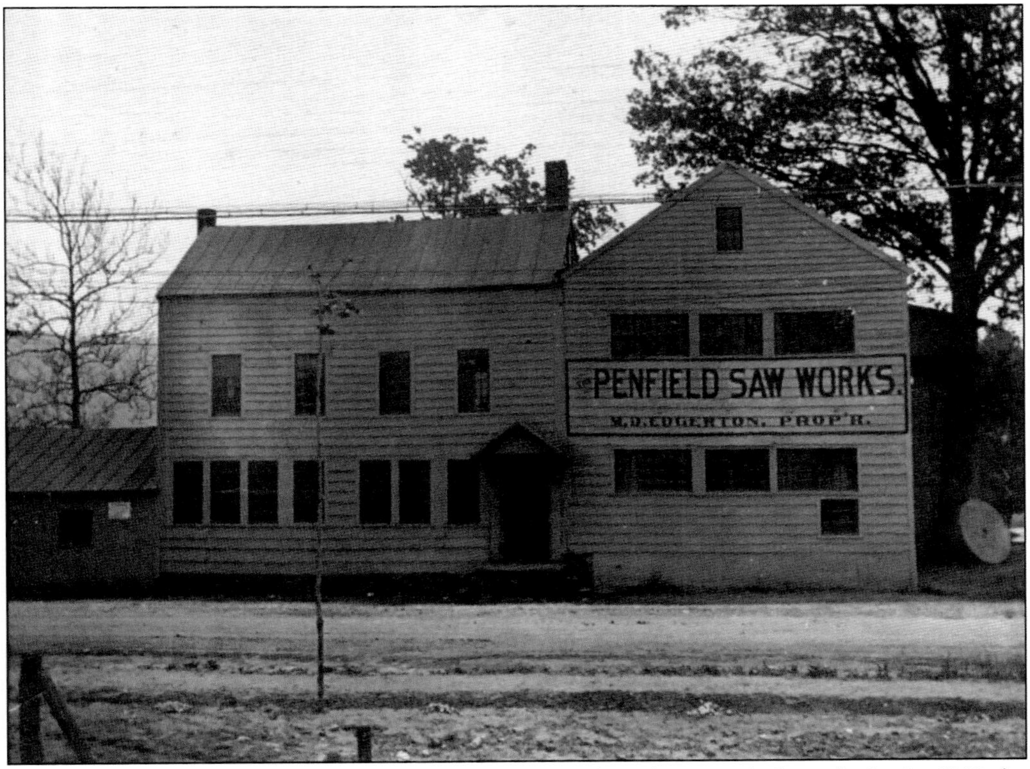

Irenus Atkins started out manufacturing various wood products, including clocks. In 1832, he formed a partnership with his brother, Rollin, making saws. Atkins sold the business, and a new business opened on Riverside Avenue called the Porter Saw Company. In 1879, it was sold to Penfield Saw Works. Besides manufacturing saws, the business made knifes, cloth, and paper. In 1899, Penfield sold the business to Marvin D. Edgerton. (Courtesy of Tom Dickau.)

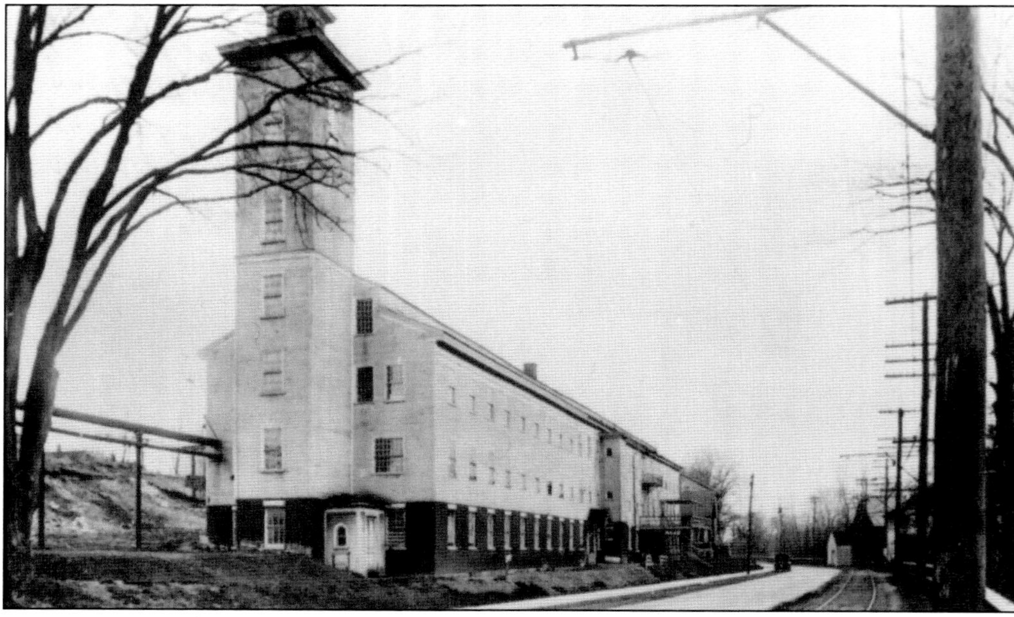

In 1837, a group of clockmakers bought land on Riverside Avenue to start Bristol Manufacturing Company. The company first manufactured "satinett," a fabric made of cotton to make wool knit underwear. In 1856, the company reorganized and changed to knit shirts and drawers. When the demand for knitted underwear ended, the business closed in 1923. This picture shows one of their buildings. (Courtesy of Bristol Historical Society.)

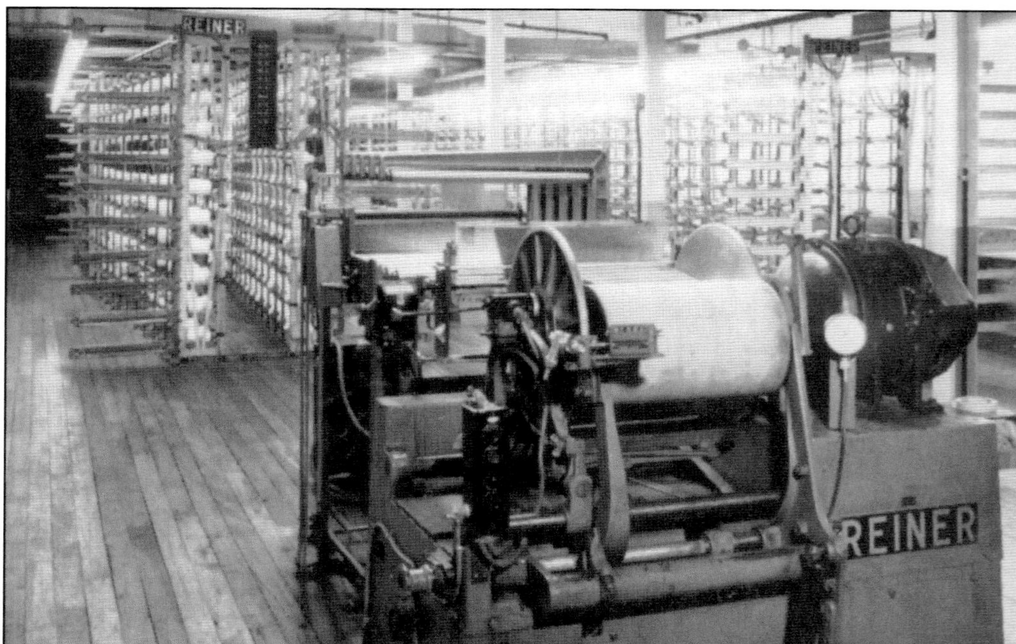

In 1945, in the old Bristol Manufacturing Company structure, a new business moved into the building from Watertown, Connecticut, called Raytric Knitting Mill. This interior picture shows the machinery used to make tricot, a warp-knit fabric made from natural and synthetic fibers. (Courtesy of Bristol Historical Society.)

Col. Edward L. Dunbar was born in 1815. In 1841, Edward started his own business purchasing the Judson and Hills Casting Shop on the corner of South and Union Streets. He manufactured clock parts and trim. In 1847, he changed to manufacturing springs. In 1858, Edward and Wallace Barnes formed a partnership called Dunbar and Barnes Company, investing $2,000 each to make springs and hoops. In 1863, Dunbar and Barnes ended their business together. (Courtesy of Bristol Historical Society.)

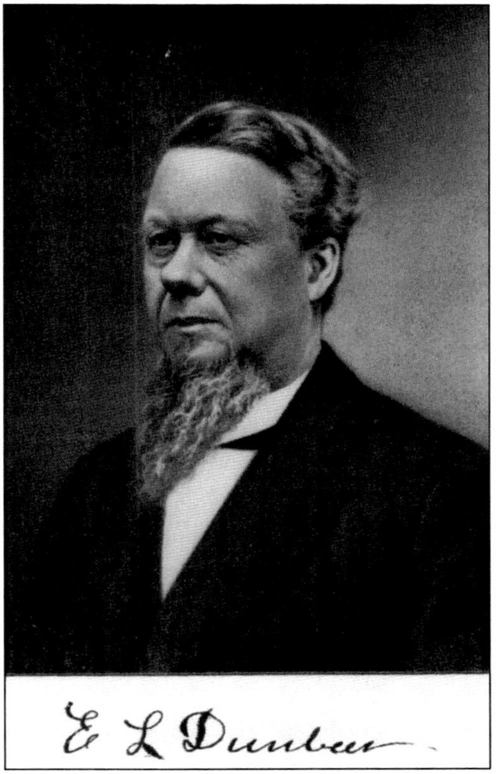

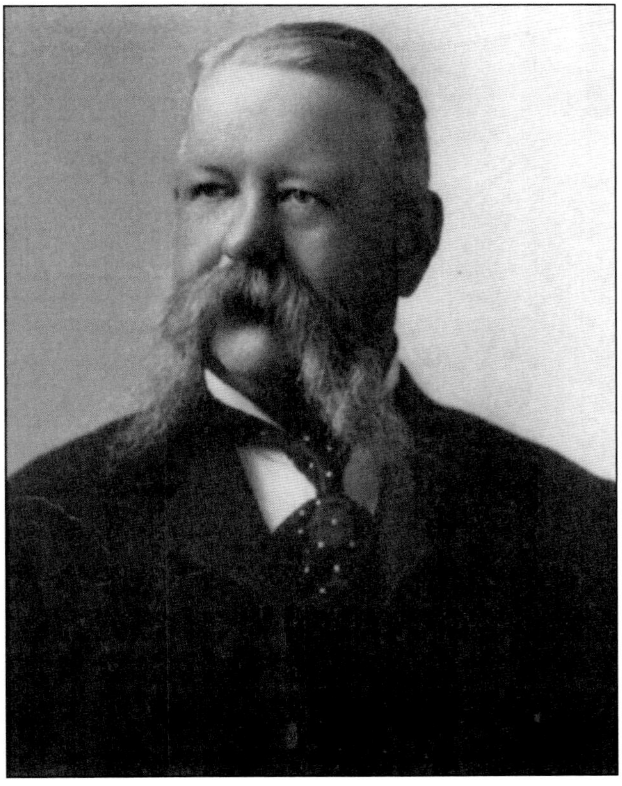

Edward Butler Dunbar, son of Col. Edward L. Dunbar and Julie Warner Dunbar, was born on November 1, 1842. In 1860, at the age of 18, Edward worked in the New York office of the Dunbar and Barnes crinoline business. He returned to Bristol to work in his father's factory making springs. When his father died in 1872, Edward and his two brothers formed a partnership that became Dunbar Brothers Company. Edward was married to Alice Giddings of Bristol. They had three children. Edward died in 1907. (Courtesy of Bristol Historical Society.)

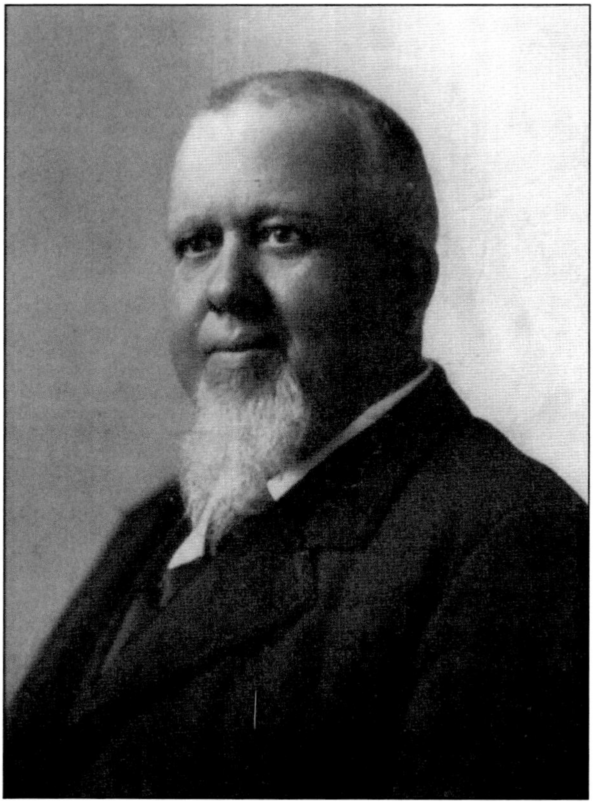

Winthrop A. Dunbar, son of Edward L. Dunbar and Julie Warner Dunbar, was born on February 25, 1841. He worked with his two brothers, Edward B. and William A., in their father's spring manufacturing company. In 1890, William sold his interest of the business to his brothers. Winthrop died on December 31, 1912. (Courtesy of Bristol Historical Society.)

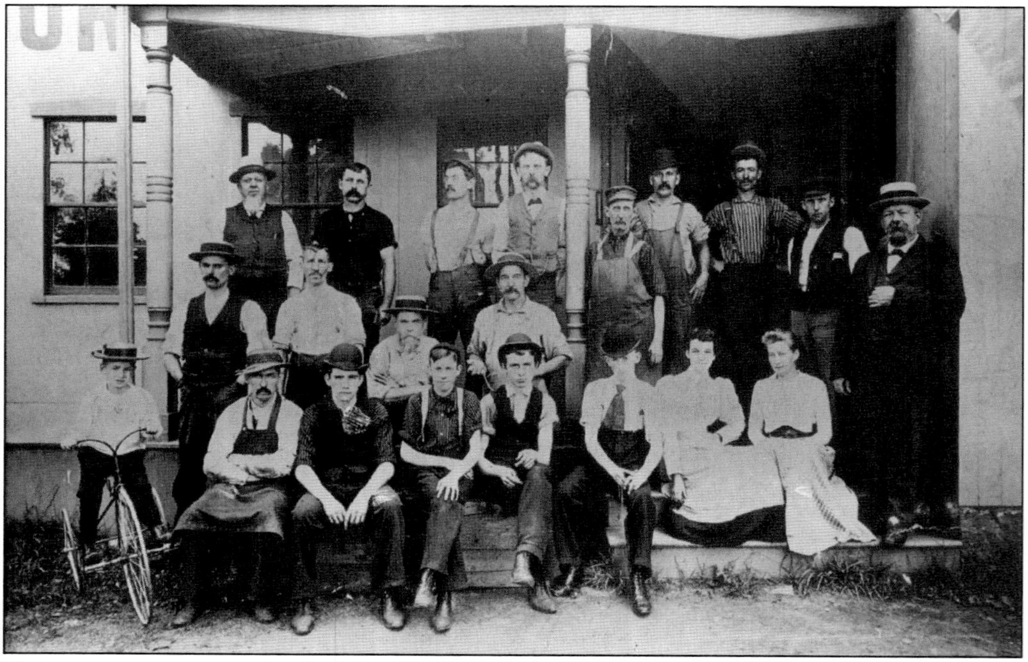

This group picture was taken by Leopold Photography of New Haven of the Dunbar factory workers at the factory located on the corner of South and Union Streets. On the left in the back row is Winthrop A. Dunbar. Edward B. Dunbar is on the right standing against the building.

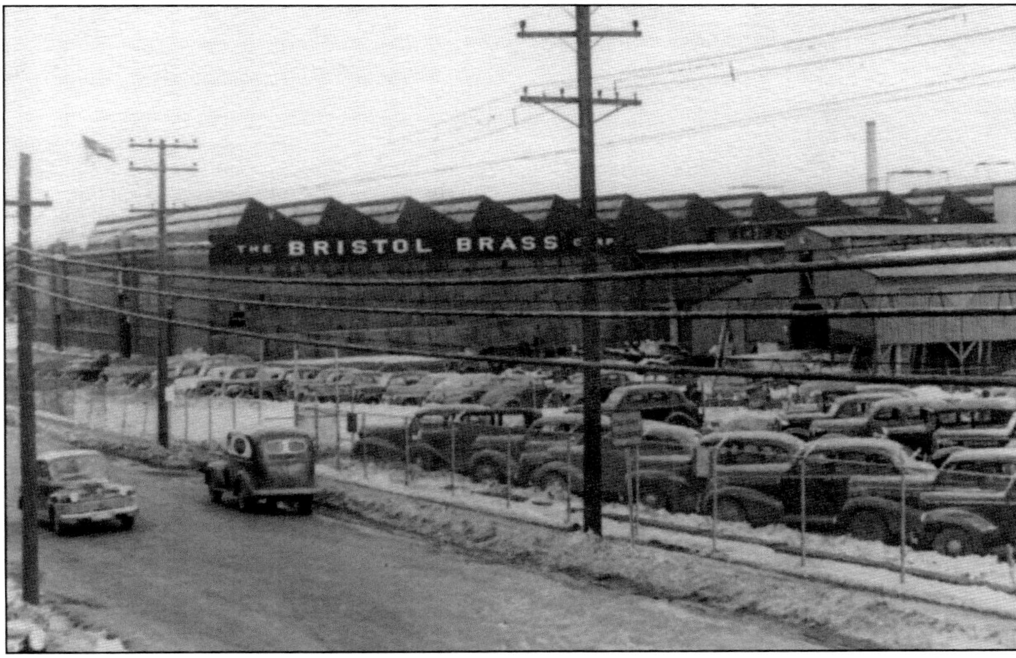

Bristol Brass and Clock Company located on Broad Street was founded in 1850 by both Bristol and Waterbury clockmakers. They made brass mechanisms for the clocks. By 1880, they became Bristol's largest employer. In 1903, the business was renamed the Bristol Brass Company. During World War I, they manufactured shells, truck parts, and brass cartridge cases. In the 1920s, they made parts for automobiles, producing radiator tanks and other parts. During World War II, they were manufacturing shell cases.

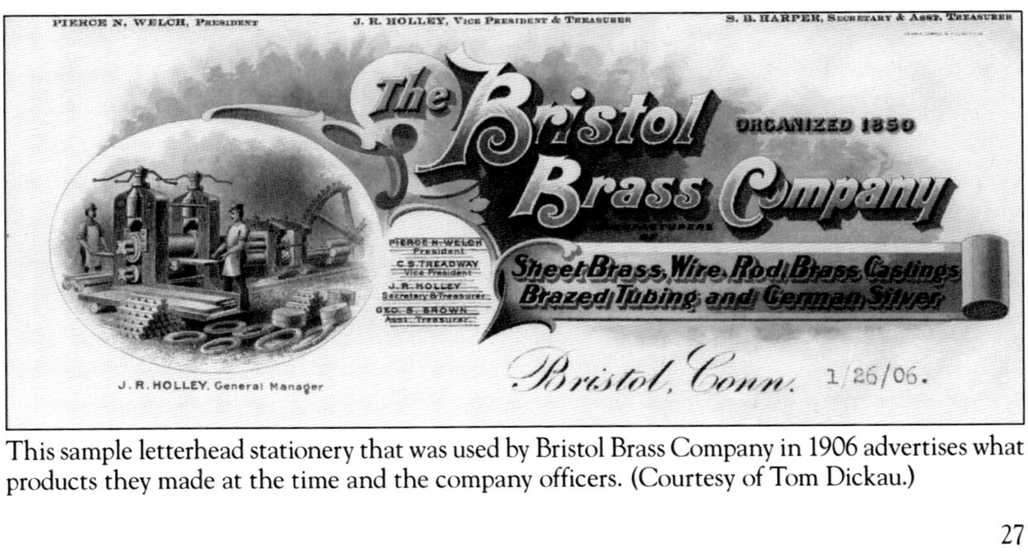
PIERCE N. WELCH, PRESIDENT J. R. HOLLEY, VICE PRESIDENT & TREASURER S. B. HARPER, SECRETARY & ASST. TREASURER

The Bristol Brass Company ORGANIZED 1850

PIERCE N. WELCH President
C. S. TREADWAY Vice President
J. R. HOLLEY Secretary & Treasurer
GEO. S. BROWN Asst. Treasurer

Sheet Brass, Wire, Rod, Brass Castings, Brazed Tubing and German Silver

J. R. HOLLEY, General Manager

Bristol, Conn. 1/26/06.

This sample letterhead stationery that was used by Bristol Brass Company in 1906 advertises what products they made at the time and the company officers. (Courtesy of Tom Dickau.)

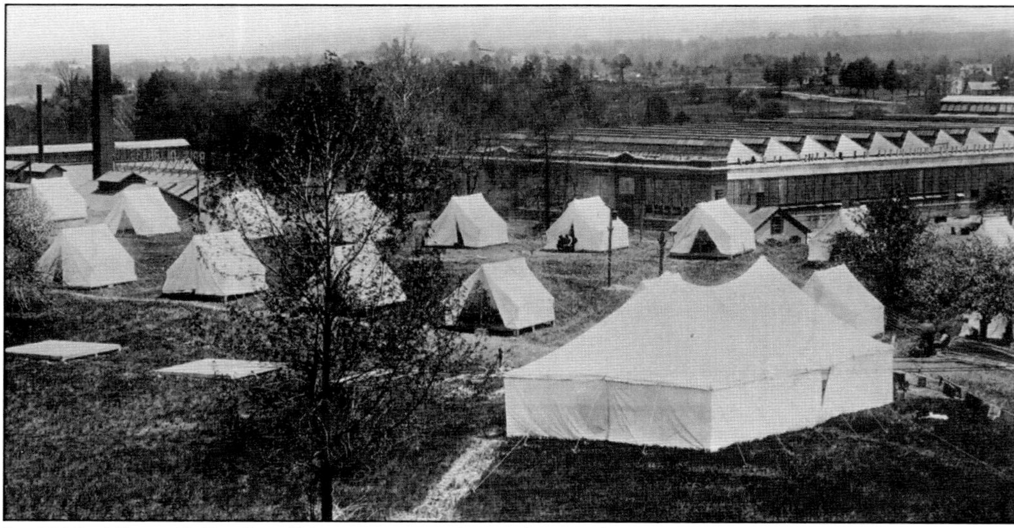

In 1913, Albert F. Rockwell became president of Bristol Brass Company. During World War I, a new rolling mill was built. Tents were set up for new workers on the hill overlooking the factory. Rockwell started a real estate subsidiary under Bristol Brass for workers to build homes. By September 1916, First, Second, and Third Streets were filled. By the end of the year, Fourth through Six Streets were built.

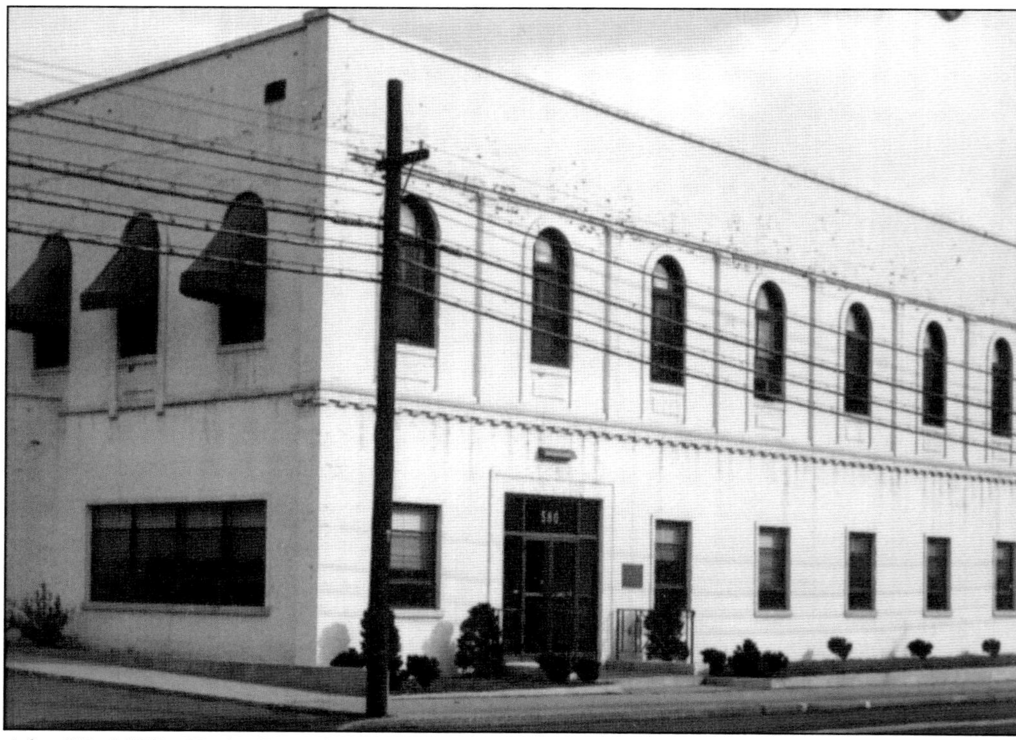

After World War II, the Bristol Brass Corporation was struggling to stay in business. The amount of brass being used in automobiles declined, and there was now foreign competition. In December 1982, after 132 years of business, the Bristol Brass Corporation closed. This building was the corporate office located on 580 Broad Street. Both this office and the old factories buildings still stand with other businesses in them now.

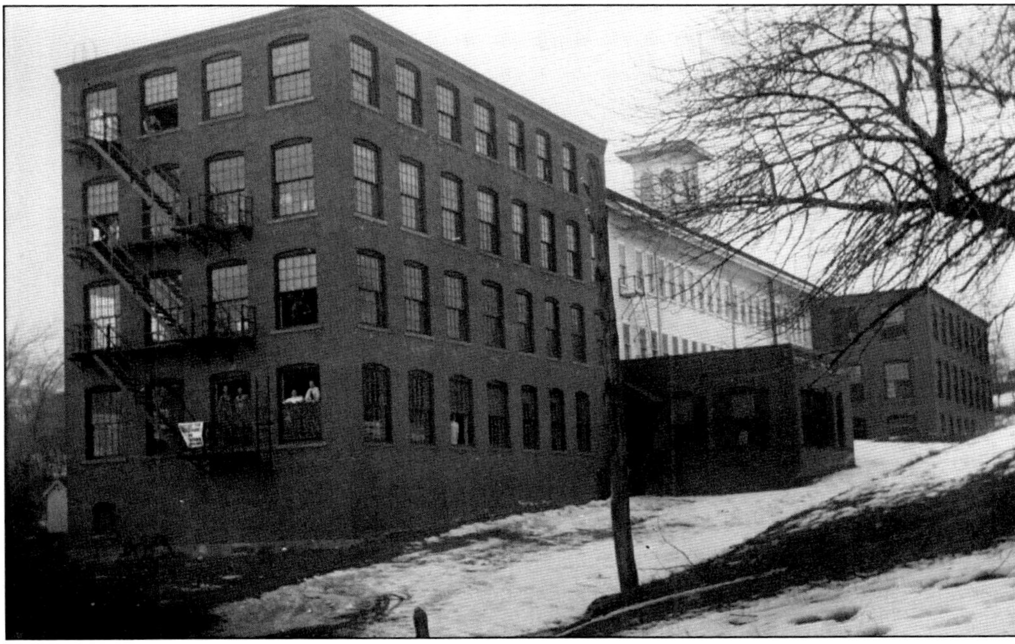

The Bristol Knitting Company was organized in 1850 by John Birge, Elisha Brewster, and Elias Ingraham. The wooden factory was located on Pond Street, later known as North Main Street. The factory made knit underwear. When a fire destroyed the original construction, a new brick building was developed when John Birge's son, Nathan L., took over the business. In 1882, Nathan's son, John, joined. In 1883, John's son, George, joined his father's business, changing the name to N. L. Birge Sons Company. In 1931, the company closed due to less demand for their products. (Courtesy of Bristol Historical Society.)

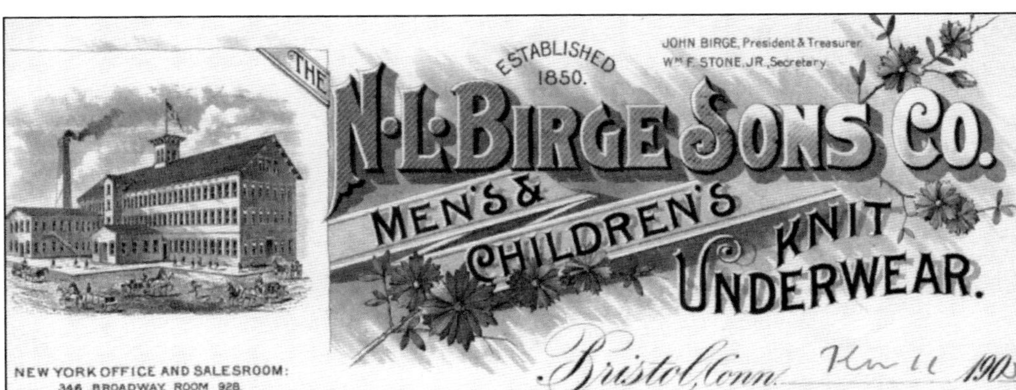

This is a sample letterhead that was used by the N. L. Birge Sons Company from 1903. (Courtesy of Tom Dickau.)

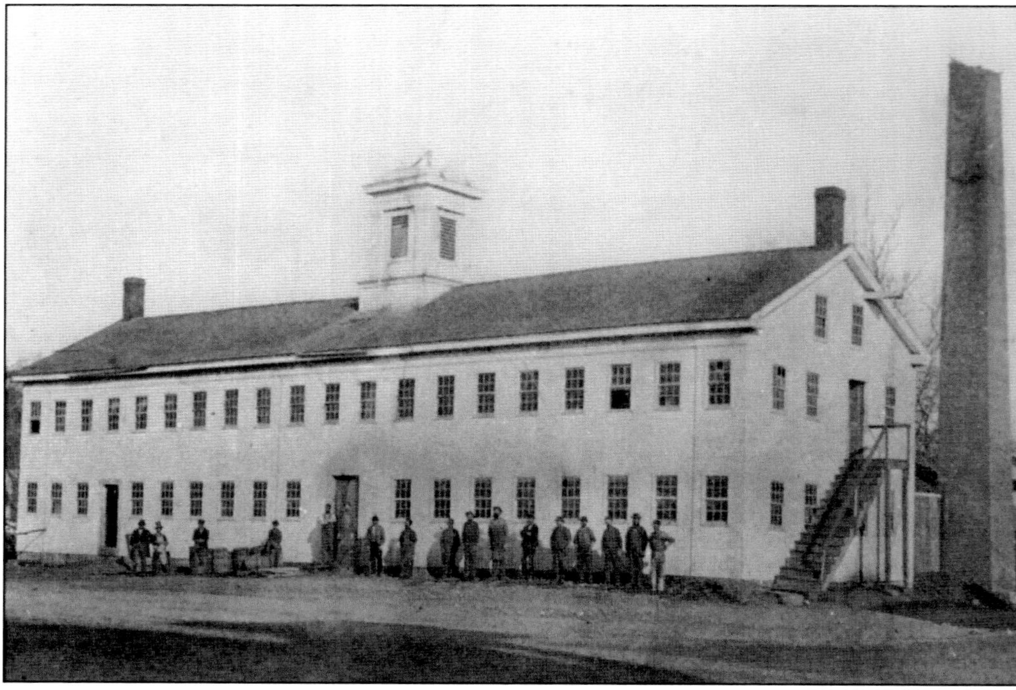

The Bristol Brass and Clock Company was making silverware and table cutlery under the name of the Holmes and Tuttle Manufacturing Company located at 120 Main Street. It became known as the "Spoon Shop." In 1901, a corporation was formed with the new name American Silver Company. As the business continued to grow, the old wooden buildings were replaced with brick ones. The business was bought by International Silver Company. The business closed in 1935 and was torn down in 1937. (Courtesy of American Clock and Watch Museum.)

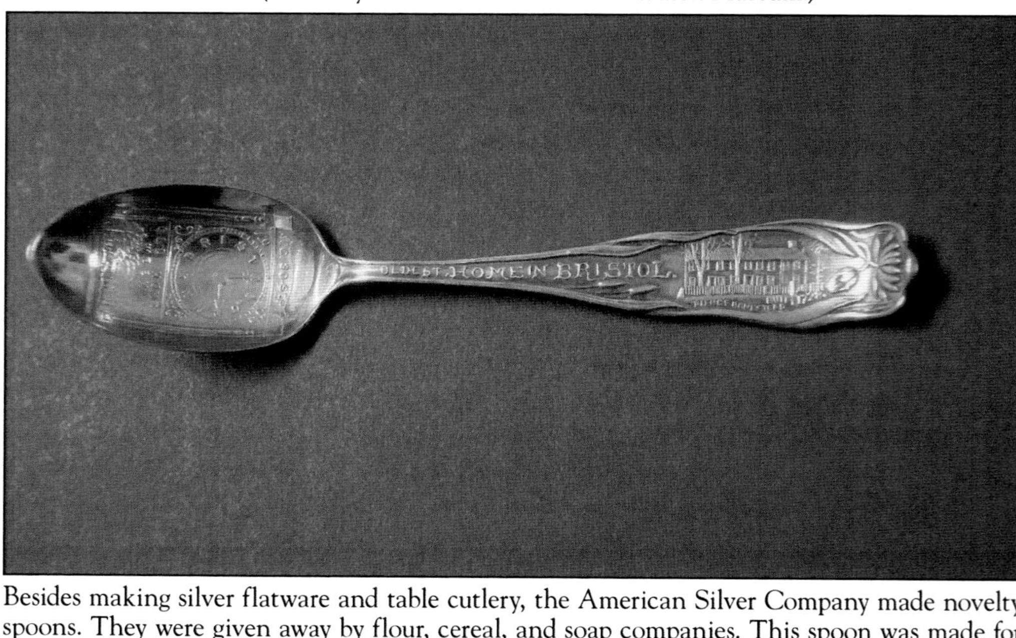

Besides making silver flatware and table cutlery, the American Silver Company made novelty spoons. They were given away by flour, cereal, and soap companies. This spoon was made for "Old Home Week," held August 30 to September 7, 1885. The handle shows the oldest home in Bristol, the Pierce home. Note the clock in the center of the spoon. (Courtesy of Gary Potter.)

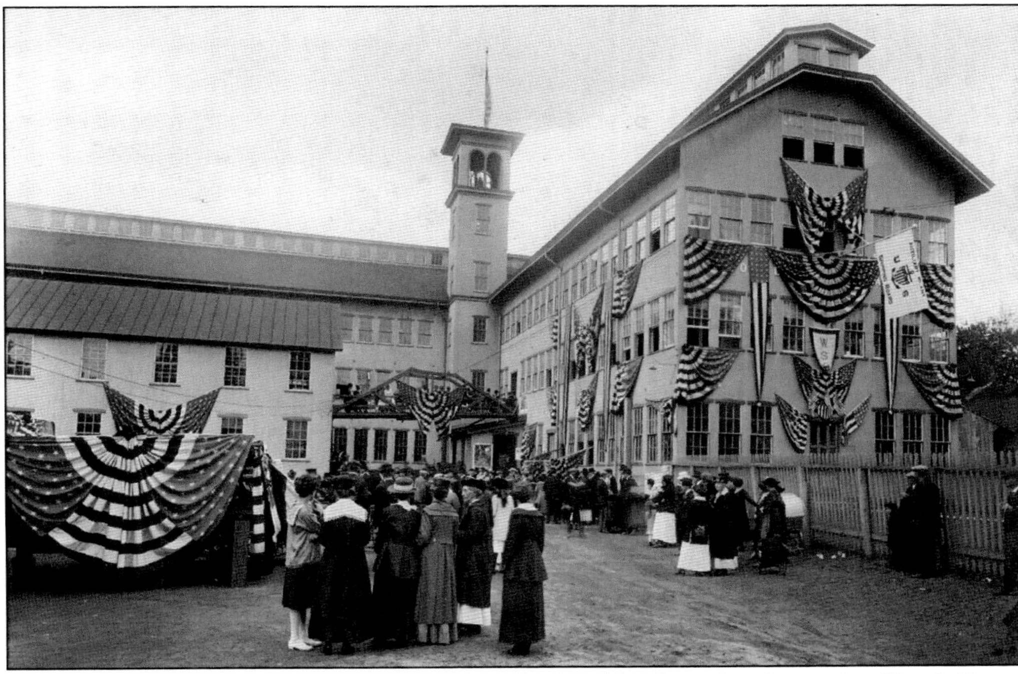

In 1868, Bristol Brass and Clock Company bought the old Atkins shop located on Brook Street. At the time, George W. Brown and Company, a toymaker, had converted his business to a lamp burner shop called the Bristol Brass Burner Company. When the building was destroyed by fire in 1881, Bristol Brass replaced it. Manufacturing the Bristol Brass Security Burner brought new profits when people were burning kerosene with wicks. When the electric lights took over, the demand for kerosene lamps ended. (Courtesy of Gary Potter.)

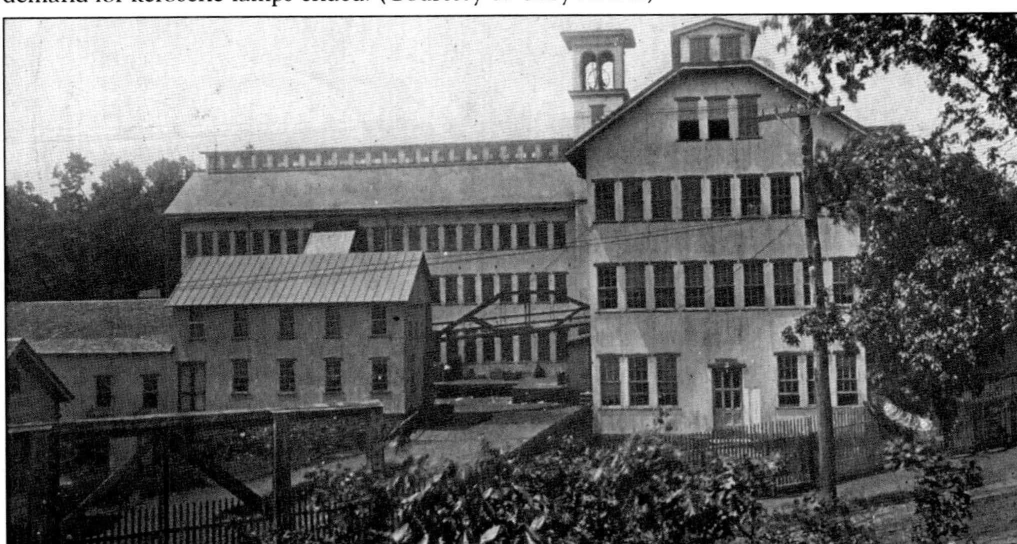

In 1912, the National Marine Lamp Company from New York purchased the Bristol Brass Burner Company building. The company incorporated in September 1912 with Frederick Perkins as president. They manufactured lamps, lanterns, brass, steel, tin, and galvanized iron. They took an active roll with shipbuilding during World War I. In 1932, the business closed due to lack of sales. (Courtesy of Gary Potter.)

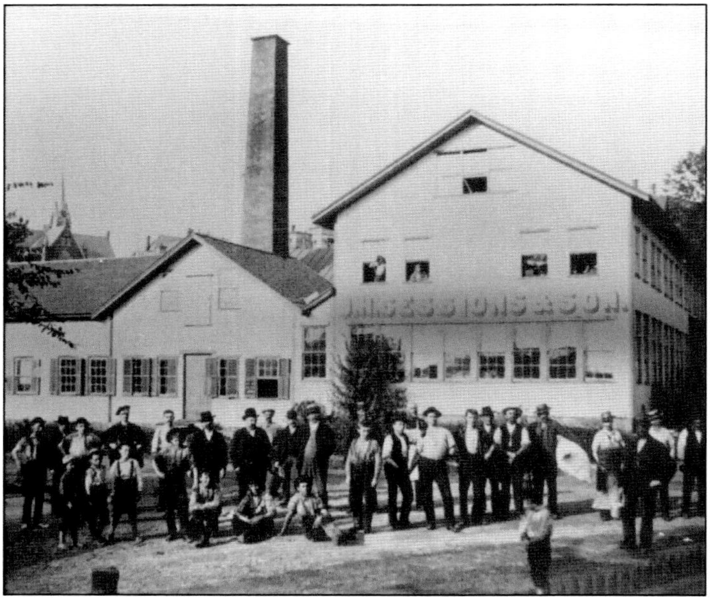

In 1854, John Humphrey Sessions and Henry Warner started a business making wooden parts. Sessions bought out Warner, moving his business on Main Street. Sessions built his factory on North Main Street in 1868. His brother, Albert, manufactured Bristol iron clamps and hinges for trunks. When Albert died in 1870, John bought Albert's business and John's son, John H., became partners in 1873. In this picture workers are standing in front of J. H. Sessions and Sons.

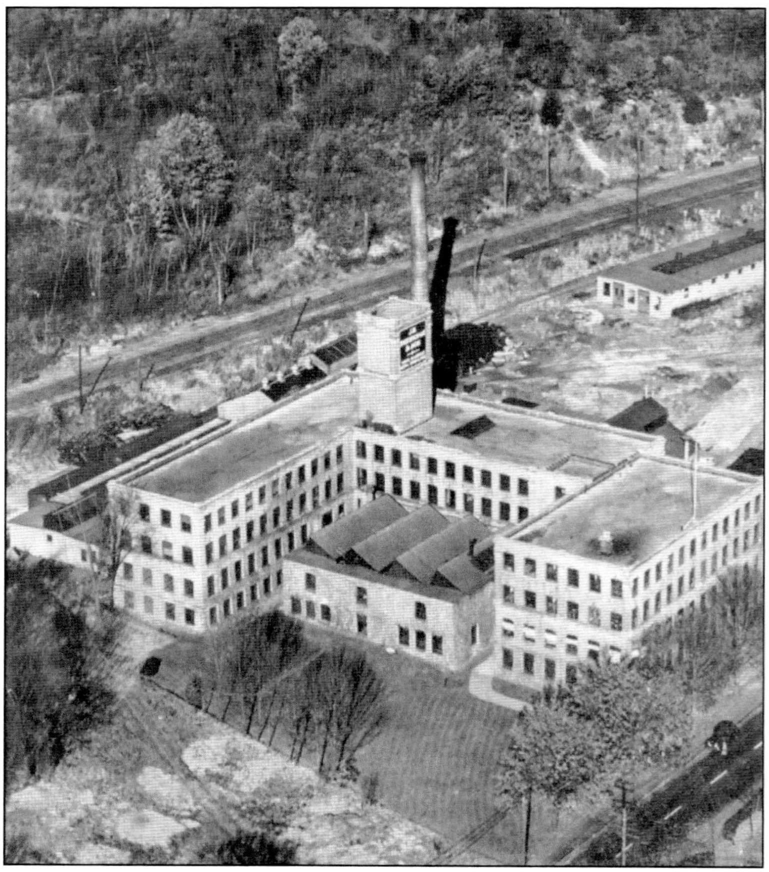

John H. Sessions, son of John Humphrey Sessions, became president when his father died in 1899. Albert, son of John H., took over the company in 1902 with his sons, Paul and John. They built a new factory on 273 Riverside Avenue in 1907. The business closed in 1994. R and B Repair Services, LLC, owned by Ray Frankowski Jr., and Brian Beals started a small engine sales and service business in 2003. In 2006, they moved into this building.

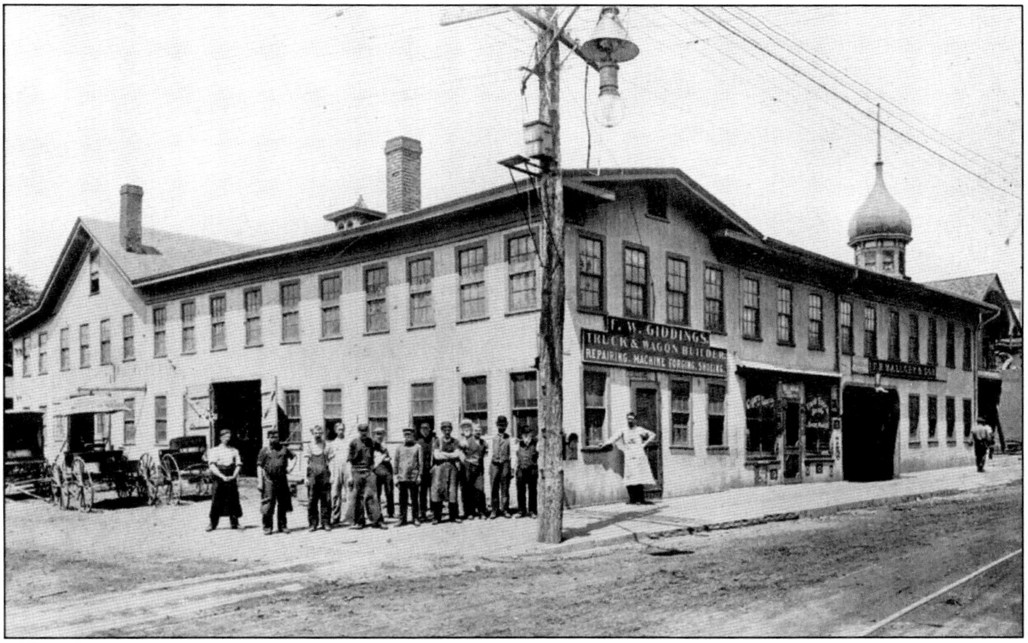

Watson Giddings and his son, Fred, established the W. Giddings and Son Company in 1874 located on 237 North Main Street. They made delivery wagons, carriages, forging, and horse shoes. In 1901, Fred took over the business, changing the name to F. W. Giddings. When New Departure Manufacturing Company set up Bristol Engineering Company in 1907, Giddings worked on the Haupt-Rockwell car and Rockwell's Yellow Cab. (Courtesy of Jerry Heresko.)

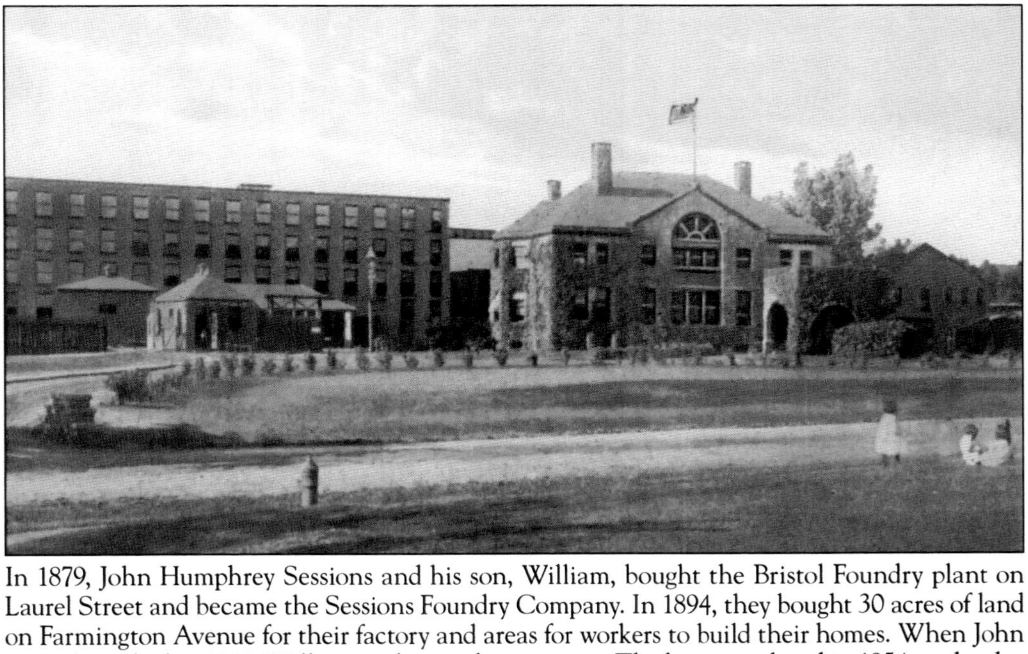

In 1879, John Humphrey Sessions and his son, William, bought the Bristol Foundry plant on Laurel Street and became the Sessions Foundry Company. In 1894, they bought 30 acres of land on Farmington Avenue for their factory and areas for workers to build their homes. When John Humphrey died in 1902, William took over the company. The business closed in 1954, and today the Bristol Commons is in its place. (Courtesy of Gary Potter.)

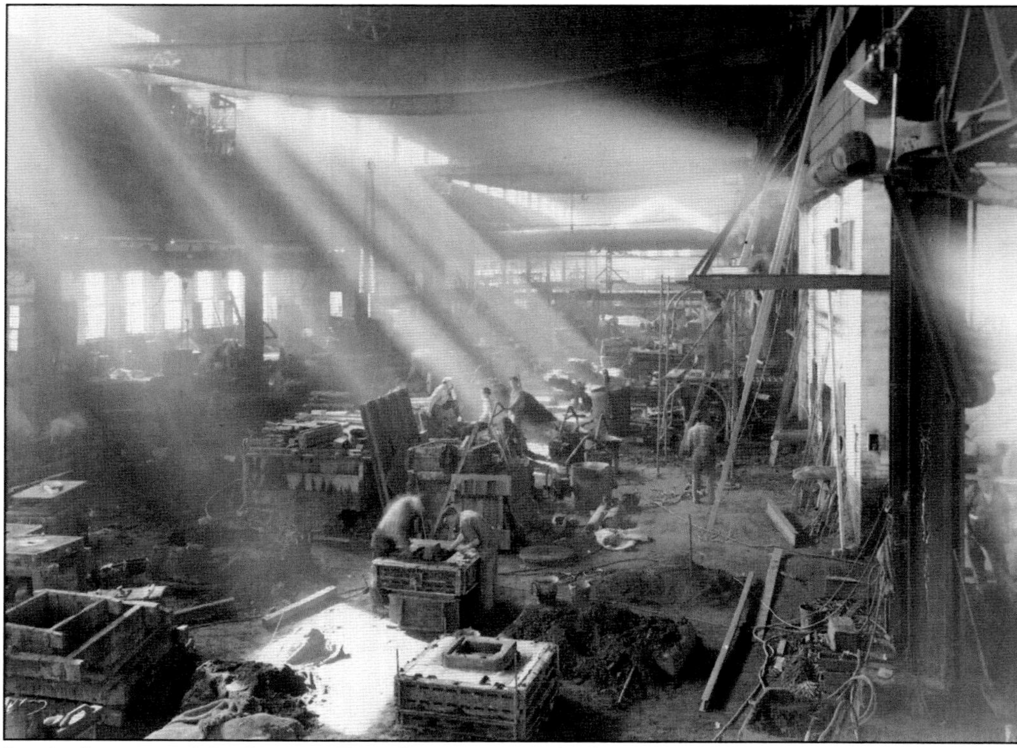

Inside this view of the Sessions Foundry Company, the business manufactured gray iron castings that were used for hand and machine tools, textile and industrial machinery, and repair and maintenance items. They also made castings for brass, copper, magnesium, and other alloys.

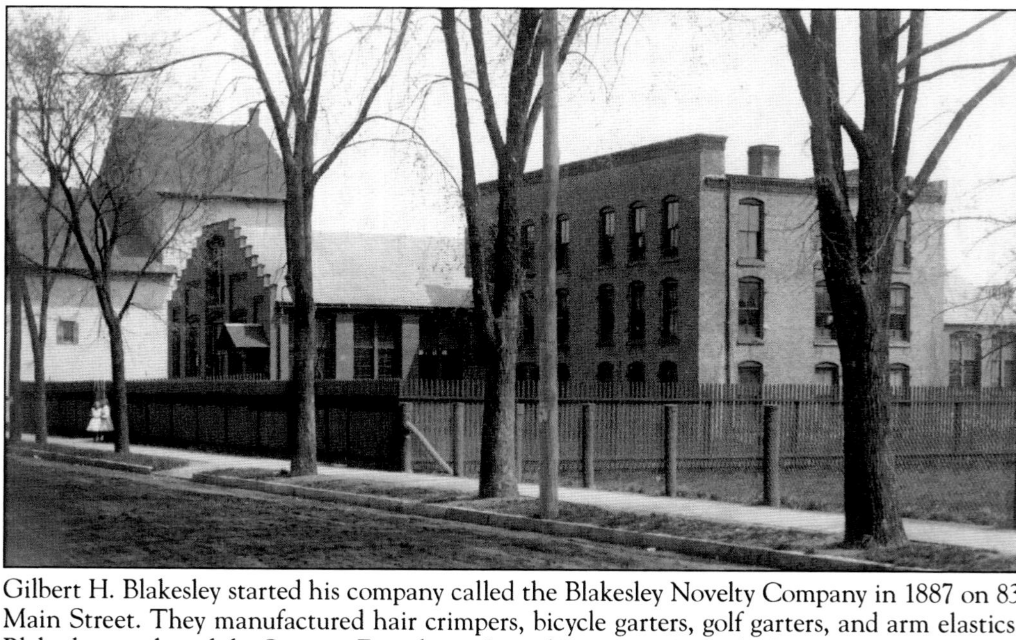

Gilbert H. Blakesley started his company called the Blakesley Novelty Company in 1887 on 83 Main Street. They manufactured hair crimpers, bicycle garters, golf garters, and arm elastics. Blakesley purchased the Sessions Foundry on Laurel Street in 1902. The business closed in 1940. In 1942, Alfred B. Nelson and his partner, Thor L. Hannon, owners of Superior Electric, bought the building. (Courtesy of Gary Potter.)

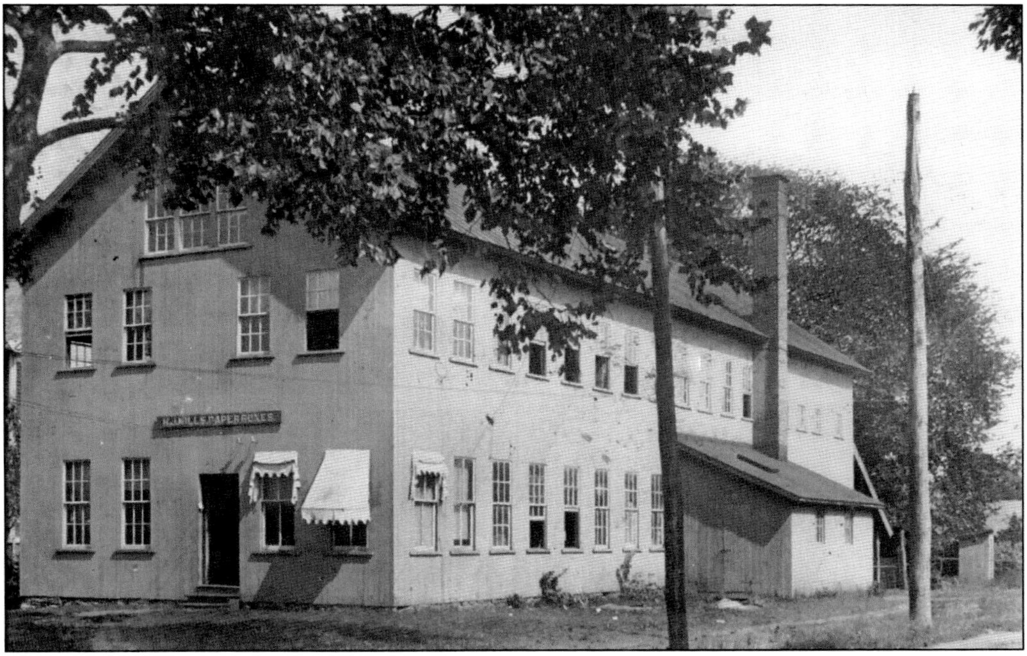

Herbert J. Mills worked with his uncle, the Reverend Benajah Hitchcock, in 1867 making boxes for matches. In 1887, Herbert and a cousin, David Mix, bought out Hitchcock. That same year Herbert bought out his cousin. In 1891, Herbert built his factory on 149 Church Street now known as H. J. Mills Company. When the business closed in 1987, it was owned by William R. Mills, a descendant of Herbert. The building no longer stands. (Courtesy of Tom Dickau.)

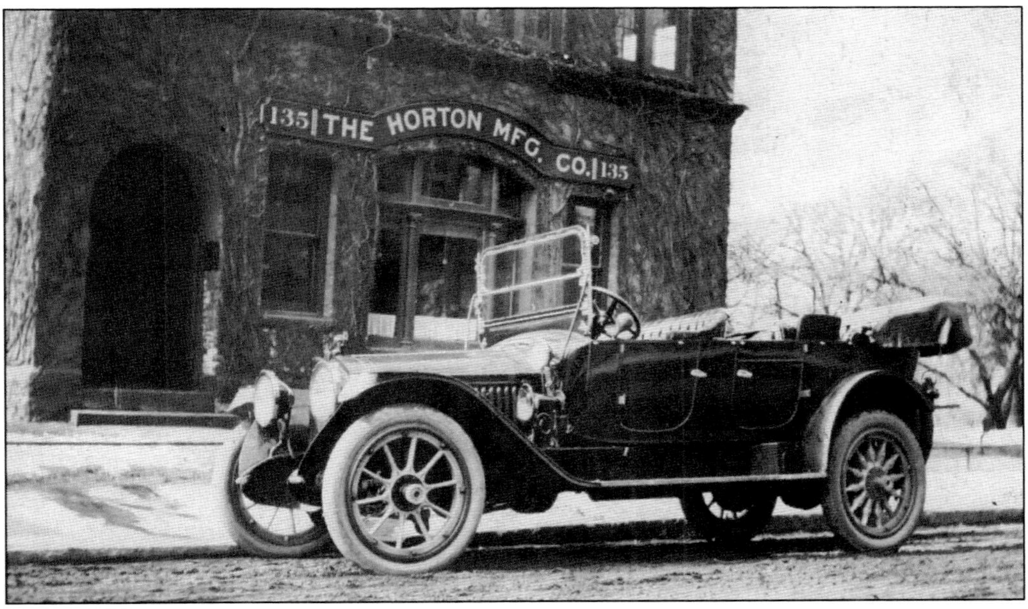

In 1887, Everett Horton invented a joined steel fishing rod that became known as the "Bristol Fishing Rod." Horton Manufacturing Company built a factory on 185 North Main Street. With the success of the fishing rods in 1921, the company added steel shafts for golf clubs. During World War II, Horton made for the government steel antenna mast sections for radios used on tanks, trucks, and ships. The business closed in 1950. (Courtesy of Tom Dickau.)

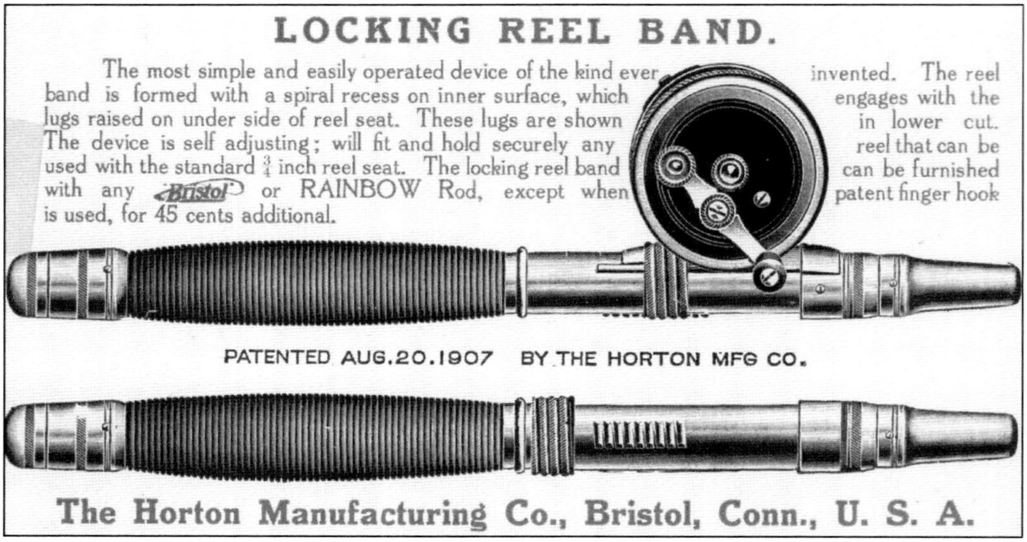

This was an advertisement used to promote the Horton Manufacturing Company locking reel band used on fishing rods. (Courtesy of Tom Dickau.)

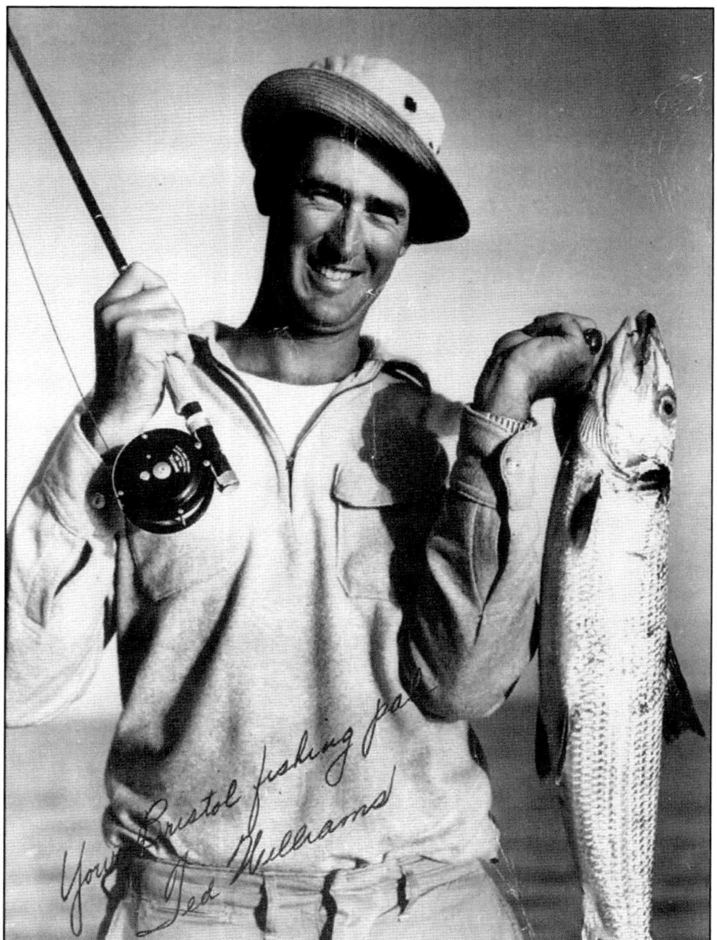

Ted Williams started his baseball career on April 29, 1939, playing his entire career for the Boston Red Sox. In this advertisement, Ted is holding a Horton fishing pole and the fish he caught. (Courtesy of Gary Potter.)

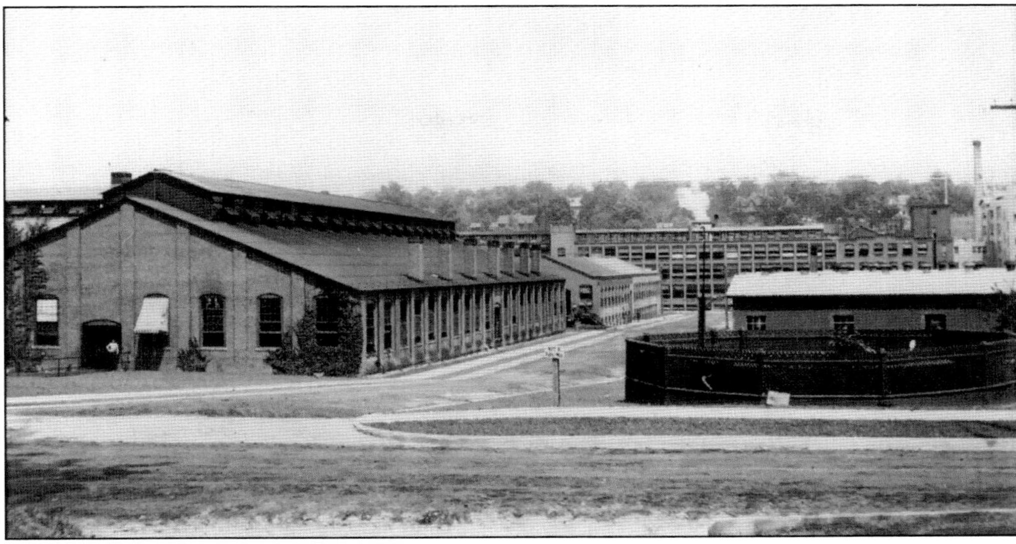

William Lawrence Barrett worked for the S. C. Monce Company whose business made glass cutters. In 1893, Barrett, whose job was general foreman, left there and started his own business called the William L. Barrett Company. The business was located in the former S. E. Root factory. In 1904, Barrett constructed this building on 30 School Street making glass cutters and glazier tools. In 1931, William retired, giving the business to his two sons, Richard and Robert. In the years ahead, they manufactured stapling machines. In 1950, the business stopped making glass cutters and turned to making metal parts for other factories. Today the business is closed, but the building still stands. (Courtesy of Charlie Nyberg.)

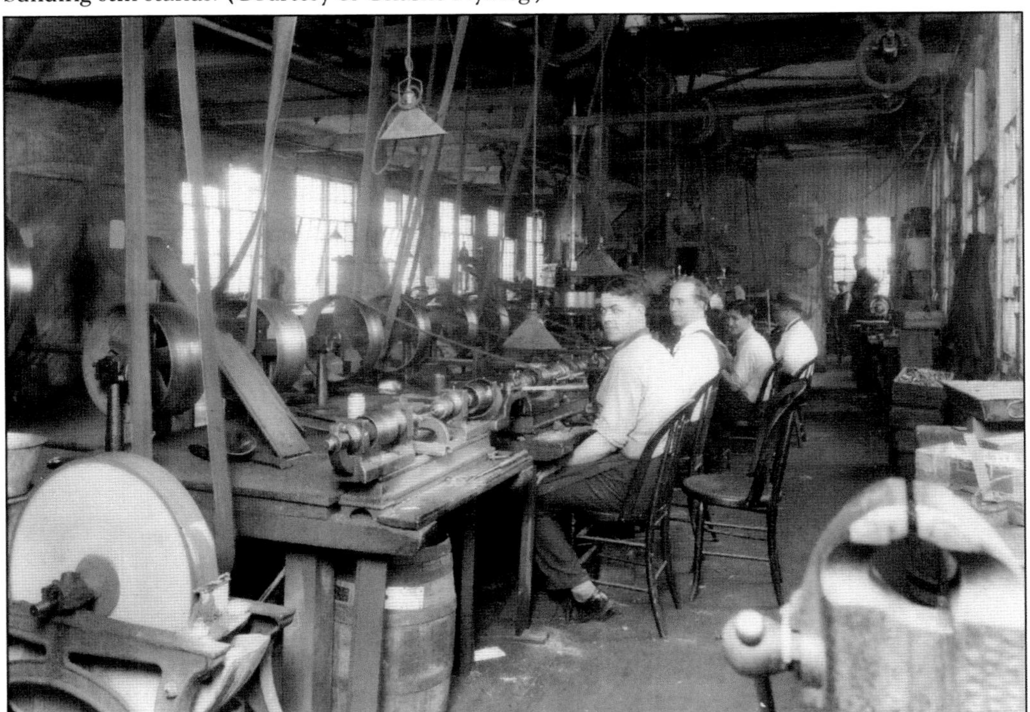

This picture, taken in the 1920s inside of the William L. Barrett Company, shows its workers as they manufacture their glass products. (Courtesy of Gary Potter.)

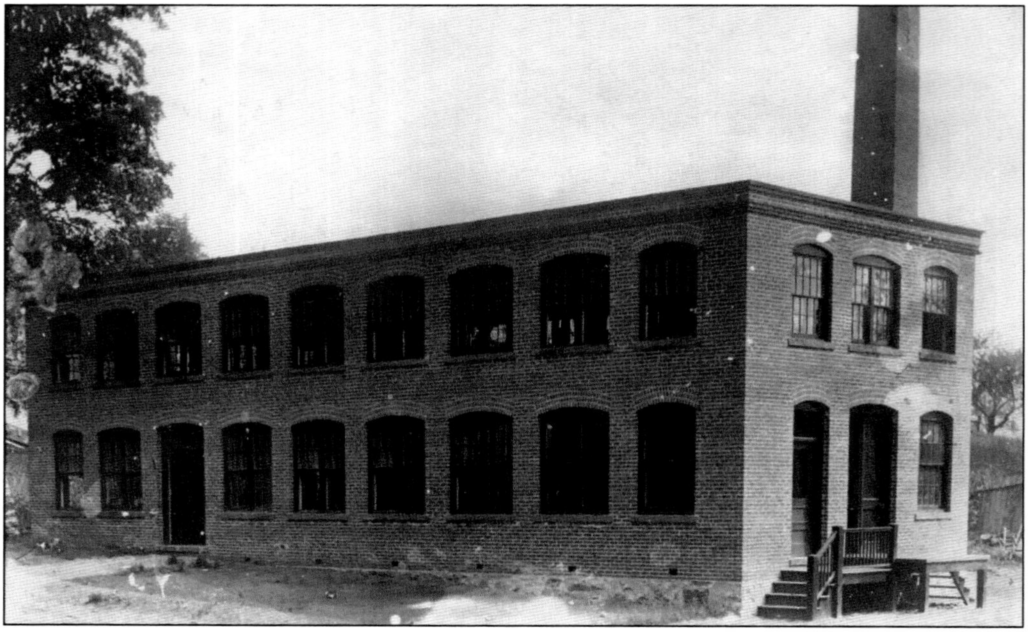

Albert Rockwell and his brother, Edward, had an idea for a new invention—to make a doorbell with a push button by using a clock mechanism instead of by hand or a battery. Hiram C. Thompson, a clockmaker in Bristol, offered to manufacture the bells for a commission. Albert and Edward left Florida and arrived in Bristol in 1888. The Rockwells rented from Thompson a 20-foot-square room to make their bell. With financial backing from Charles S. Treadway and Thompson providing them space and equipment, the Rockwells were able to start their company called the New Departure Bell Company. (Courtesy of American Clock and Watch Museum.)

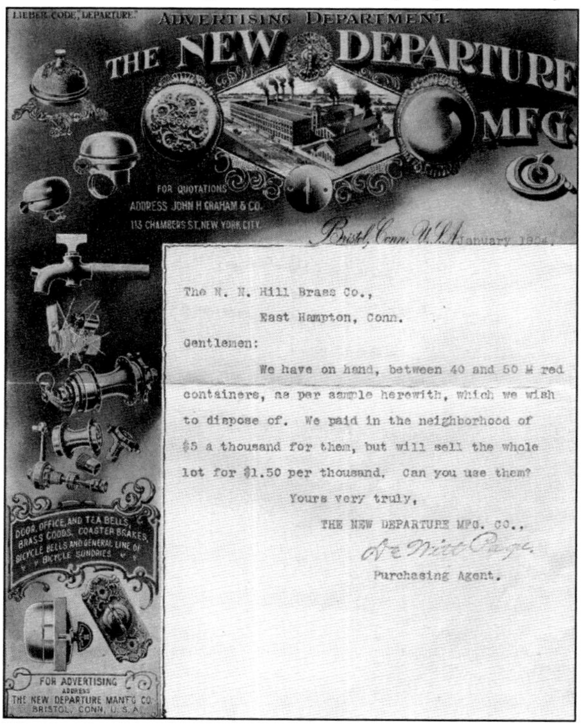

LIEBER CODE, "DEPARTURE."
ADVERTISING DEPARTMENT.
THE NEW DEPARTURE MFG. CO.
FOR QUOTATIONS ADDRESS JOHN H GRAHAM & CO. 113 CHAMBERS ST. NEW YORK CITY.
DOOR, OFFICE, AND TEA BELLS, BRASS GOODS, COASTER BRAKES, BICYCLE BELLS AND GENERAL LINE OF BICYCLE SUNDRIES.
FOR ADVERTISING ADDRESS THE NEW DEPARTURE MANF'G CO. BRISTOL, CONN. U. S. A.

Bristol, Conn. U.S.A. January 1904.

The N. N. Hill Brass Co.,
East Hampton, Conn.

Gentlemen:

We have on hand, between 40 and 50 M red containers, as per sample herewith, which we wish to dispose of. We paid in the neighborhood of $5 a thousand for them, but will sell the whole lot for $1.50 per thousand. Can you use them?

Yours very truly,
THE NEW DEPARTURE MFG. CO.,
DeWitt Page.
Purchasing Agent.

By 1890, New Departure Bell Company had moved into the old Jones Clock factory building and was making door, alarm, and bicycle bells. By 1892, fifteen thousand bicycle bells were being produced a day. Shown on New Departure stationery, dated 1894, are the products made by the company. The purchasing agent then was DeWitt Page who later would take over the company. (Courtesy of Tom Dickau.)

Harry Townsend invented the coaster brake for bicycles to replace the hand brake found on the front tire. New Departure received the patent, calling it the New Departure Coaster Brake. P. F. Corbin in 1898 made the product for New Departure until 1899. Albert Rockwell changed the design so his company could produce the coaster brake. With the new dynamo (electric generator) from the Bristol and Plainville Tramway Company, New Departure was able to manufacture over 5,000 brakes a day. This poster was one of many that advertised the New Departure Coaster Brake both here in the United States and in Europe. (Courtesy of Neil LeDuc.)

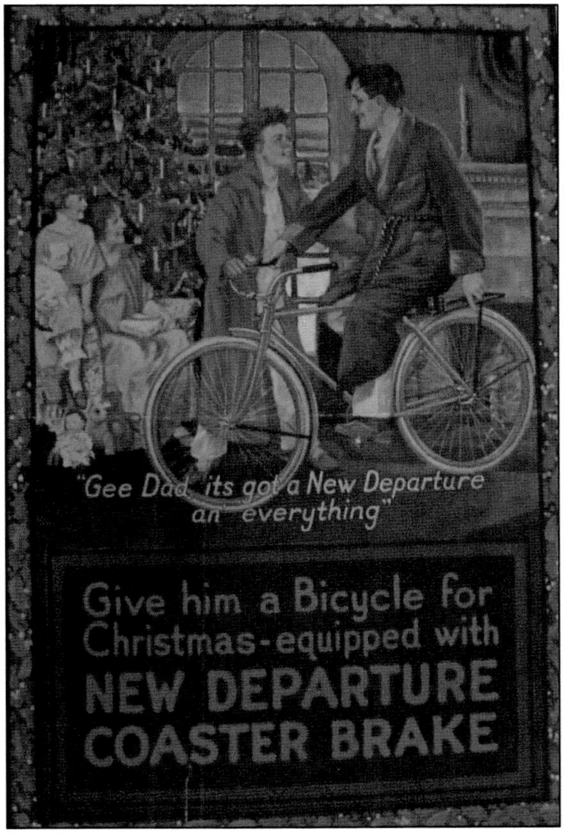

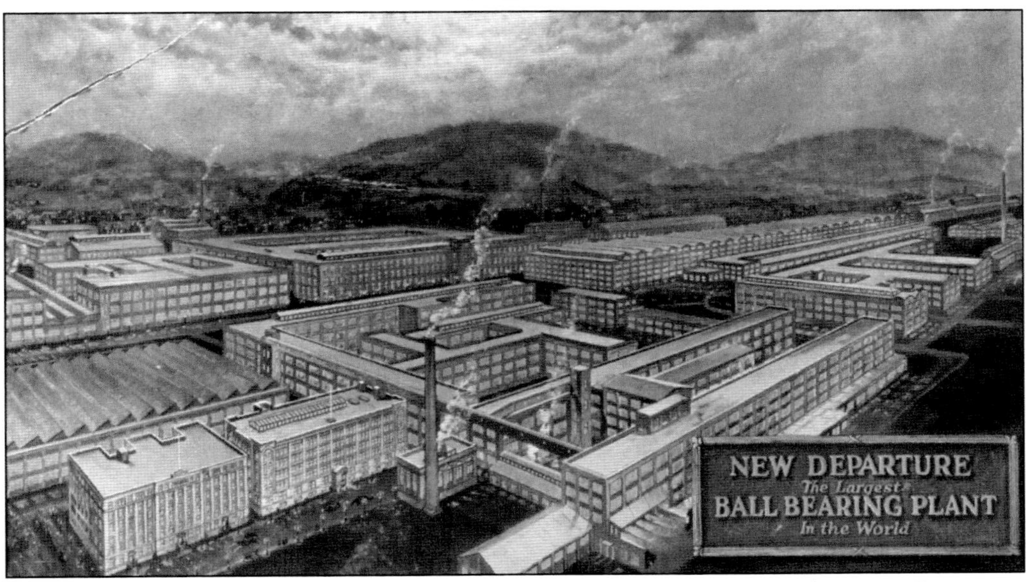

On June 17, 1901, the New Departure Bell Company's name was changed to New Departure Manufacturing. Albert Rockwell designed a new type of ball bearing to be used in automobiles. New Departure was able to compete with Europe to produce a design that both American and European cars could use. This 1927 picture shows how New Departure Manufacturing has expanded its operation with added buildings. (Courtesy of Tom Dickau.)

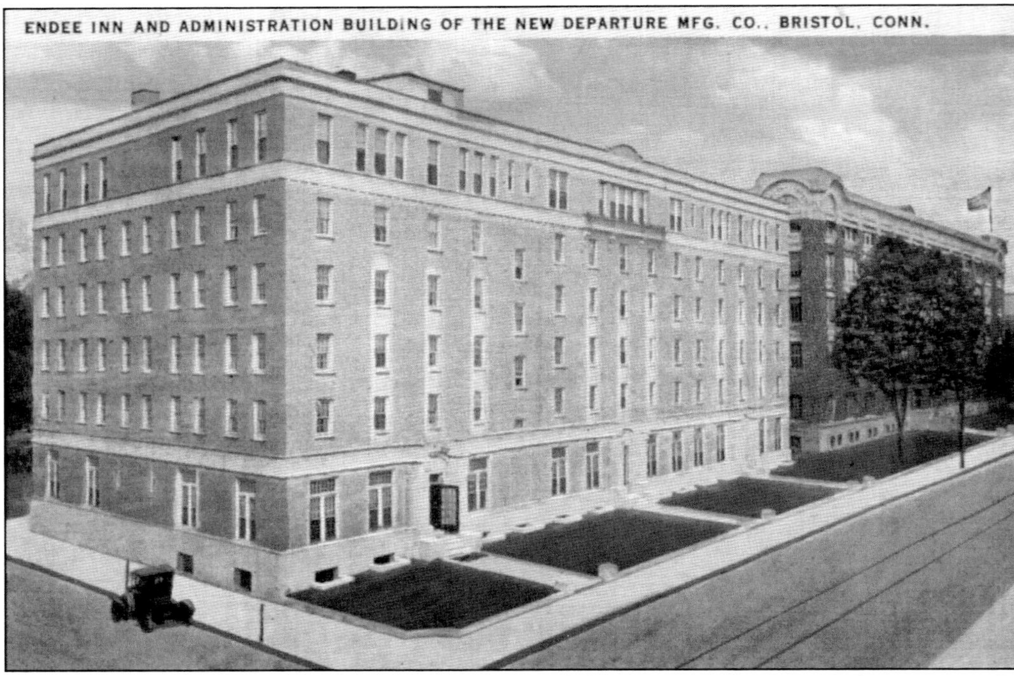

The Endee Inn and Administration Office were built by New Departure Manufacturing in the former location of F. W. Giddings and Jennings Market stood on North Main Street. Employees and their families of New Departure could stay at the inn. Today only the administration building stands owned by the Carpenter Realty Company.

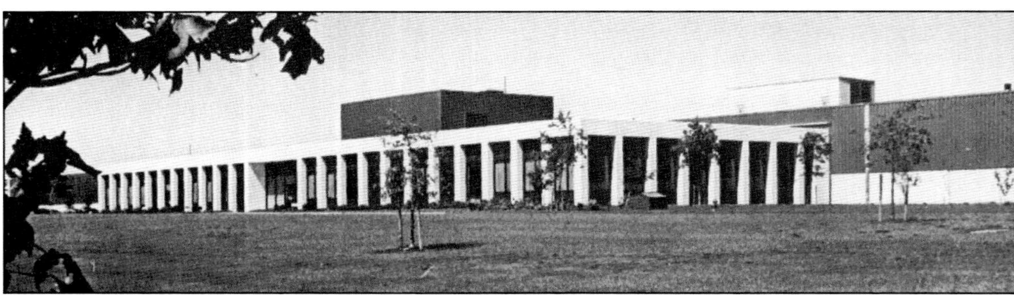

In 1916, New Departure Manufacturing Company was sold to the United Motors Corporation. In 1919, United Motors was reorganized to General Motors Corporation. In 1965, General Motors was planning to consolidate both New Departure Manufacturing in Bristol and Hyatt Bearings from Meriden into one plant. With the help of Bristol's mayor, city boards, and the Bristol Chamber of Commerce, the New Departure-Hyatt Bearings Division of the General Motors Corporation built a factory on 300 acres on Chippens Hill. It was the largest single-floor plant in New England.

Three

PROGRESS

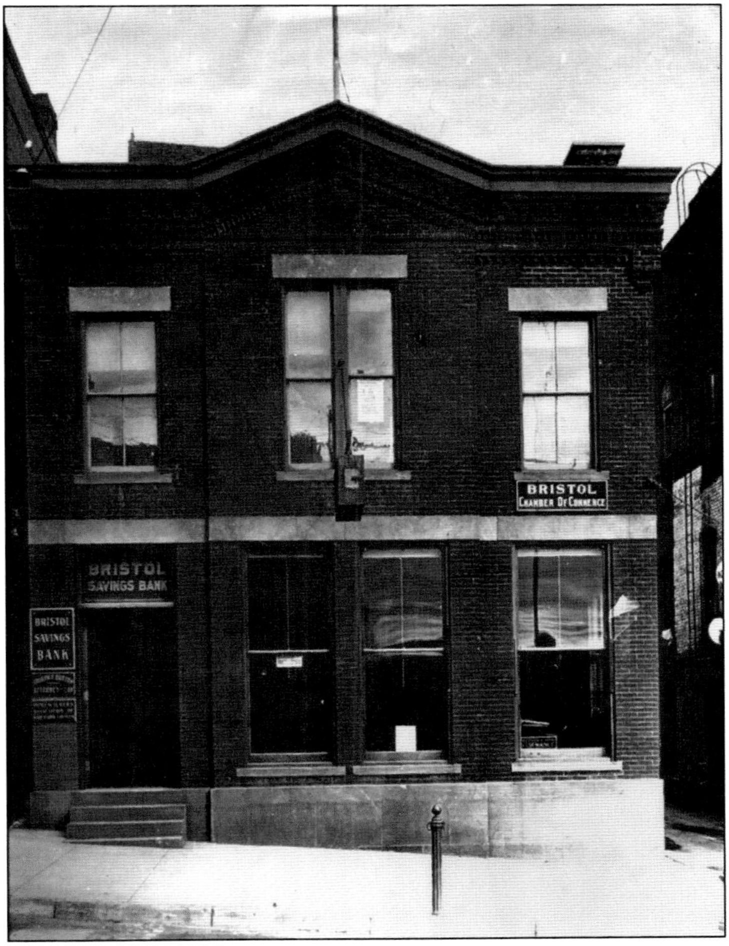

On July 4, 1870, Bristol Savings Bank opened for business in the Nott-Seymour building. Henry Seymour was the bank's first president, and Josiah T. Peck was treasurer. When the structure burned down, the bank constructed a building at 242 Main Street. The second floor was rented by the town for their offices until 1906. In 1915, the chamber of commerce rented space. Today the Shaffer Company has their business there. (Courtesy of Bristol Chamber of Commerce.)

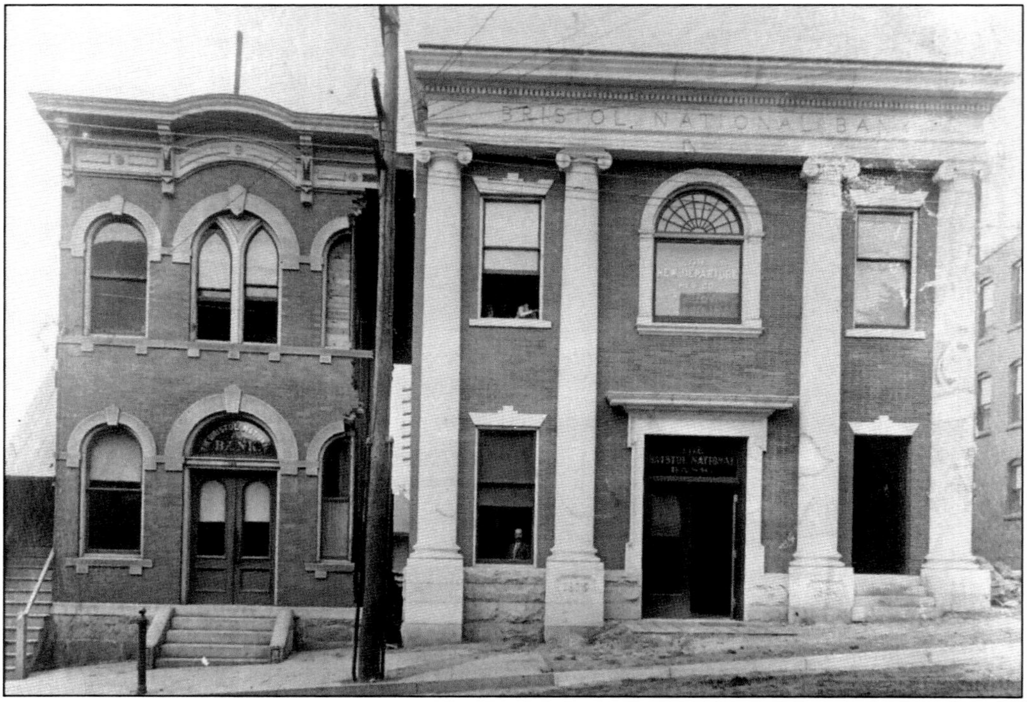

John Humphrey Sessions, Miles Lewis Peck, Nathan Birge, and Edward Ingraham invested money to establish a commercial bank. On May 5, 1875, Bristol National Bank opened for business. John H. Sessions became president, and Charles S. Treadway was cashier. In 1878, they moved into their building on Main Street and in 1904 built a larger bank next door. The American Trust Company was organized in 1919. In 1932, the bank consolidated to become Bristol Bank and Trust. (Courtesy of Gary Potter.)

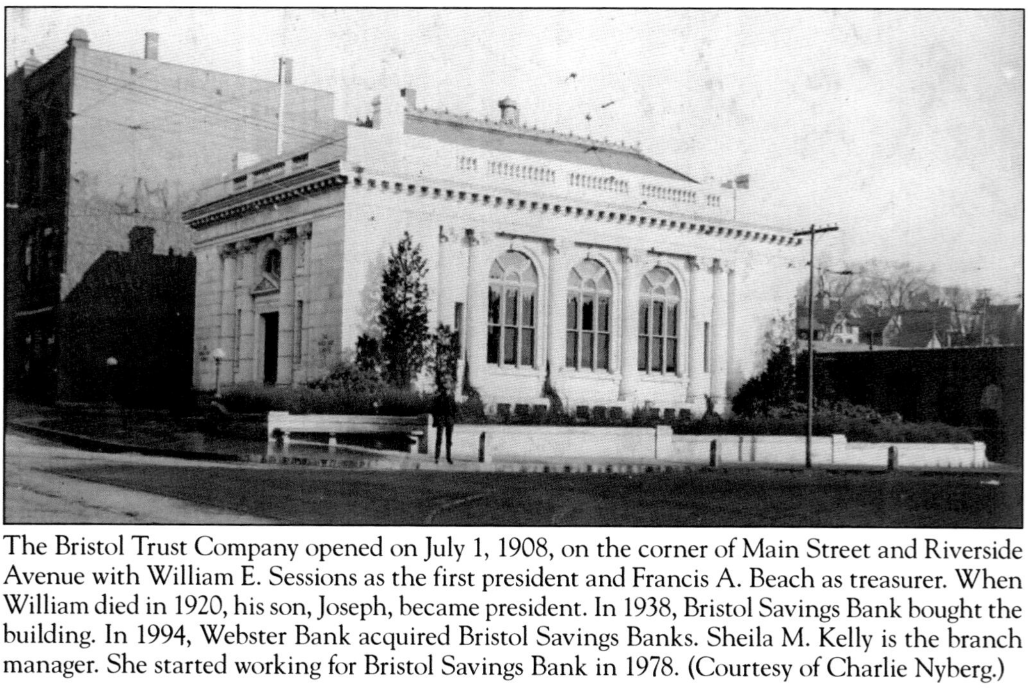

The Bristol Trust Company opened on July 1, 1908, on the corner of Main Street and Riverside Avenue with William E. Sessions as the first president and Francis A. Beach as treasurer. When William died in 1920, his son, Joseph, became president. In 1938, Bristol Savings Bank bought the building. In 1994, Webster Bank acquired Bristol Savings Banks. Sheila M. Kelly is the branch manager. She started working for Bristol Savings Bank in 1978. (Courtesy of Charlie Nyberg.)

The *Bristol Press* published its first weekly newspaper on March 9, 1871. Rev. Charles Hart Riggs was the editor and proprietor of the paper. The paper's first location was in a structure next to the Nott-Seymour building on Main Street. In 1875, the *Bristol Press* moved into its own building located in the rear of Gale Photography Studio. In 1891, it became the Bristol Publishing Company. This picture shows the downtown in 1875 from Riverside Avenue looking north on Main Street.

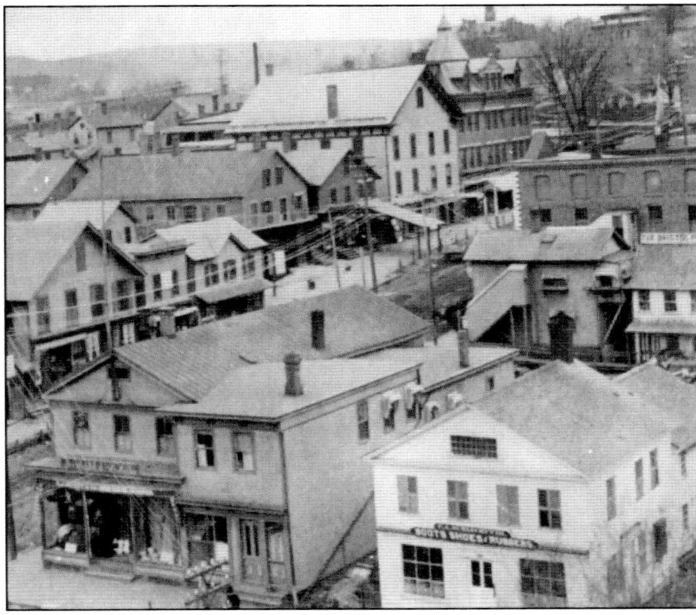

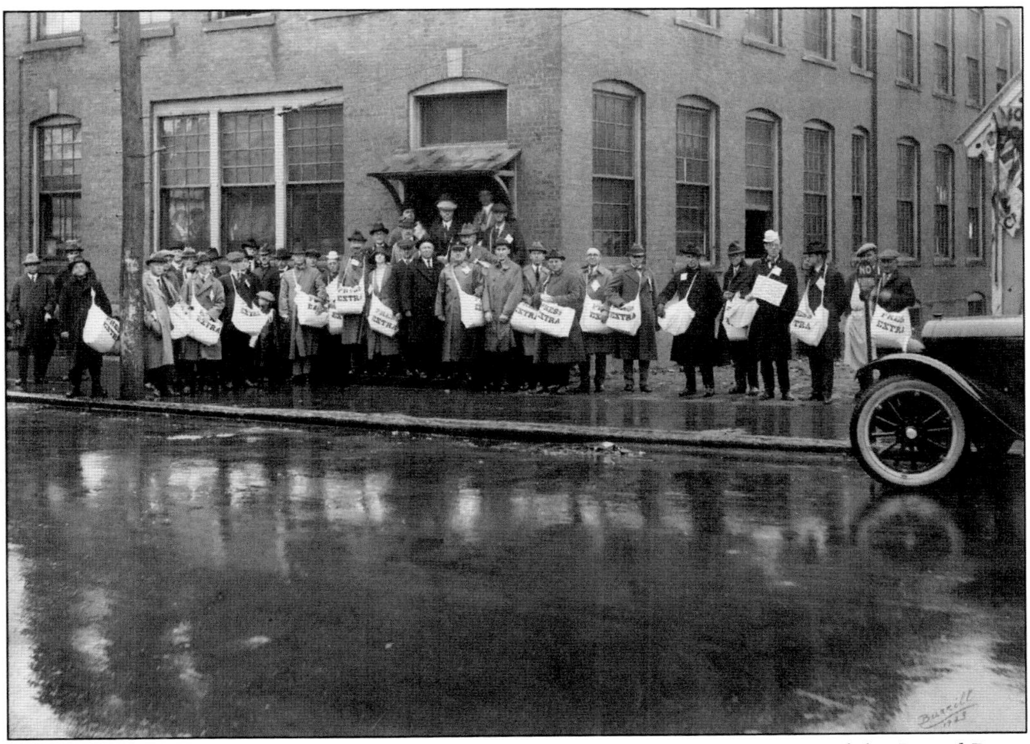

In 1902, Arthur S. Barnes, son of clockmaker Seth Barnes, became manager of the *Bristol Press*. Under his leadership on January 1, 1910, the paper became a semiweekly publication and on October 25, 1916, changed to a daily paper. The Barnes family owned the paper until 1985. The *Journal Register* bought the paper in 1994. Michael E. Schroeder purchased the paper in 2009. This picture shows the building when it was located at 99 Main Street with newspaper carriers standing out front. In fall 2009, the *Bristol Press* moved to its present location at 188 Main Street.

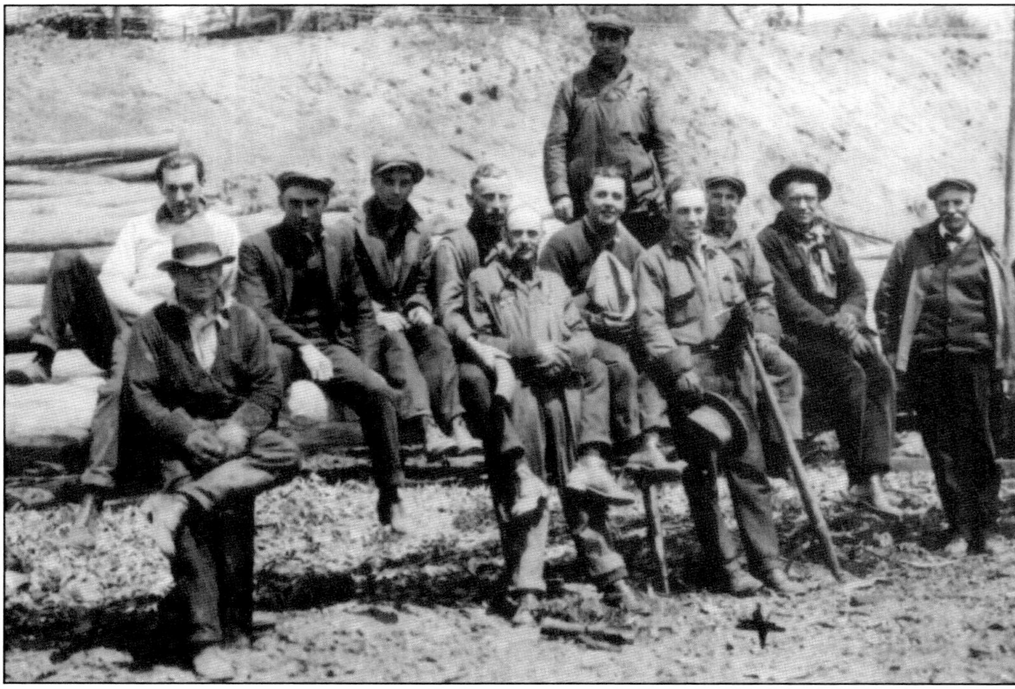

The Bristol Electric Light Company became a business in 1886. The first lighting was for streets before it expanded to homes and businesses. In 1897, the Bristol Electric Company combined with the Bristol and Plainville Tramway Company and in 1927 became part of the Connecticut Light and Power Company. This is a 1920s photograph of the Connecticut Light and Power crew. On the far right with the bow tie is foreman Samuel Dutcher and his son, Earl, is fourth from the right, holding his hat.

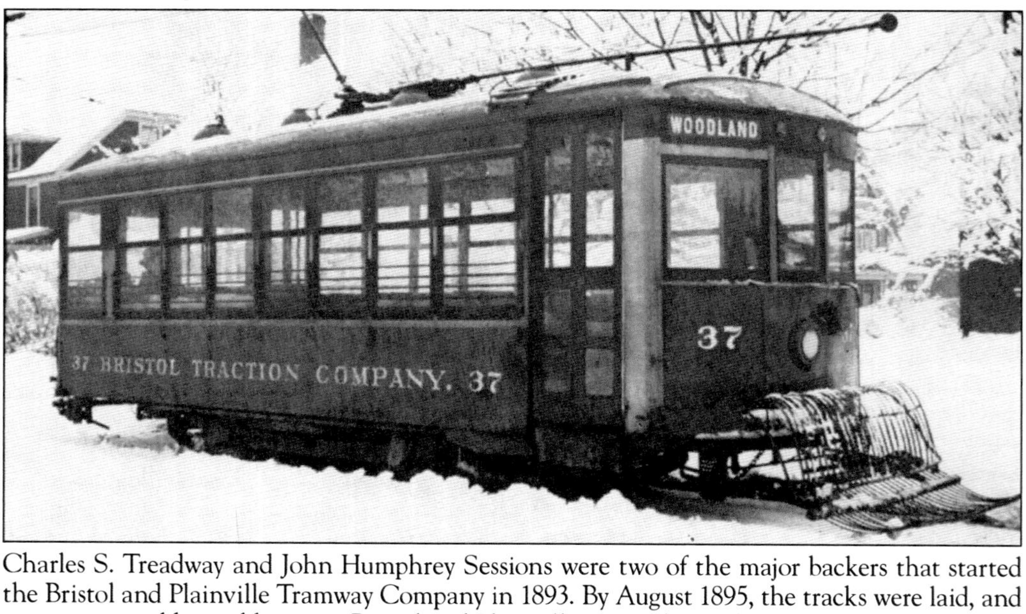

Charles S. Treadway and John Humphrey Sessions were two of the major backers that started the Bristol and Plainville Tramway Company in 1893. By August 1895, the tracks were laid, and passengers could travel between Bristol and Plainville. Later the trolley lines went to Terryville and to Lake Compounce. This Birney trolley car was used for Woodland Street. The trolleys ended in 1932. (Courtesy of Gary Potter.)

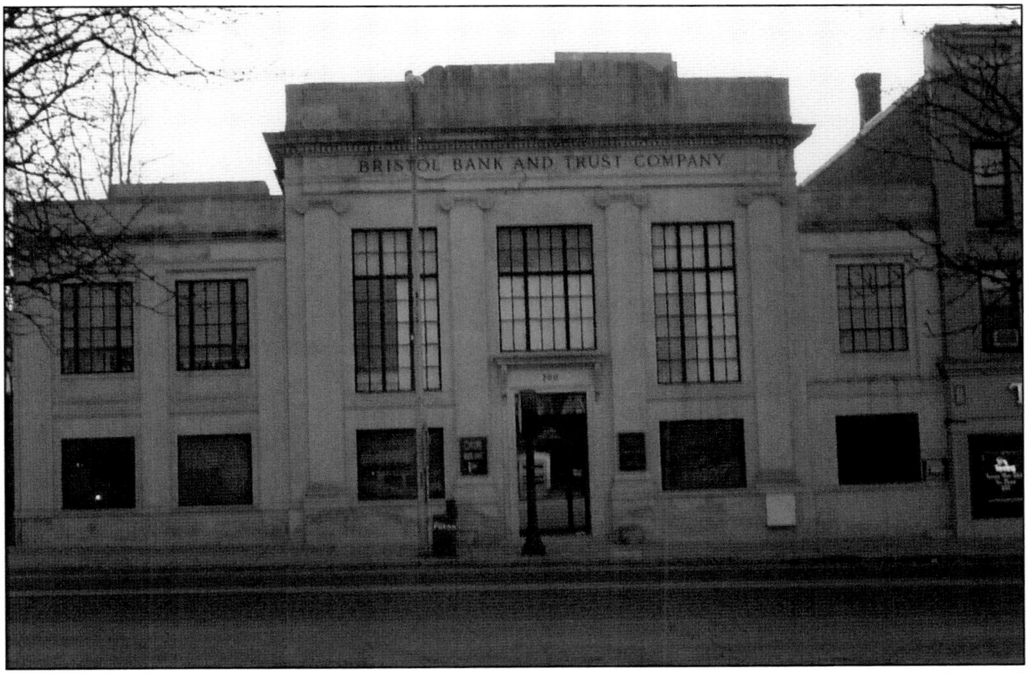

On February 7, 1889, Miles L. Peck, Walter Woodruff, and Carlton Ives started the Bristol Board of Trade. That same year the Merchant Association was formed. In 1901, the Bristol Businessmen's Association was formed. On April 8, 1915, these groups became the Bristol Chamber of Commerce. The chamber's mission was to promote civic, business, and social welfare. At the 120th annual meeting in 2009, Michael Nicastro, president of the chamber of commerce, introduced its new slogan "One Region One Voice" to promote businesses. The chamber is in the former Bristol Bank and Trust at 200 Main Street. (Courtesy of Bristol Chamber of Commerce.)

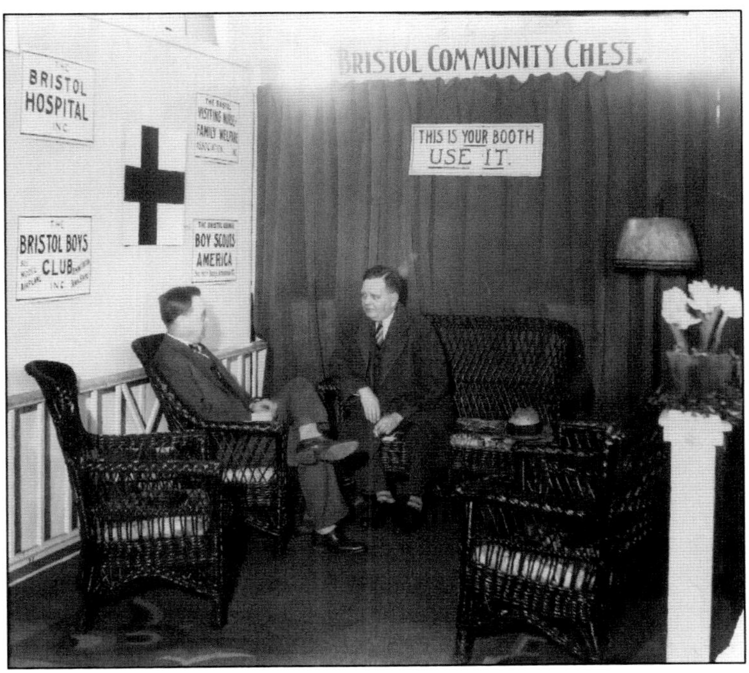

The Bristol chamber held a show to promote businesses called "The Progress Show" at the Bristol Armory from April 25 through 27, 1929. In this Bristol Community Chest booth, they were promoting the Bristol Hospital, Bristol Boys and Girls Club, Bristol Visiting Nurses, Family Welfare, and the Boy Scouts of America. Sitting on the left is Edward Ingraham and on the right Carl Carlson. (Courtesy of Bristol Chamber of Commerce.)

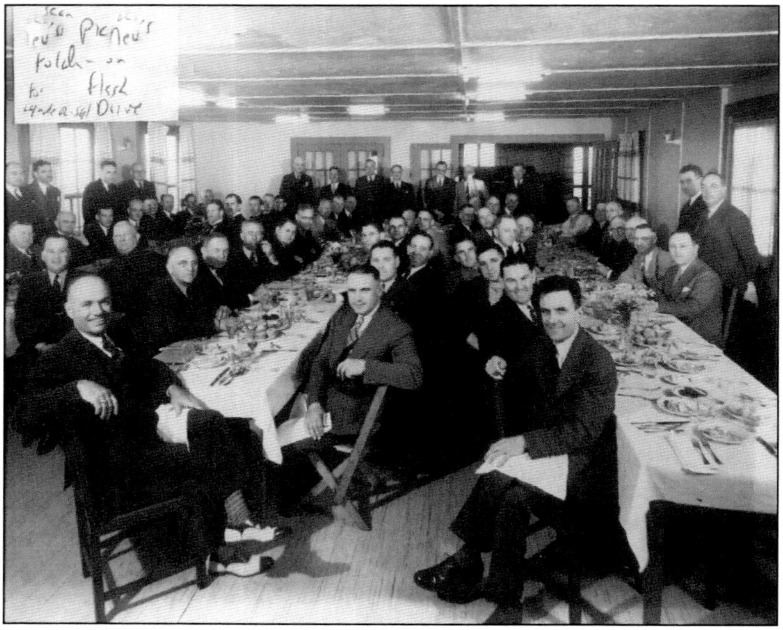

At a 1939 Bristol Chamber of Commerce banquet sitting in front on the left is Jeffrey J. Hammel, executive secretary of the Bristol chamber, and in front on the right is Ludger Valentine, a chamber member. (Courtesy of Bristol Chamber of Commerce.)

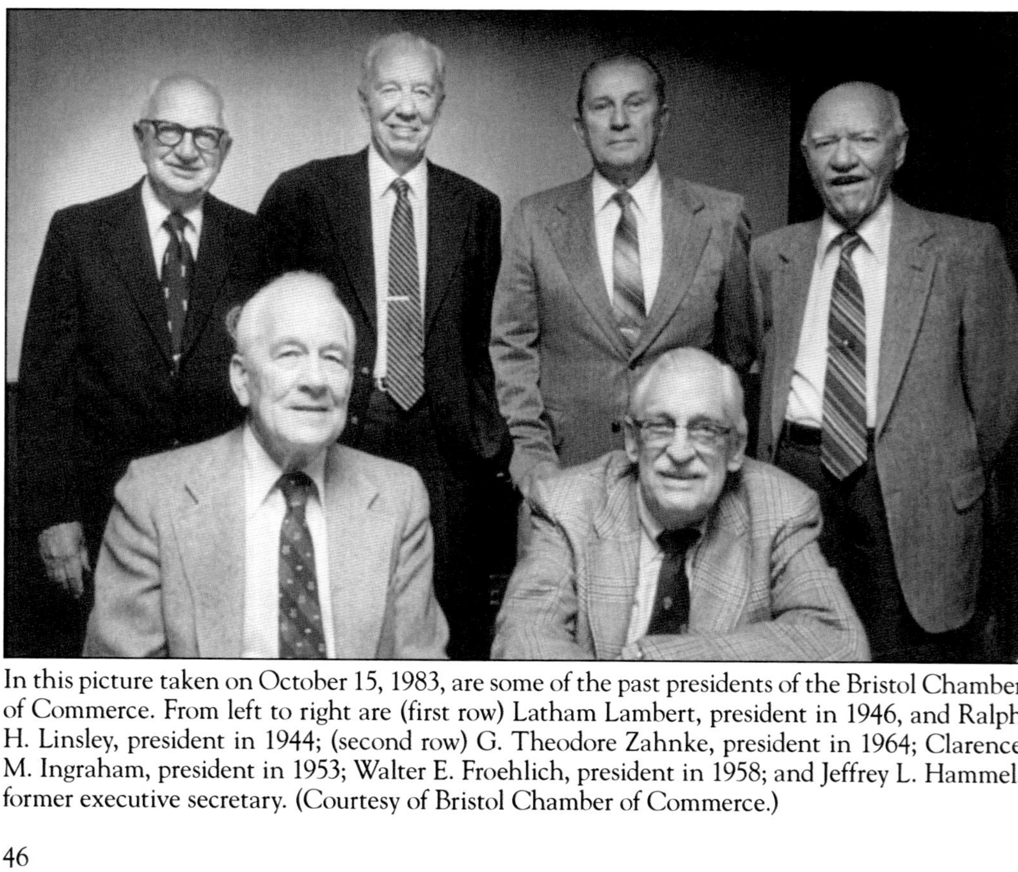

In this picture taken on October 15, 1983, are some of the past presidents of the Bristol Chamber of Commerce. From left to right are (first row) Latham Lambert, president in 1946, and Ralph H. Linsley, president in 1944; (second row) G. Theodore Zahnke, president in 1964; Clarence M. Ingraham, president in 1953; Walter E. Froehlich, president in 1958; and Jeffrey L. Hammel, former executive secretary. (Courtesy of Bristol Chamber of Commerce.)

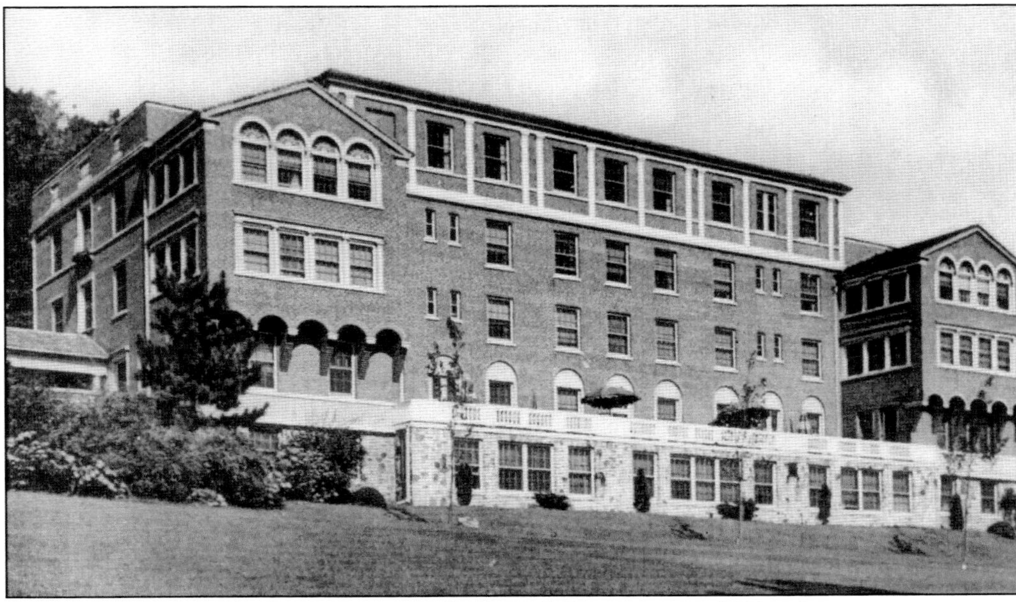

When the influenza broke out in 1918, the Bristol Congregational Church set up a temporary hospital. In 1919, the chamber of commerce organized a fund with Fuller Barnes. In 1920, Bristol Hospital, Inc., was formed. Judge Roger S. Newell donated land near Queen Street. A house on South and George Streets became a temporary hospital. In 1921, Fuller Barnes became president. On October 4, 1925, the hospital opened on Newell Road. Barnes served for 51 years as president. In 1948, the Barnes Medical building was added.

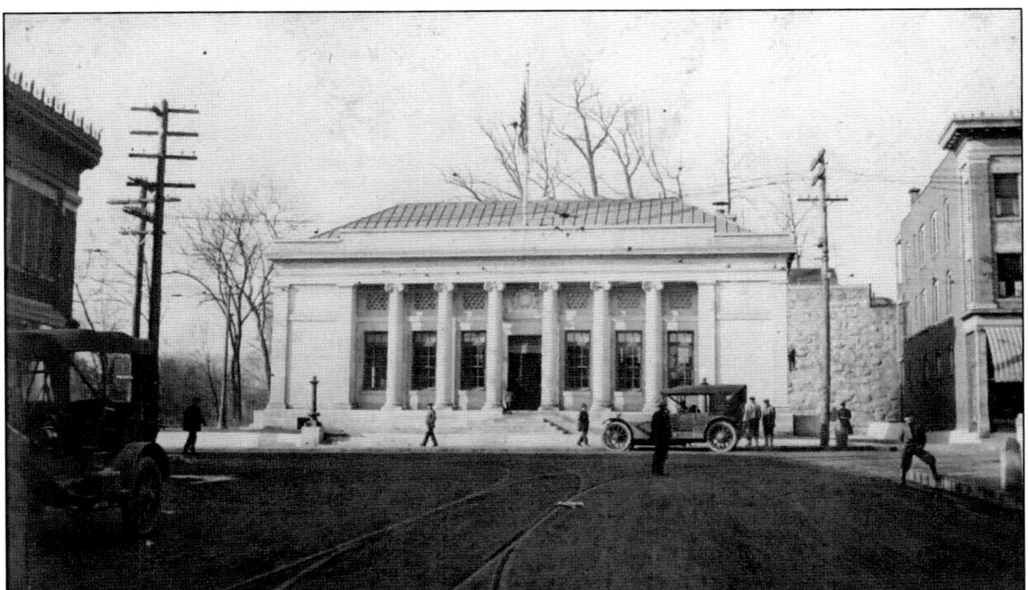

Prior to 1820, the mail came once a week to Bristol. The first postmaster was Lott Newell followed by George Mitchell. Until 1913, the U.S. government leased space in the Seymour Block on Main Street and then moved to Judd's Block on North Main Street. In 1913, the government purchased land on Main Street and erected the post office. This picture taken from Riverside Avenue shows the post office on Main Street in the 1920s. (Courtesy of Charlie Nyberg.)

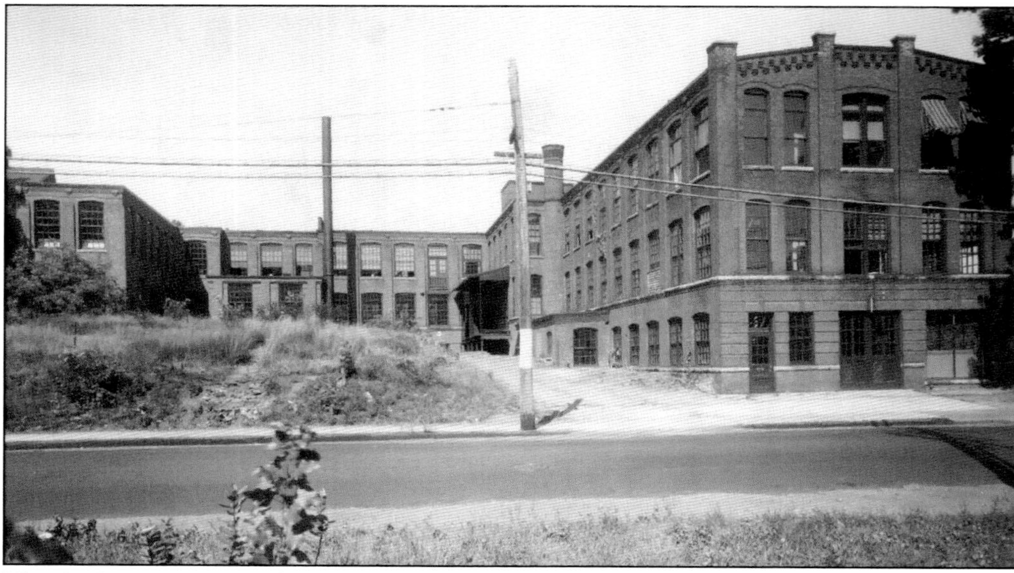

The C. G. Garrigus Machine Company building was constructed in 1908 and located at 165 Riverside Avenue. The business did machine work for other companies. One of the companies they did machine work for was Albert Rockwell's Bristol Engineering Company for his "Yellow Cabs." Wallace Barnes, a division of Associated Spring, took over the factory during World War I in 1917. A new administrative building was added so Barnes could make springs for machine guns. In 1932, Associated Spring closed the Garrigus Plant. They rented the building to the Harry I. Bartholomew Company.

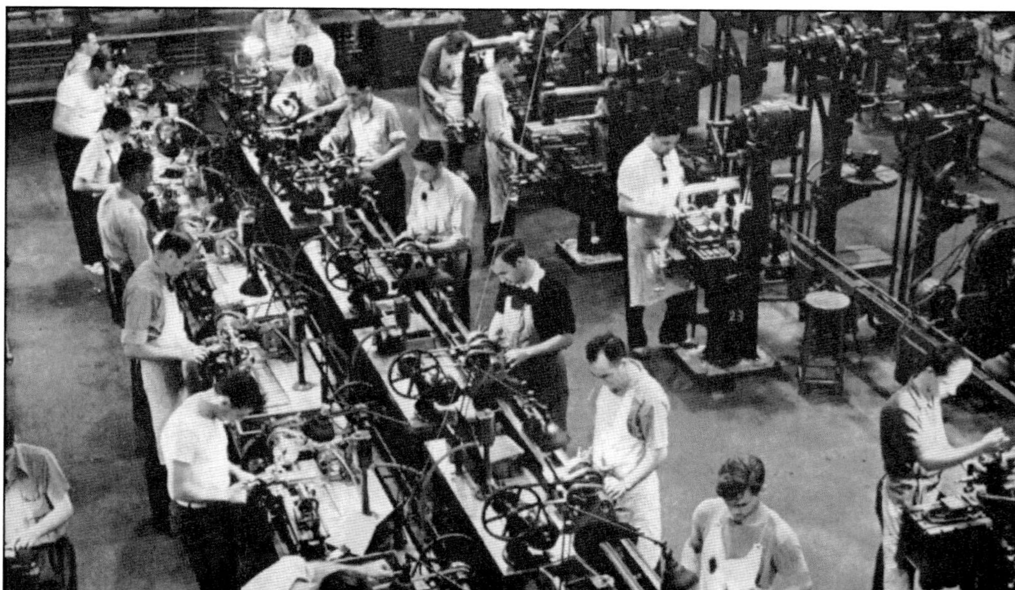

In 1936, the building was donated to the city to be used as a technical department for the high school. Both New Departure Manufacturing and E. Ingraham Company donated machinery and tools. It became Bristol Technical High School. In 1960, Stanley Bitel, owner of Rowley Spring Company, purchased the building for his business. Rowley Spring stayed there until 1994 when they moved to the former Bussman Building on Red Stone Hill Road.

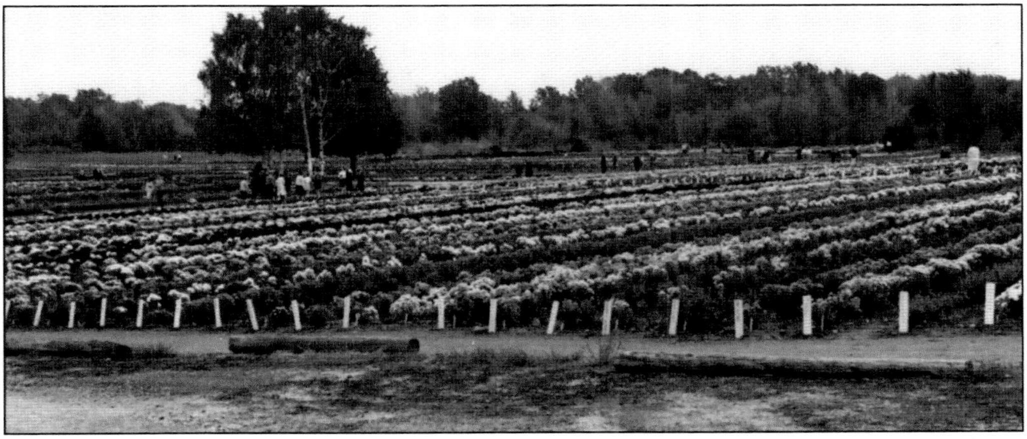

Paul Hubbard started a floral shop on North Main Street in 1916 and owned property on Pinehurst Road. Alex Cummings Jr., an authority on the propagation, joined Hubbard in 1920. Cumming began crossing mums. In 1925, the Bristol Nurseries hired Arthur Bird. In 1948, Paul Hubbard sold his interest in the business to Arthur Bird. Jerry Heresko began working at Bristol Nurseries in 1965. He worked with Rod Cumming, son of Alex, learning to propagate mums. The Chrysanthemum Festival started as a combined effort of the Bristol Nursery and the Bristol Chamber of Commerce. In 1985, Jerry Heresko purchased some of the original Bristol Nursery and renamed it Bristol Mums, Inc. (Courtesy of Jerry Heresko.)

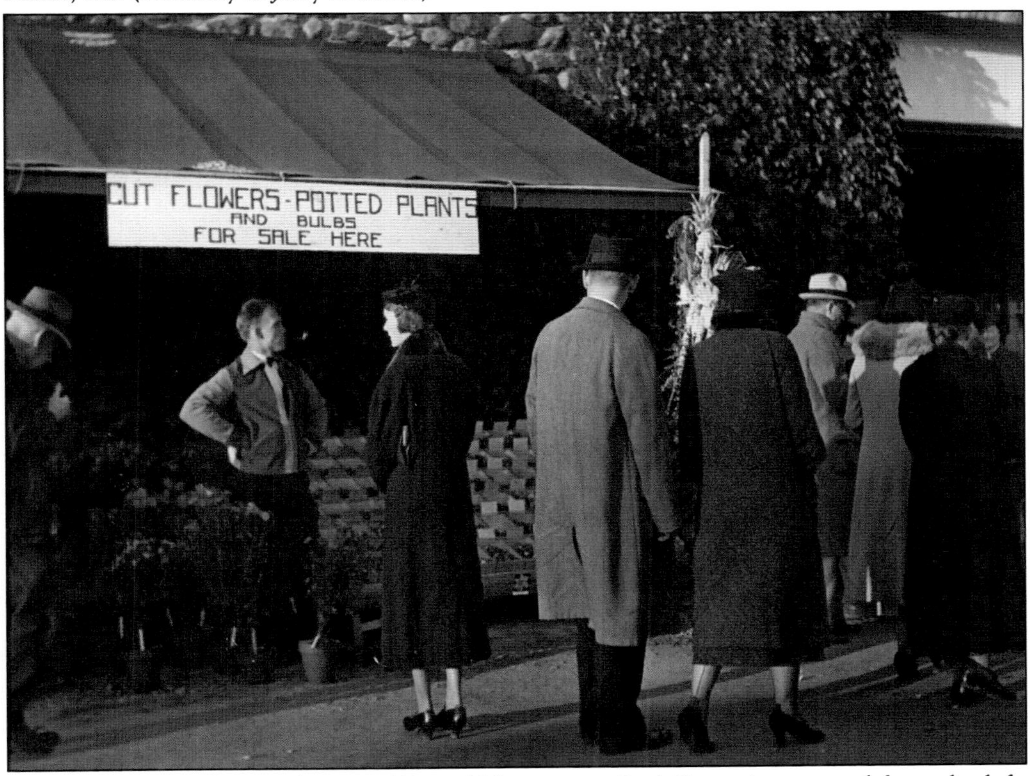

Standing outside the retail store of Bristol Nurseries is Rod Cumming, second from the left. He continued the propagation of mums as his father, Alex, had. Through Paul Hubbard, Alex Cumming, and the Bird family, they made the chrysanthemum famous for Bristol so much so that Bristol adopted the name "Bristol, the Mum City." (Courtesy of Jerry Heresko.)

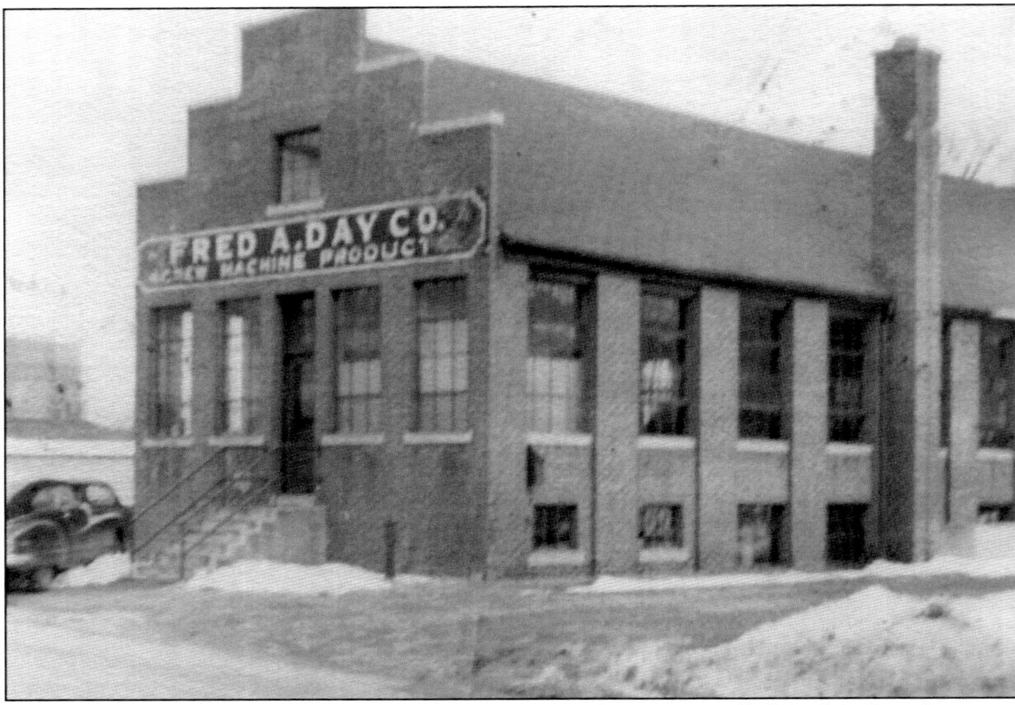

In 1926, Frederick A. Day built a factory on 300 Riverside Avenue called Fred A. Day Company. Starting with 11 employees, the company made screw-machine products. During World War II, they manufactured gun and instruments parts for the navy and air force. When Fred died in 1936, the business was continued by his children. Today the business, under new owners, continues to make precision-machined products.

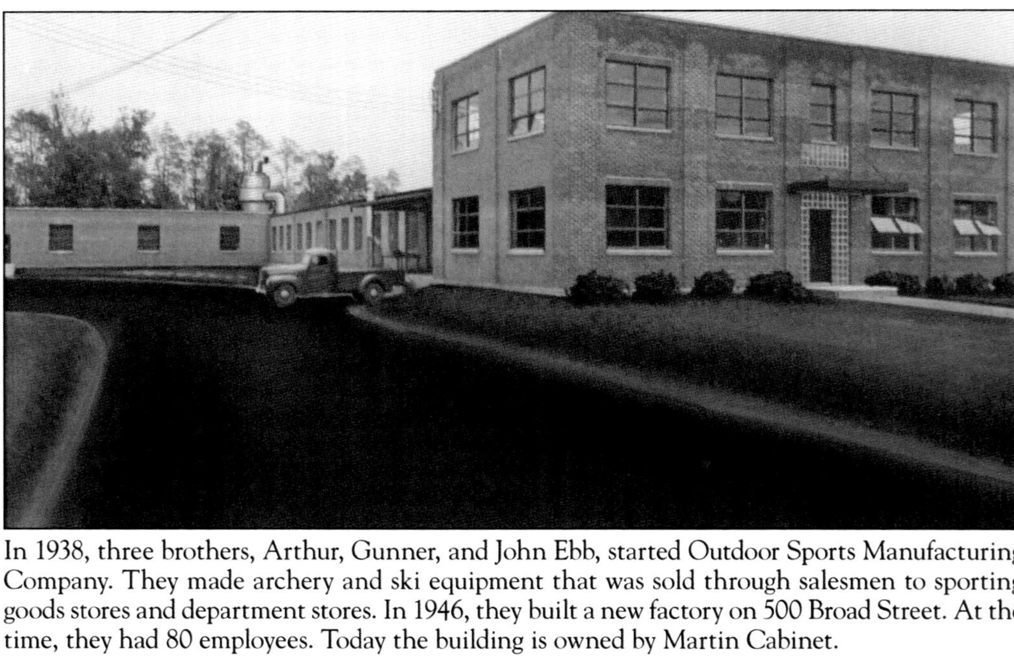

In 1938, three brothers, Arthur, Gunner, and John Ebb, started Outdoor Sports Manufacturing Company. They made archery and ski equipment that was sold through salesmen to sporting goods stores and department stores. In 1946, they built a new factory on 500 Broad Street. At the time, they had 80 employees. Today the building is owned by Martin Cabinet.

The old Bristol Airport located on Middle Street was know as Stephenson Field after Arthur B. Stephenson, an early aviator from Bristol who died in a plane crash in 1918. In 1925, the Bristol chamber organized Bristol's first air show to help convince the City of Bristol to own the airport. The 84 acres was purchased by Arthur S. Barnes, Fuller F. Barnes, and Morton Treadway, who offered this property to the city at cost. In October 1929, the voters decided against spending $45,000 for the city to buy it. This 1947 picture shows the administration building on the left and one of the hangers.

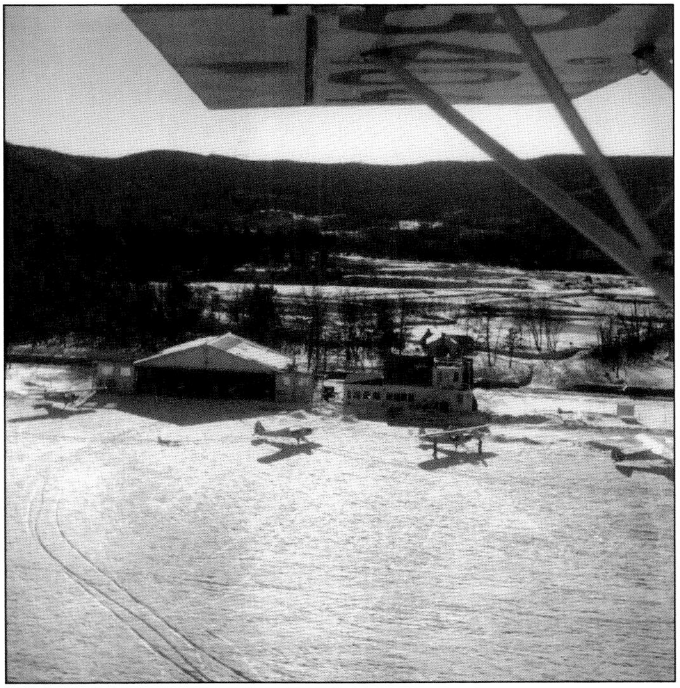

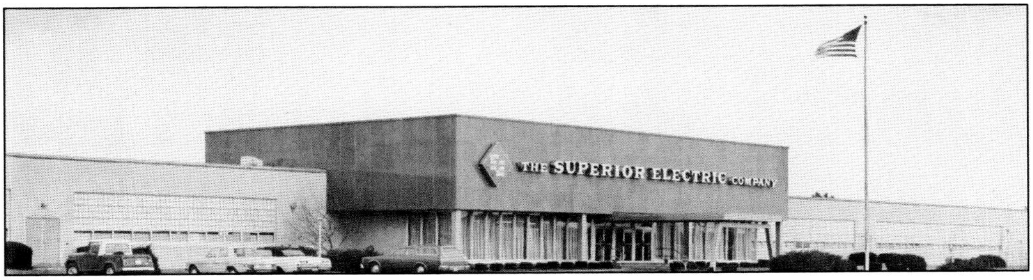

Superior Electric Company was started in 1938 by Alfred B. Nelson and Thor Hannon. They made a variable transformer to control electrical energy. In 1939, they got their first order for Powerstat variable voltage transformer for the Campbell X-ray Company of Boston. In 1942, the company bought the former Blakeslee Novelty Company building on Laurel Street. During World War II, they were making components for the government's submarines and aircraft radars. In 1953, the company bought the former Bristol Airport and built a 325,000-square-foot structure on Middle Street. The company moved in 1961 with 700 employees. In 1989, Superior Electric was sold to Dana Corporation of Ohio.

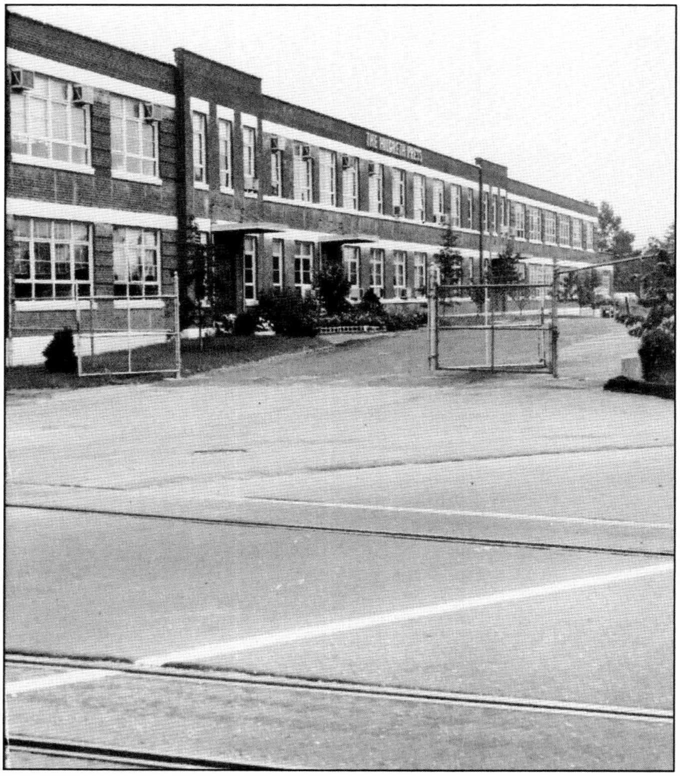

This building was originally constructed by the Springfield Ordinance District called the East Bristol Ordinance Facility. When World War II started, New Departure Manufacturing needed a larger location to manufacture the tank bearings and used this building until 1945. The building was sold in 1949 to Hildreth Press from Brattleboro, Vermont, a publisher of trade magazines. In 1950, there were 300 employees and over 30 publications being printed. In 1968, Domonel Press from Meriden became part of Hildreth Press, Inc. The building is now owned by R. G. D. Technologies, Inc. (Courtesy of Bristol Historical Society.)

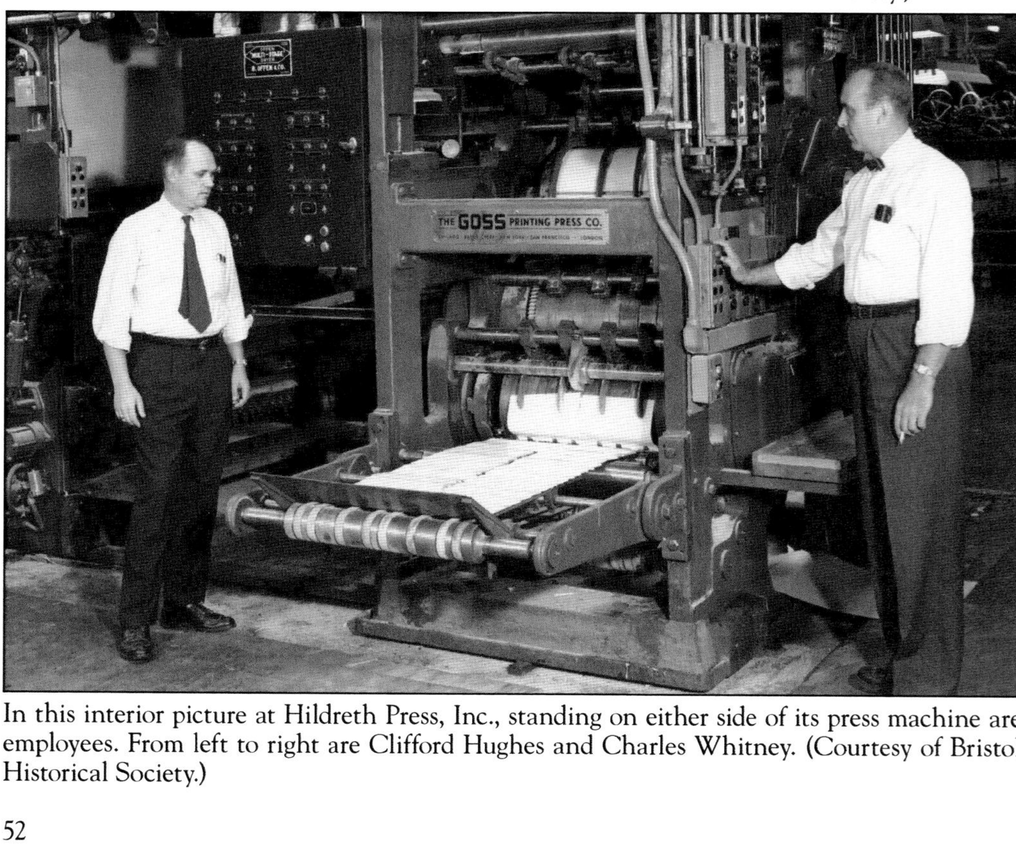

In this interior picture at Hildreth Press, Inc., standing on either side of its press machine are employees. From left to right are Clifford Hughes and Charles Whitney. (Courtesy of Bristol Historical Society.)

Four

FAMILY BUSINESSES

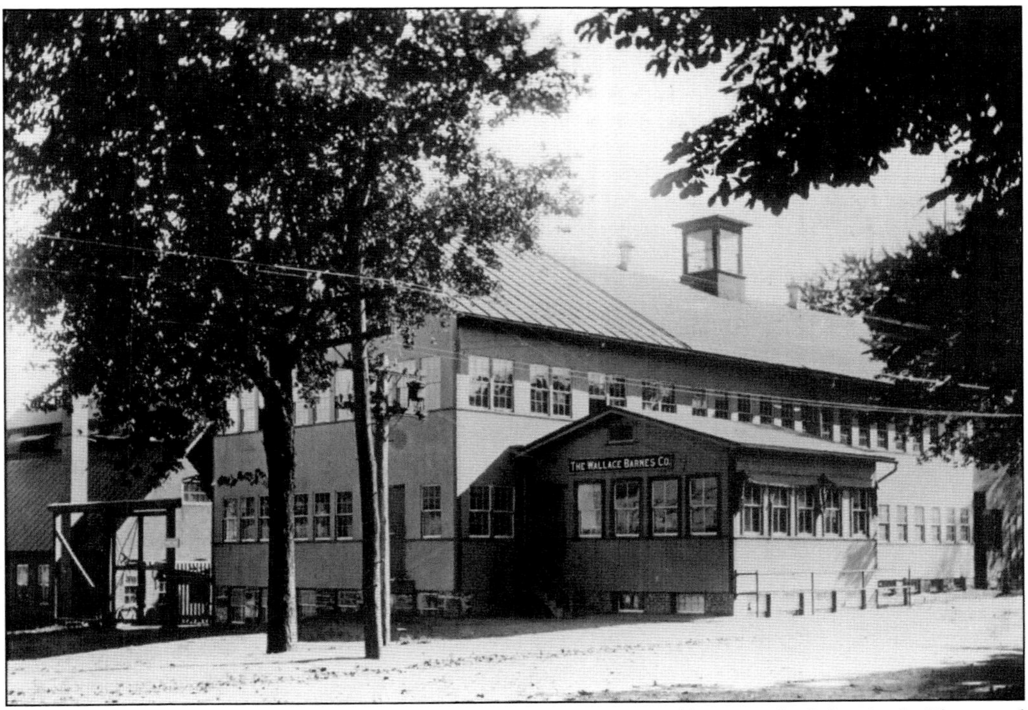

Wallace Barnes was born on December 25, 1827. In 1856, Wallace worked for A. S. Platt and Company, makers of clocks, clock springs, and wire hoops. Barnes began manufacturing clock springs in 1857. On January 11, 1858, Wallace and E. L. Dunbar Spring Company formed the Dunbar and Barnes Company. Demand for hoopskirts took over springs. To accommodate the demand, they constructed a new building, calling it "Crinoline Hall" in 1860. In 1861, the partnership ended between Dunbar and Barnes. Wallace and his wife, Eliza Fuller Barnes, had five children. Their oldest son, Carlyle, took over the business when his father died in 1893.

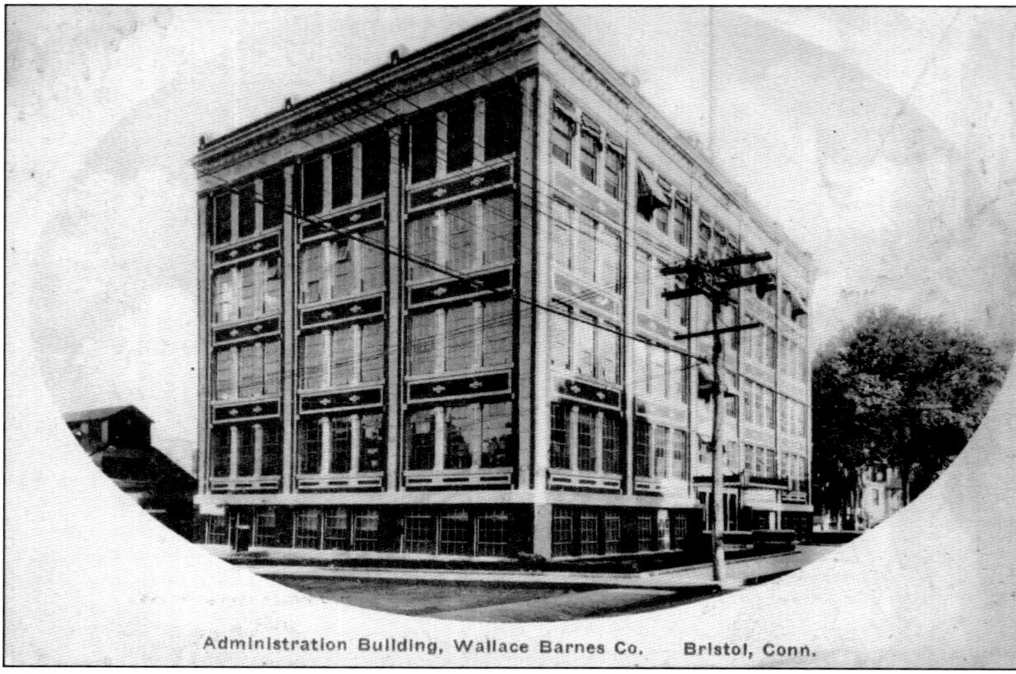

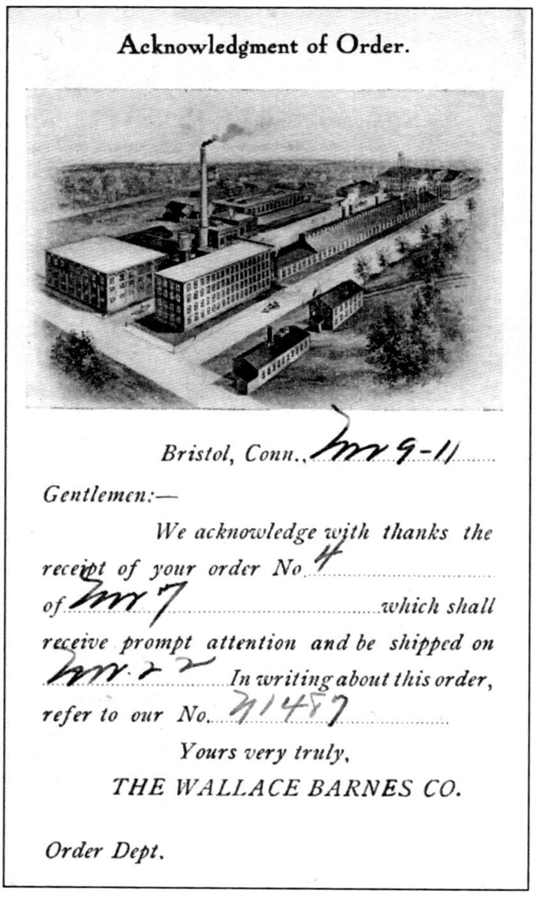

Acknowledgment of Order.

Bristol, Conn., Nov 9-11

Gentlemen:—

We acknowledge with thanks the receipt of your order No 4 of Nov 7 which shall receive prompt attention and be shipped on Nov 22 In writing about this order, refer to our No. 71457

Yours very truly,

THE WALLACE BARNES CO.

Order Dept.

When Carlyle Fuller Barnes took over Wallace Barnes Company in 1893, he incorporated the business. Through the bicycle era, the company made trouser guards and springs for automobiles along with springs for other products. In 1923, the name was changed to Associated Spring Corporation. Carlyle and his wife had two sons, Fuller Forbes and Harry C. Barnes. When Carlyle died in 1926, his son, Fuller, took over the company. This picture shows the Wallace Barnes Administration Building. This building still stands at 10 Main Street and is being used by Webster Bank. (Courtesy of Gary Potter.)

A view of the Wallace Barnes Company is shown in this acknowledgement order sent on November 9, 1911, to New York Electric Tool Company from West Newton, Massachusetts. (Courtesy of Gary Potter.)

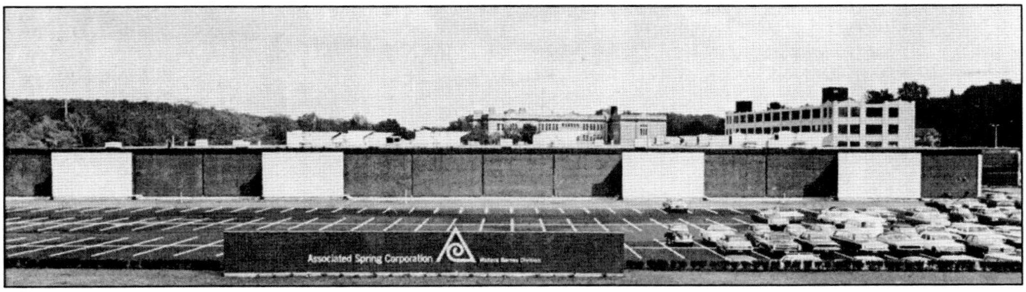

Memorial Boulevard was prepared for developing once buildings were torn down during the 1960s. In 1970, Associated Spring Corporation built a new 221,000-square-foot manufacturing plant for the Wallace Barnes Division on Memorial Boulevard. The City of Bristol provided $500,000 worth of utilities and other improvements as part of the redevelopment program.

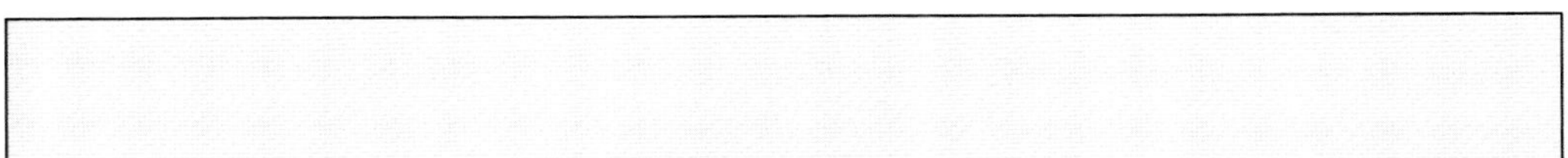
In 1976, Associated Spring's officers changed the company's name to Barnes Group. In April 2007, Barnes Group renamed its Associated Springs business to Barnes Industrial. The company has a presence in over 65 locations in the United States and internationally. This building is the Barnes Group International Headquarters building constructed in 1979 and is located on Main Street.

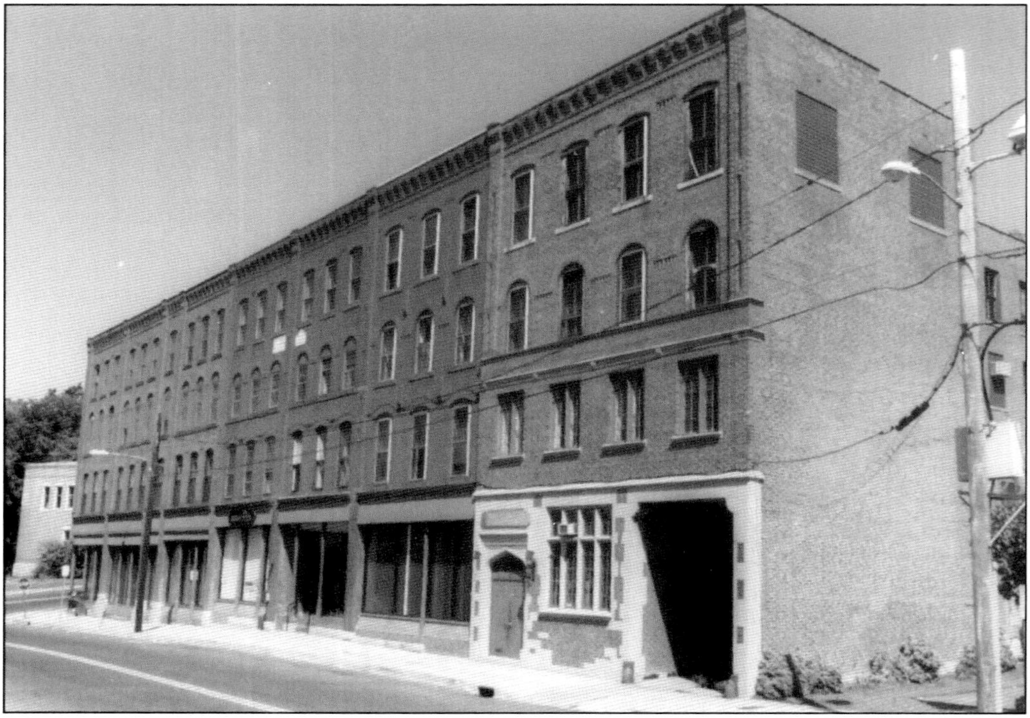

Christian Funck was born in Germany in 1810. In 1846, Christian and his family came to the United States through New York. Christian went to work at E. Ingraham Company. In 1865, Christian started a furniture business with his son, Augustus, at Doolittle's corner called C. Funck and Son. Besides making furniture, coffins were made to order. In 1889, the new Funck Block was built on Prospect Street. Augustus became president when his father died in 1888. In this picture taken on Prospect Street, C. Funck Company used the first floor of the building to sell furniture and carpet and for their undertaking business. (Courtesy of Funk Funeral Home.)

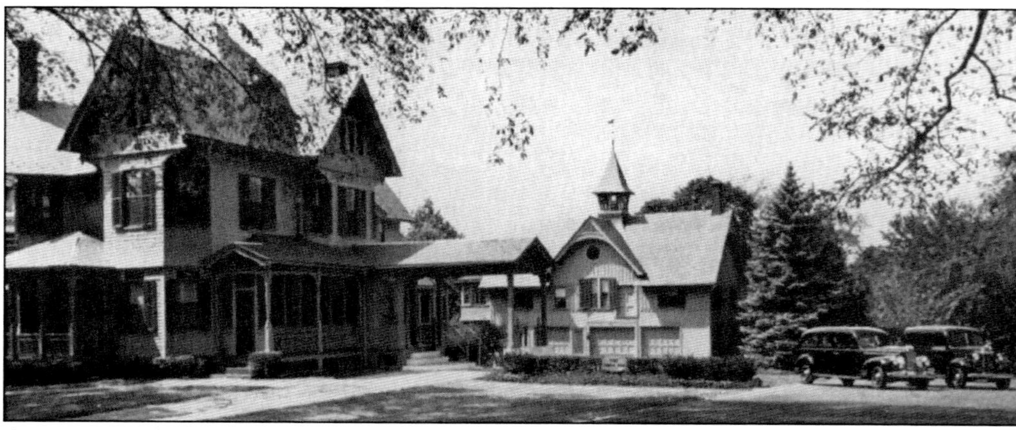

Augustus Funk's sons, George, Emil, and Louis, continued making furniture and running the undertaking business. In 1940, Emil Funk moved the funeral business to 35 Bellevue Avenue in the original George W. Mitchell house. Ronald F. Duhaime and his wife, Emilie, purchased the Funk Funeral Home business in 1980 from Augustus G. Funk. Ron and Emilie's son, Christopher, joined his parents business in 1985. In 1990, the Duhaimes purchased the Duhaime Funeral Home on 250 West Street that was started by Ron's parents, Edgar and Dorothy Duhaime, in 1950. (Courtesy of Funk Funeral Home.)

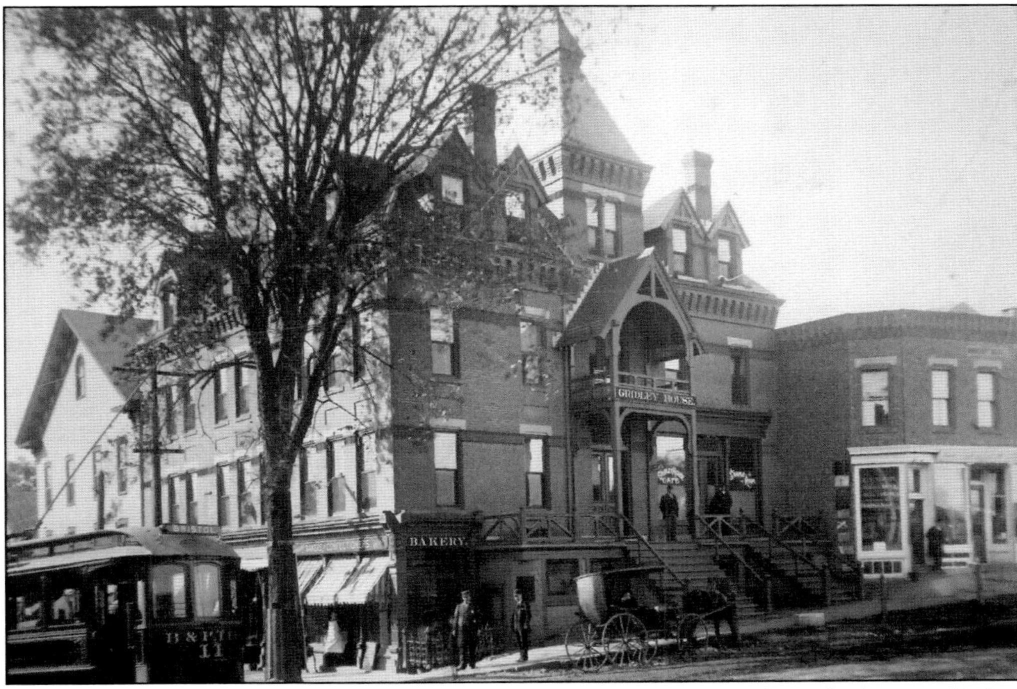

Carlos V., son of Carlos L. Mason, was born in Unionville in 1863. Carlos L. had an established insurance business in Unionville. In 1882, Carlos V. came to Bristol and opened up another office in the first Muzzy's Department Store. On October 25, 1883, C. L. Mason and Son advertised in the *Bristol Press* as a fire, life, and insurance agency. In the 1890s, the business moved to North Main Street next to the Gridley House. Carlos V. changed the name to C. V. Mason and Company. Carlos V. married Alice M. Dunbar and had three children: Florence, Anna, and Carlos H. Carlos V. died in 1937, and his son, Carlos H., took over his father's business. This picture taken in 1895 shows that C. V. Mason Real Estate and Insurance Company is next to the Gridley House on the right.

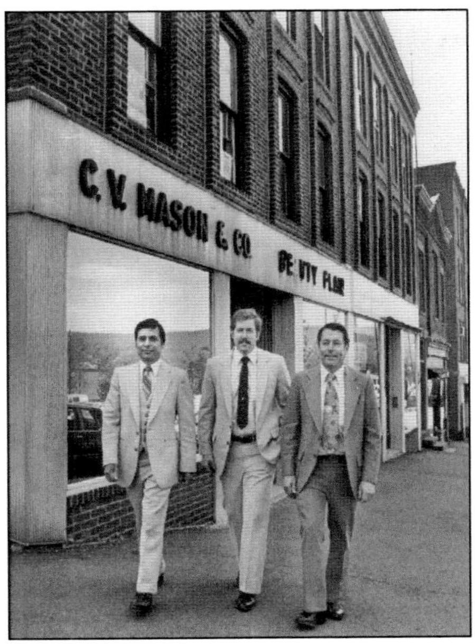

In this 1983 picture taken outside of the C. V. Mason, Inc., office at their present location at 254 Main Street were the officers of the company. From the left to right are Vice Pres. Robert Van Gorder; secretary Christopher Wilson, son-in-law of Carl E. Mason; and Pres. Carl E. Mason. Gerry Letizia joined the agency in 1979. In 1994, Chris Wilson became president, and Gerry became secretary in 1998. Today Chris is president and general manager, Gerry is the personal lines manager, and Tim Wilson, son of Chris, is the marketing director as they start their 127th year in business in Bristol.

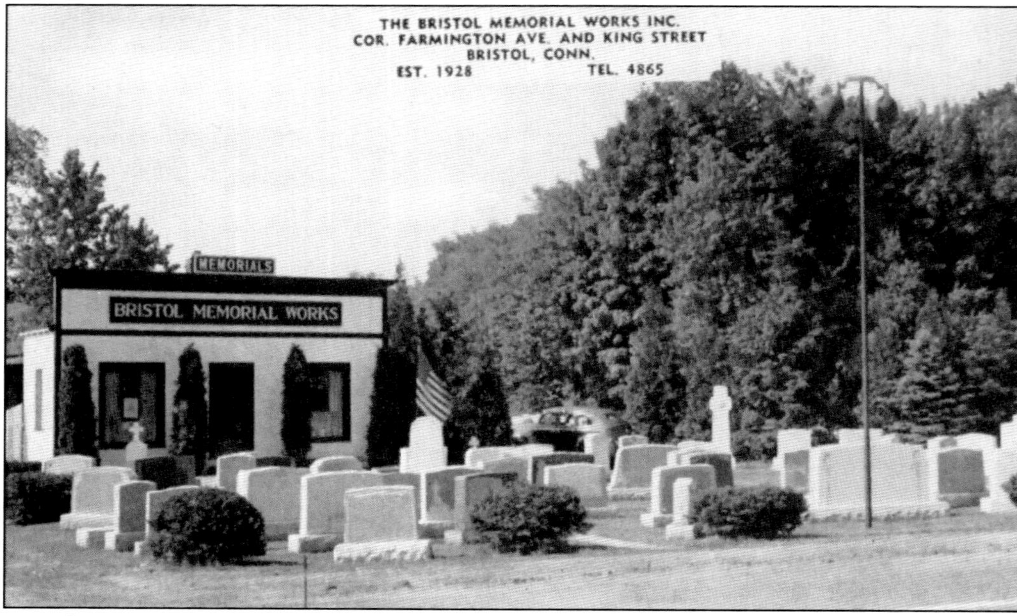

Bristol Memorial Works, located at 508 Farmington Avenue, was established in 1928 by Ross O. Reed, Louis Dainty, and LeRoy W. Greeno and incorporated in 1930. In 1937, Milton W. Slade started working as a sales representative. The business had 14 employees, including craftsmen that did the design work on the monuments. In 1971, Milton W. Slade was president and treasurer, Helen L. Dainty was vice president, and Milton's son, M. Williams Slade, was secretary. Today the business is owned by Barry W. Slade, grandson of Milton, and located on 729 King Street. This picture at 508 Farmington Avenue shows monuments in front of their building.

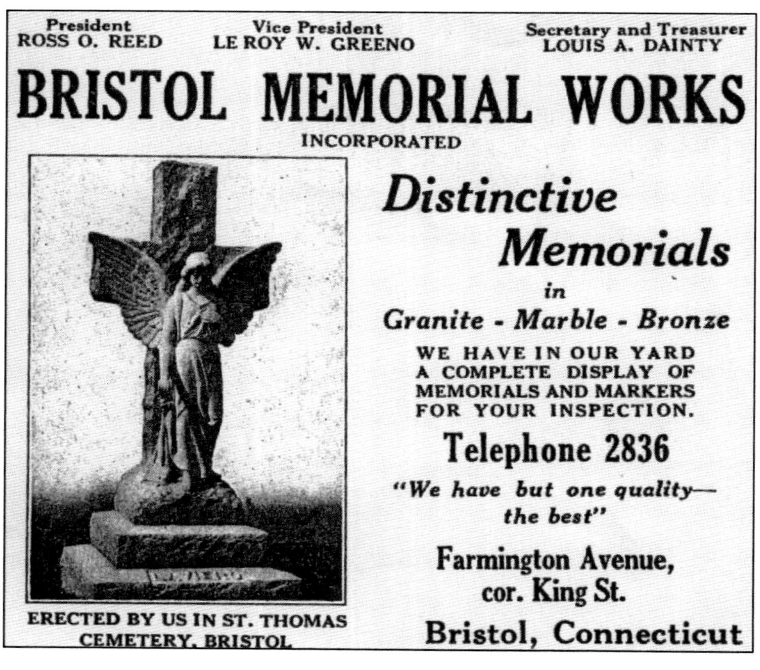

This 1930 advertisement of Bristol Memorial Works shows the type of products they sold.

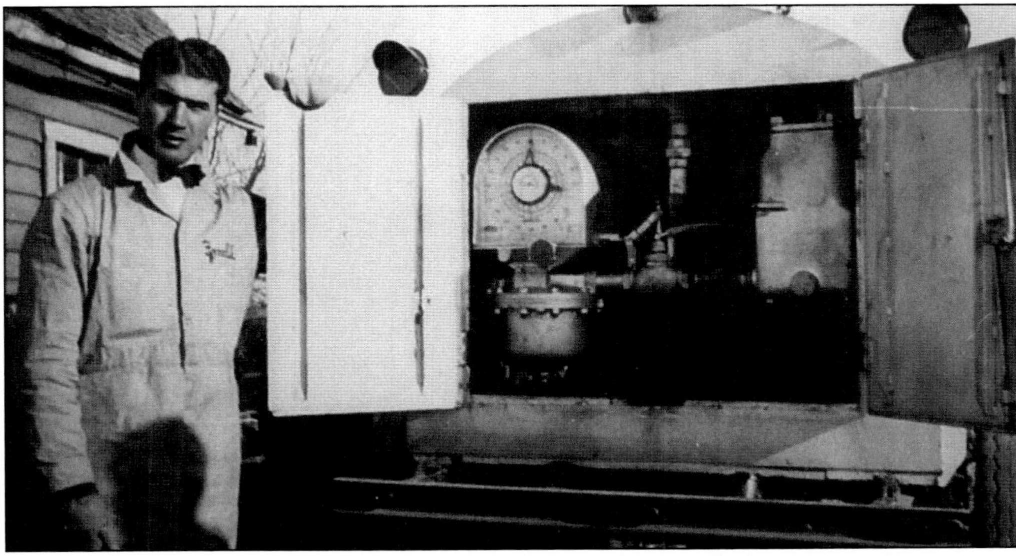

In 1931, Paul J. Fanelli, son of Vito and Domenica Fanelli, started a business on Crown Street in his parent's backyard barn. He delivered ice to homes and added range oil that was used to heat the kitchen range stove. In 1940, Paul's wife, Anna "Joan," took customer orders and did the bookkeeping. During World War II, Paul became partners with Angelo Spinelli, naming their company Spinelli and Fanelli. They added petroleum to their deliveries. After the war, the business was renamed Crown Oil Company for the street where Paul grew up. In 1948, Paul and Angelo bought land on 347 Riverside Avenue and installed storage tanks for their petroleum. In this picture, Paul is standing next to his oil delivery truck in the 1940s. (Courtesy of Crown Oil Company.)

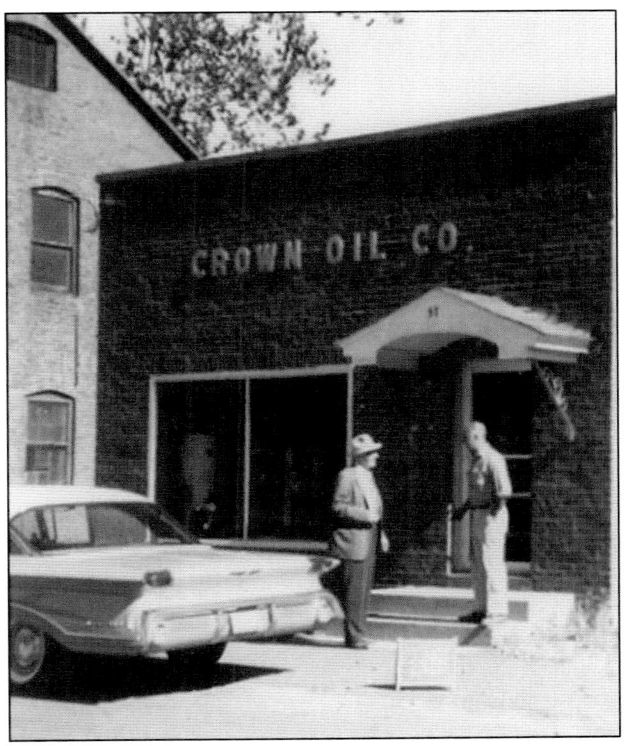

In 1951, Crown Oil Company moved into 57 Church Street from Crown Street. In 1958, Paul's son, Paul Jr., joined the business. The business remained here until 1971, when it moved to their 347 Riverside Avenue location and constructed a building next to the storage tanks. Since Paul Jr. was a certified licensed contractor, the company became a full service oil company. In 1979, Paul Sr. died leaving Angelo, Paul Jr., and Joan to operate the business. Angelo retired in 1985, and the business incorporated, leaving the Fanelli family owning the business. Joan died in 2008; her children, Paul Jr., Catherine F. Guerriere, and Deborah F. Yarde continue the traditions of personal service and integrity that their parents passed down to them. (Courtesy of Bristol Town Clerk Office.)

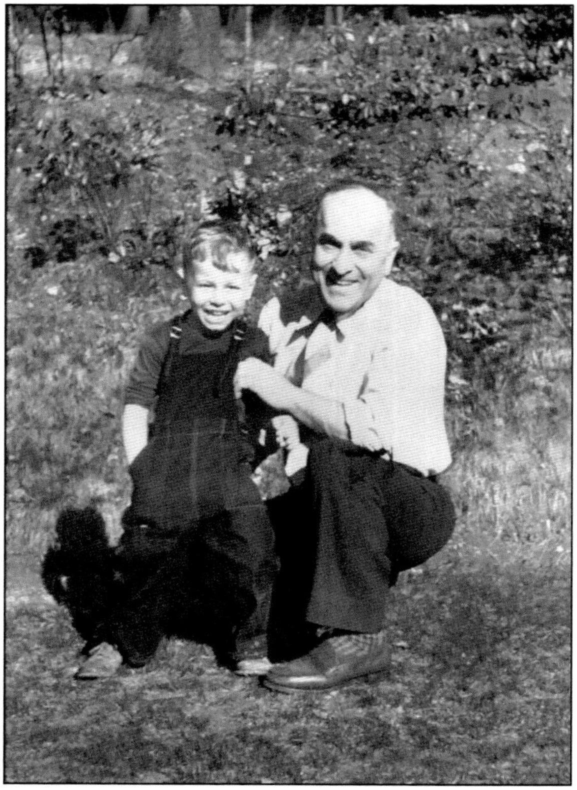

Born in Bristol on March 24, 1893, Spartacus "Spark" Carpenter, the son of Giacchino "Jack" and Carmella Carpentieri, lived at 45 Gaylord Street. In 1929, Spark started his own company called Carpenter Construction. In 1936, Spark married Lillian La Course, and they had two children, George T. and Mary Ann. George T. joined his father's business building new construction on retail and commercial structures. The business moved in 1970 from Gaylord Street to 67 Race Street. In 1977, Spark died, leaving the business to his son, George T. Carpenter Construction continues as a family business with George T. and his children, George E. and Sarah Carpenter Warner (secretary). This picture was taken in 1944 of George T. with his father, Spark Carpenter. (Courtesy of Carpenter Construction Company.)

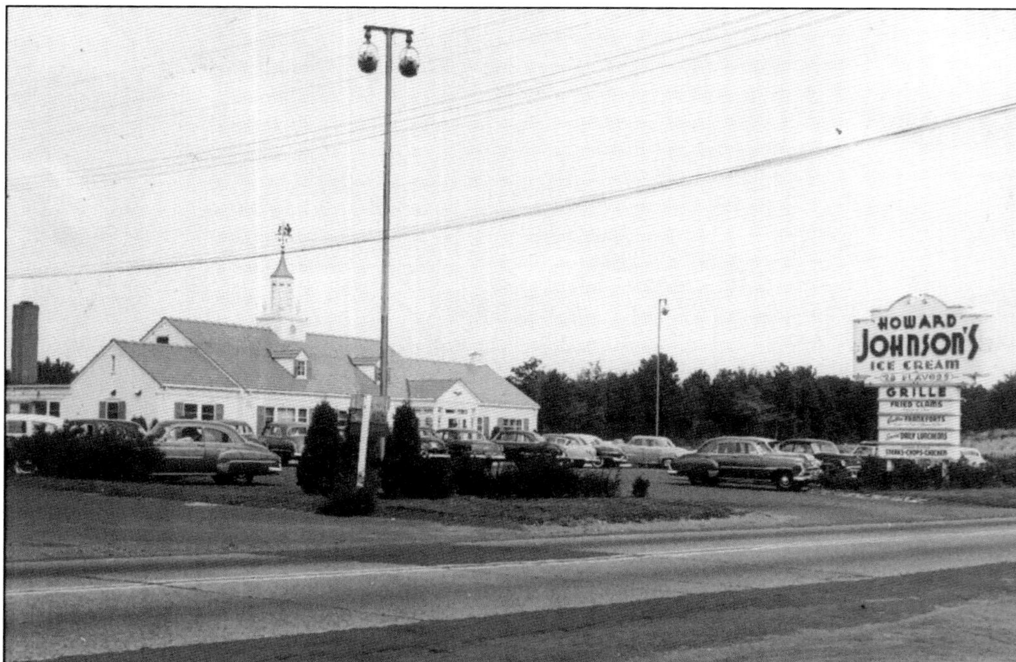

Prior to 1960, Howard Johnson Restaurant and the Bristol Motel were the two businesses on Farmington Avenue that would be torn down when Carpenter Construction built the Bristol Shopping Plaza in their place.

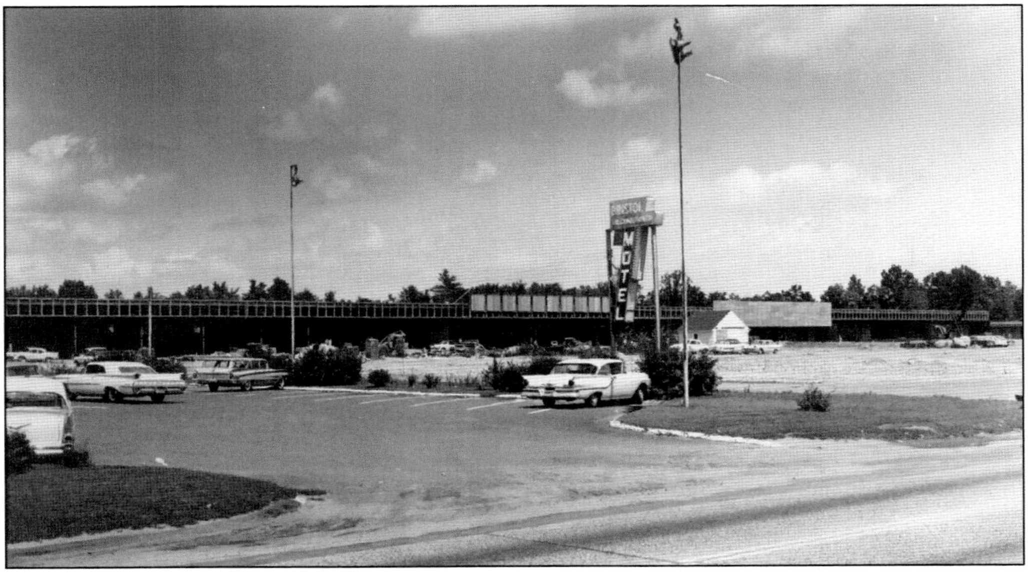

In 1960, under construction by developer Carpenter Construction, the first shopping center was built on Farmington Avenue. Prior to opening the plaza, both Bradlees Department Store and Stop and Shop grocery store signed up to become the first tenants. In this picture, the sign is still up for the Bristol Motel. The Howard Johnson Restaurant building was where the parking lot is in the picture. (Courtesy of Bristol Chamber of Commerce.)

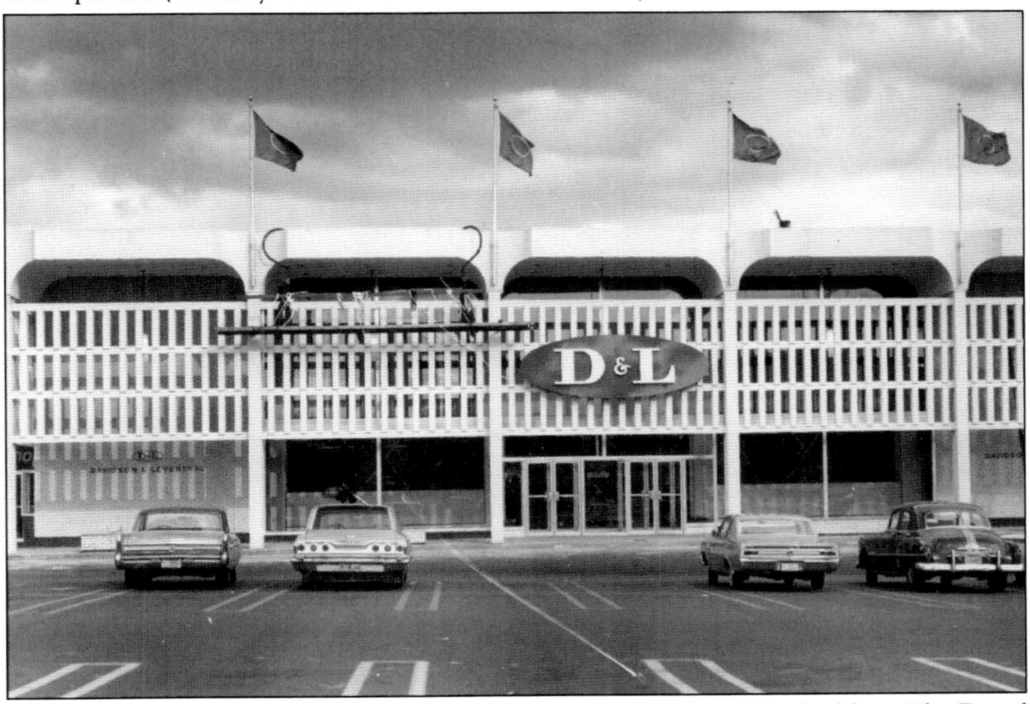

In 1966, Carpenter Construction enlarged the Bristol Plaza adding this building. The D and L Venture Corporation from New Britain opened this store called D and L department store. When D and L closed, T. J. Maxx went into building. Today Ocean Job Lot, a discount outlet store, is here. The Bristol Plaza is made up of 30 businesses today. (Courtesy of Bristol Chamber of Commerce.)

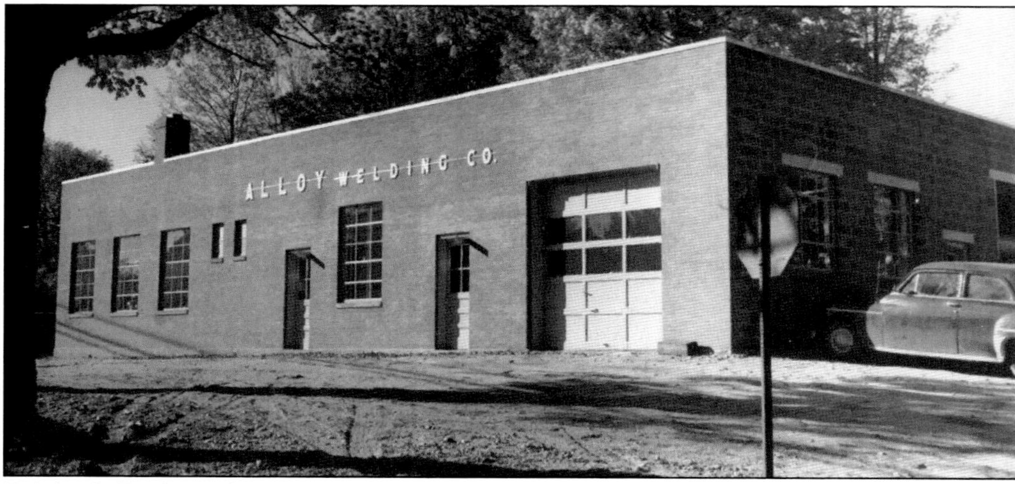

Delphis J. Frechette, born in Canada in 1910 and raised in Maine, moved to New Britain. Del learned a new method of joining metals called electric welding. In 1937, Del quit his job and started his business called Alloy Welding on 30 Church Street. Del started with a portable welder that he mounted on a truck. In 1941, Del constructed a building at 116 Riverside Avenue. During World War II, the company did fabricating on ball bearings for Marlin Rockwell in Plainville. In 1955, they constructed a larger building at 233 Riverside Avenue and moved in 1956. In 1960, Alloy Electric Welding Company became Alloy Welding and Manufacturing Company, Inc. Del's son, Alfred, joined his father's business in 1960 and took over the business when his father died in 1973. Al's son, Darren, joined the business and became general manager of the company in 2005. (Courtesy of Alloy Welding.)

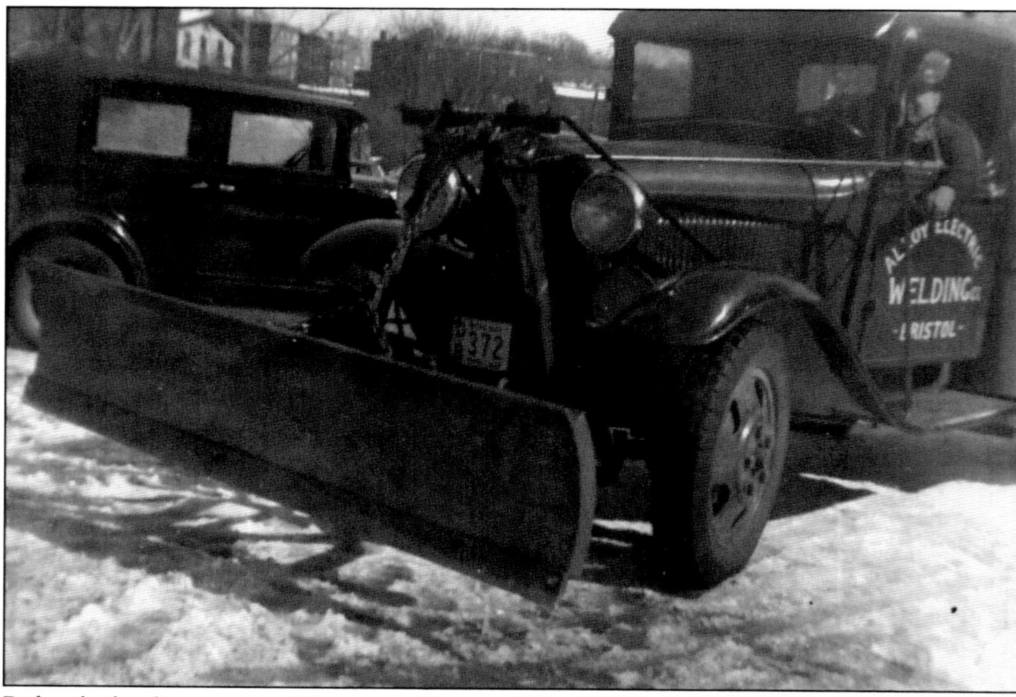

Before hydraulics were used for snow plowing, Alloy Welding's truck driver would put his arm out of the window and turn a wheel mounted on the door that would make the plow go up or down. (Courtesy of Alloy Welding.)

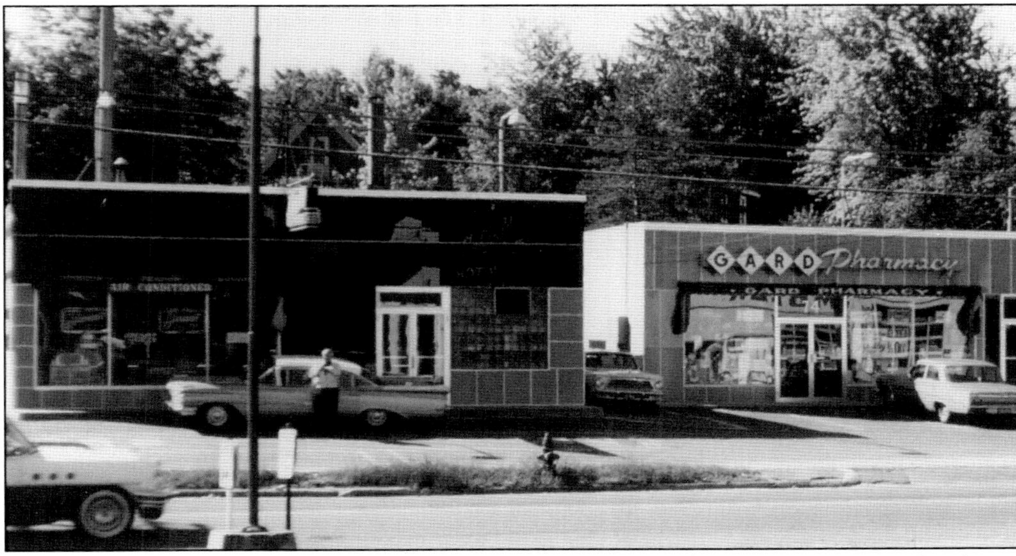

In 1927, Albert and Natalie Kasica opened a bakery on 562 North Main Street. Louis Barth and his wife, Anne, bought the business from Natalie in 1941. While at this location, the Barths built their business up by serving the local factories during World War II. In 1948, Louis and Anne moved Harvest Bakery into its present location at 84 Farmington Avenue. Their daughter, Barbara, and her husband, Payson Hurwitz, joined the business in 1949. Their son, Marty, and his wife, Jackie, own the business and continue to provide the same quality in their baked good for their customers that Harvest Bakery has been known for. In this picture from left to right are Harvest Bakery, Gard Pharmacy, and Home Meat Center. (Courtesy of Harvest Bakery.)

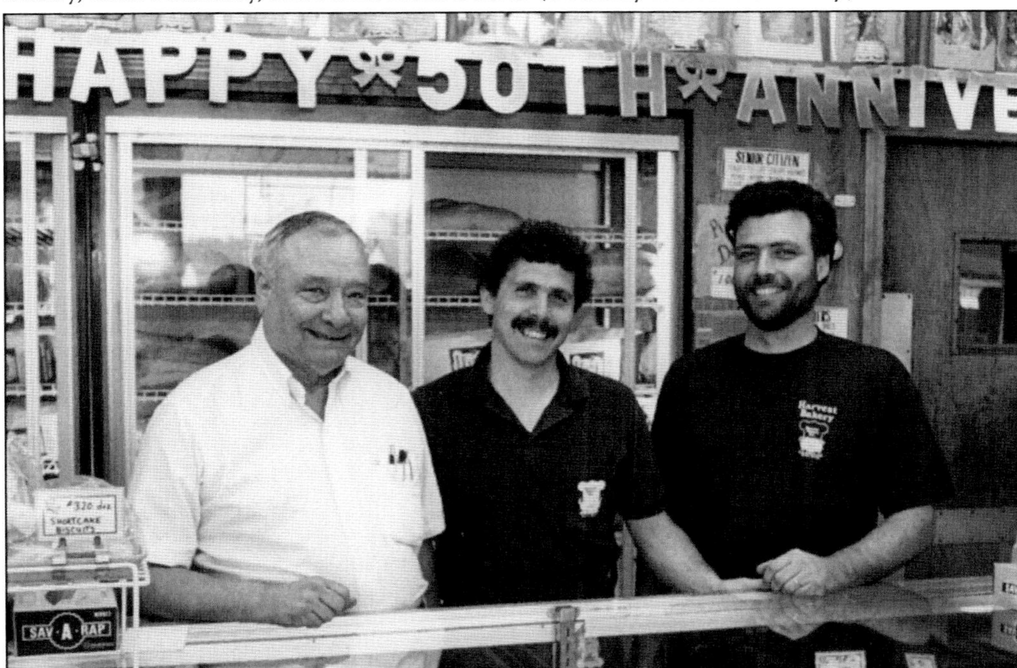

This picture was taken in 1991 when Harvest Bakery was celebrating their 50th year in business. From left to right are (standing behind the counter) Payson Hurwitz; his son, Marty; and employee Dave Belanger. (Courtesy of Harvest Bakery.)

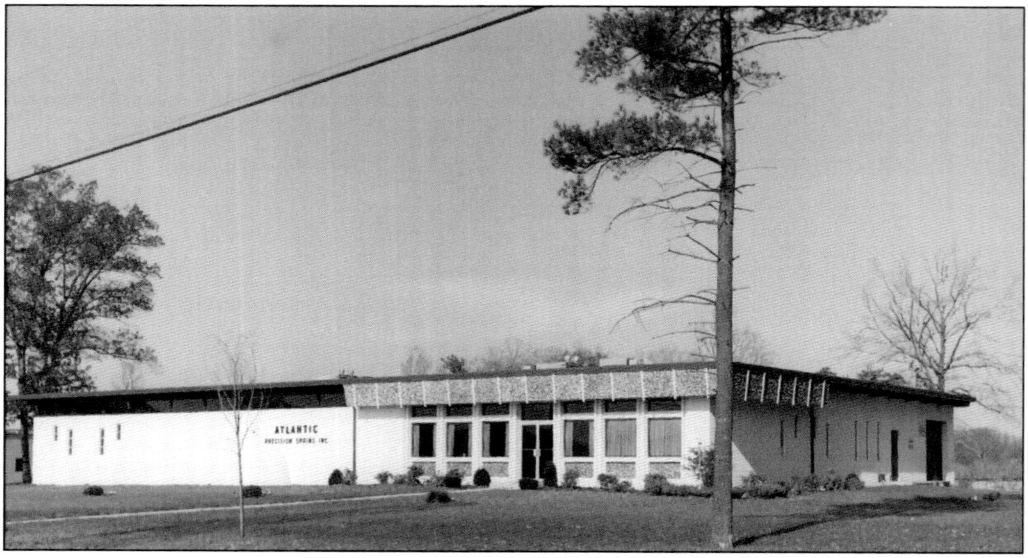

In 1958, Henry Tracz, Lawrence Budnick, John Kozikowski, and Benedict Tracy formed a company to start Atlantic Precision Spring, Inc. They manufactured flat springs and wire forms for clocks, sewing machines, and consumer products manufactured on fourslide equipment and manual foot presses. In 1969, the business moved to their building on 125 Ronzo Road. In 1992, the business was purchased by Neil Fries, an employee of the company since 1964. In 1996, the company achieved ISO certification. To keep up with the requirements, they added computerized equipment for the tooling, production, and inspecting departments. Today their customers include medical, electronic, and aerospace. In 2008, they celebrated their 50th year. Neil Fries and his sons, Brian and Michael, are committed to providing quality products and service to their customers. (Courtesy of Industrial Builders and Realty Company.)

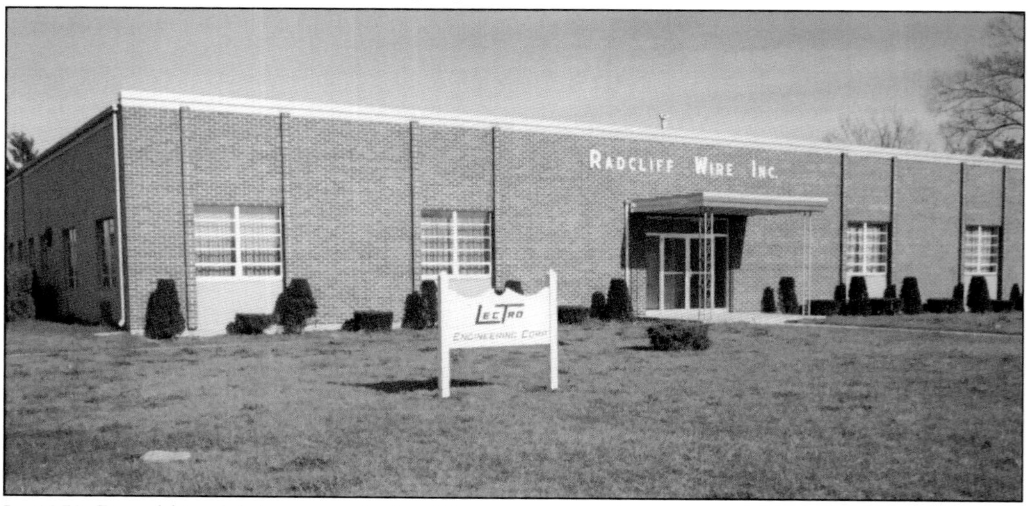

In 1959, Donald Radcliff started Radcliff Wire, Inc., in Plantsville. The company produces flat wire, square wire, and special-shaped wire in 40 different metals and alloys. On June 21, 1965, the business moved to its present location on 97 Ronzo Road. It was one of the first companies to build in Bristol's first industrial park. In 1976, Donald's daughter, Jeanne Radcliff, joined the business, succeeding her father as president in 1984. Her brother, Charlie, also joined the company and became president in 2001. In 2009, Radcliff Wire, Inc., celebrated 50 years as a major supplier to many different industries. (Courtesy of Industrial Builders and Realty Company.)

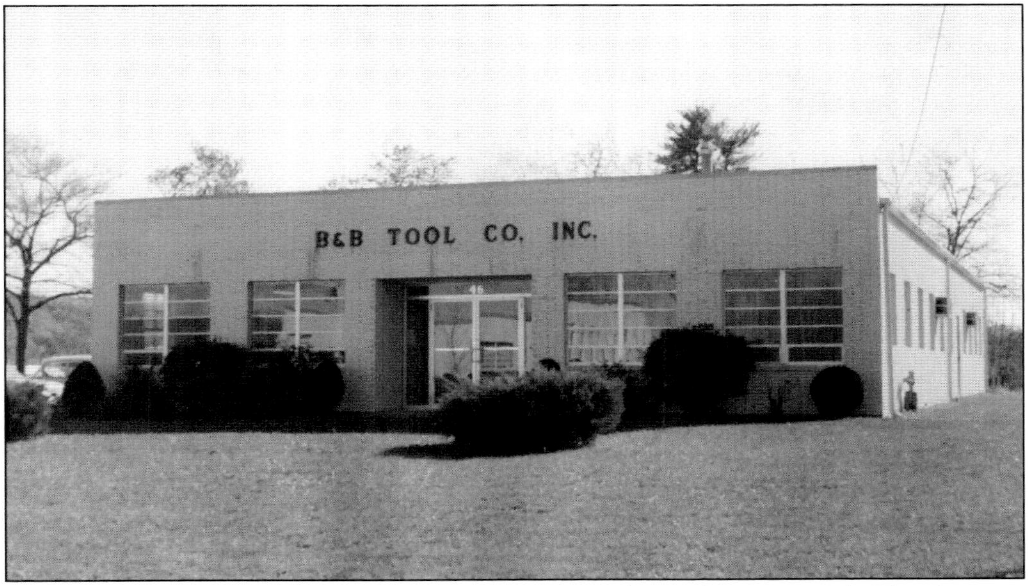

Anthony Bettua started his own business with a partner, John Witkewicz, in 1961. Their business was called BeWitt. In 1963, Anthony and his wife, Adele, took over the business, renaming it B&B Tool Company, Inc. They first started working out of a garage until 1964, when they moved to the former J. H. Sessions factory on Riverside Avenue in Bristol. In 1967, they moved into this building at 46 Ronzo Road. In 1973, when Anthony died, his wife, Adele, continued ownership of the business until 1987 when her son, Bob, took over the company. (Courtesy of Industrial Builders and Realty Company.)

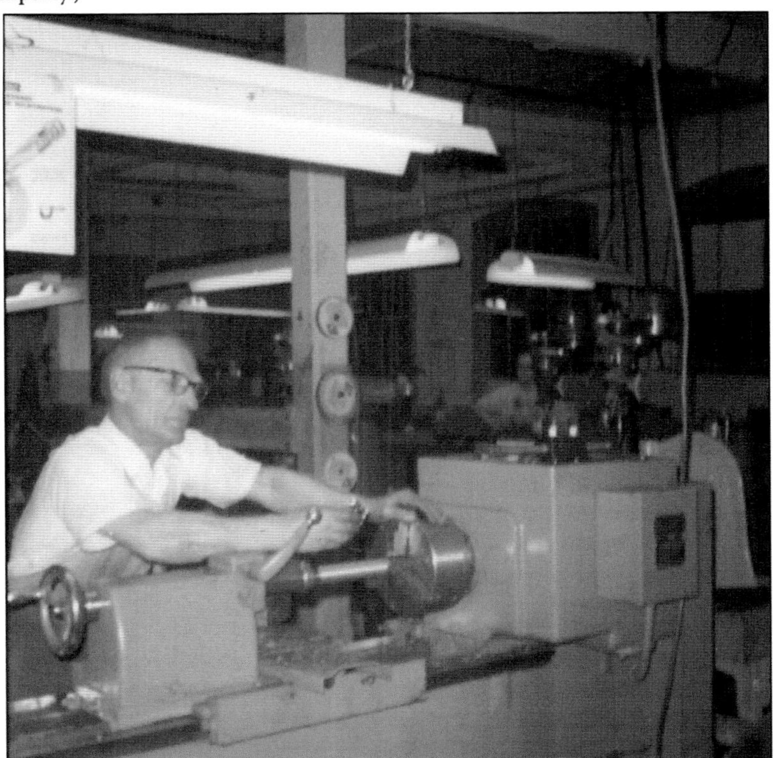

B&B Tool Company, Inc., makes parts for commercial machines. Some jobs might require one or two pieces to be made while others could be hundreds of parts. In this picture, Anthony Bettua, founder of the company, is using a lathe. (Courtesy of B&B Tool Company, Inc.)

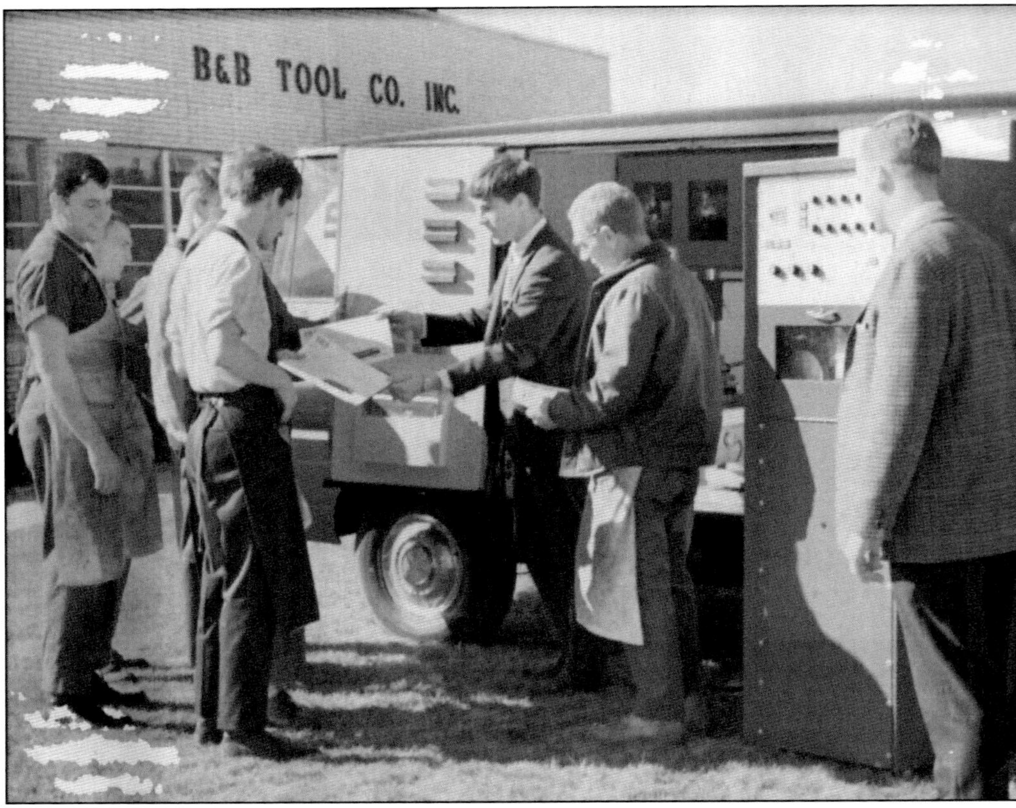

Representatives of Superior Electric are going over a product they need made with B&B Tool Company, Inc., in 1968. From left to right are B&B Tool employee Reggie L'Heureux, Bob Bettua, two employees of B&B Tool, a sales representative from Superior Electric (in a suit), Anthony Bettua (in an apron), and a Superior Electric sales representative at B&B Tool's building on Ronzo Road. (Courtesy of B&B Tool Company, Inc.)

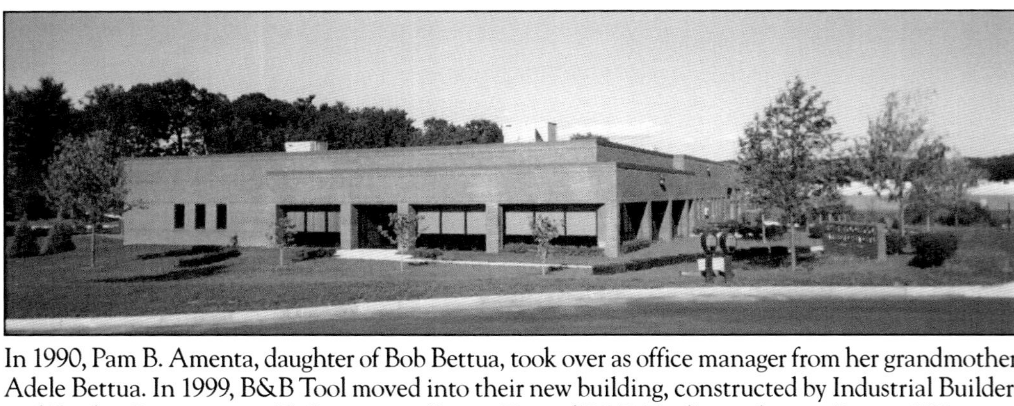

In 1990, Pam B. Amenta, daughter of Bob Bettua, took over as office manager from her grandmother, Adele Bettua. In 1999, B&B Tool moved into their new building, constructed by Industrial Builders and Realty Company, at 35 Commerce Drive. Two of B&B Tool's employees, Reggie L'Heureux and Paul Le Clair, have been with the company over 40 years. This picture shows B&B Tool Company, Inc., in their present location. (Courtesy of B&B Tool Company, Inc.)

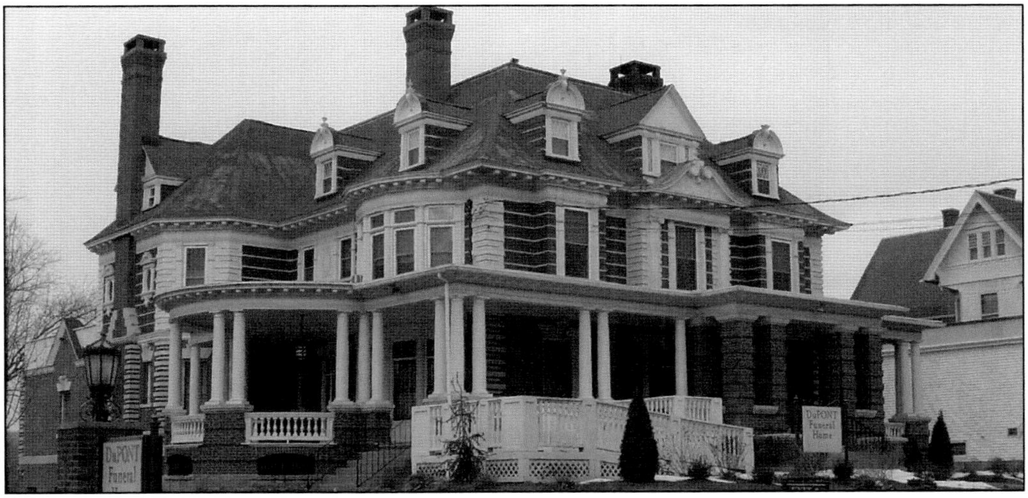

This was the home of industrialist Albert Leslie Sessions, which was built in 1903 on 25 Bellevue Avenue. In 1940, it became the town club. In 1960, the building was bought by Pretzman G. Young who turned it into a funeral home called Young Funeral Services, Inc. In 1980, Robert and Diane DuPont purchased the business, continuing as DuPont Young Funeral Service until they incorporated and renamed it DuPont Funeral Home, Inc. Their daughter, Dana Ballard, became office manager in 1996, and their son, Ryan, become a funeral director in 1999. This year they will celebrate 30 years in business. (Courtesy of DuPont Funeral Home.)

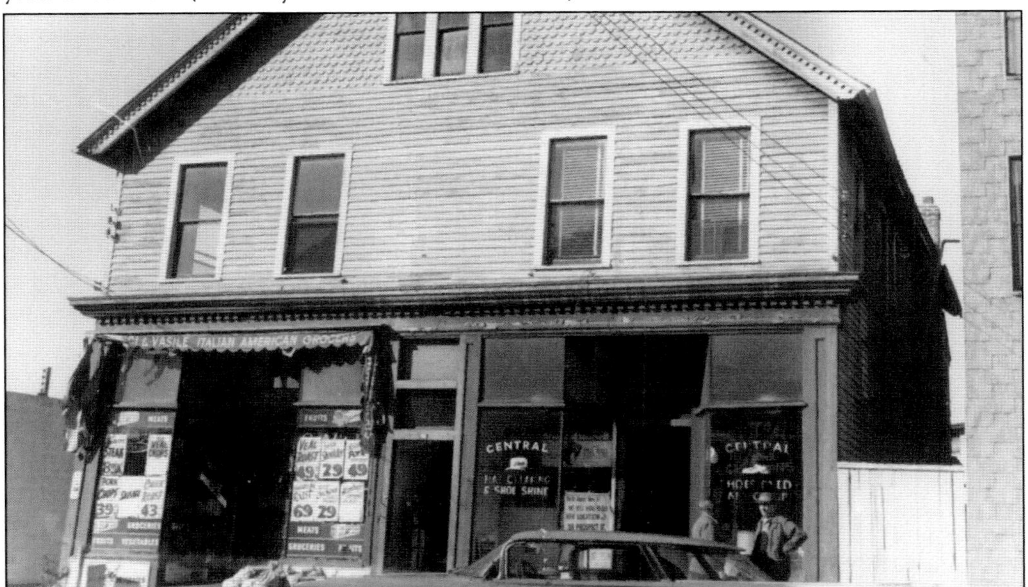

Samuel Vasile was born in Bristol in 1918. In 1947, Samuel and Anthony Raucci opened a business called Raucci and Vasile Market on Laurel Street. In 1962, they moved to 76 South Street and changed the name to South Side Market. In 1976, when Anthony died, Samuel became partners with John Gallant. In November 1989, Samuel Vasile died. In 1992, Samuel's son, Sammy, and John Gallant's sons, Steve and John, became partners and moved the business to its present location at 145 West Street. The three partners continue the values and traditions set by their fathers as South Side Market celebrates 63 years of business in April 2010. In this picture was the first location of Samuel and Anthony's business on Laurel Street. (Courtesy of South Side Market.)

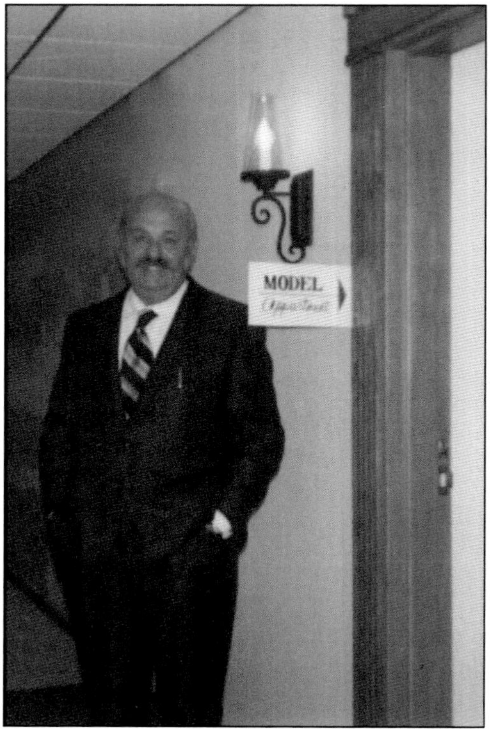

Angelo Delfino was born in Bristol in 1917. In the 1950s, Angelo formed a business with Manfred Stein of Hartford called D and S Builders, Inc., constructing several hundred homes in Bristol. In 1964, their name changed to Industrial Builders and Realty Company. Angelo's son, William, joined the company. On Angelo's family's land, the company built Ronzo Road and developed commercial buildings along that street as well as Middle Street. Their company was responsible for bringing more than 60 businesses to this area. Industrial Builders and Realty Company on 785 Middle Street is owned by William and Tom Delfino, sons of Angelo, and Martin Stein, son of Manfred. In this picture, Angelo is standing next to one of the model luxury apartments for the elderly built on Stafford Avenue. (Courtesy of Industrial Builders and Realty Company.)

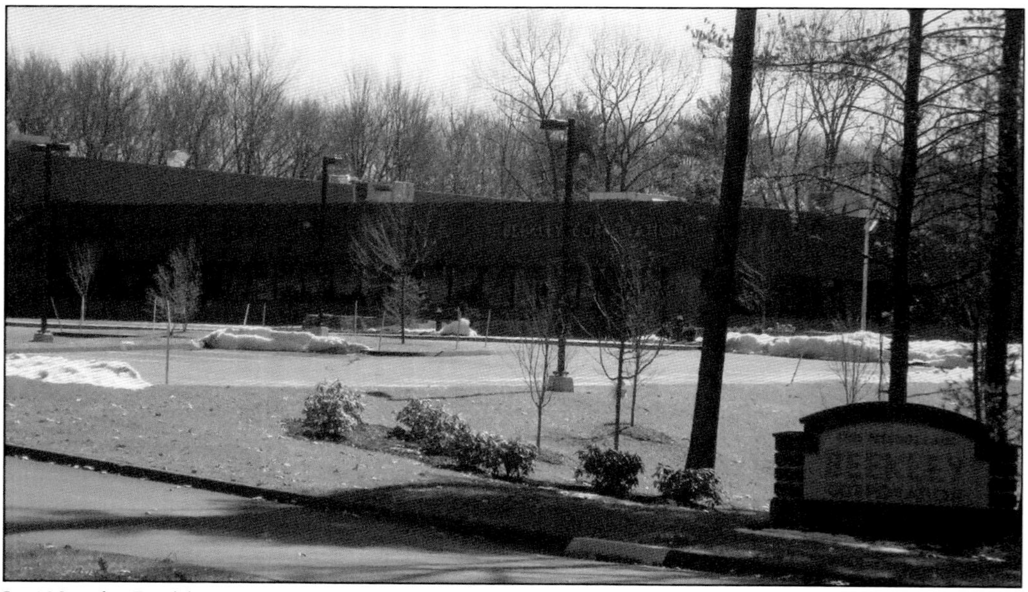

In 1934, the Beekley Corporation was founded by F. Cheyney Beekley in Farmington. In 1982, the company moved to Bristol on Dolfin Road. Beekley's son, W. Mason Beekley, became president in 1969 when his father died. In 1977, Ayn LaPlant joined the company. Her career progressed so that in 1990, she became president and then CEO in 2001. Beekley Corporation manufactures medical products, including skin markers, biopsy systems, and patient-care devices. In 1981, Beekley added their hospitality division, which manufactures and markets hotel luggage, valet, and promotional tags. In 2009, Industrial Builders and Realty Company constructed Beekley's new corporate headquarters on 1 Prestige Lane. (Courtesy of Beekley Corporation.)

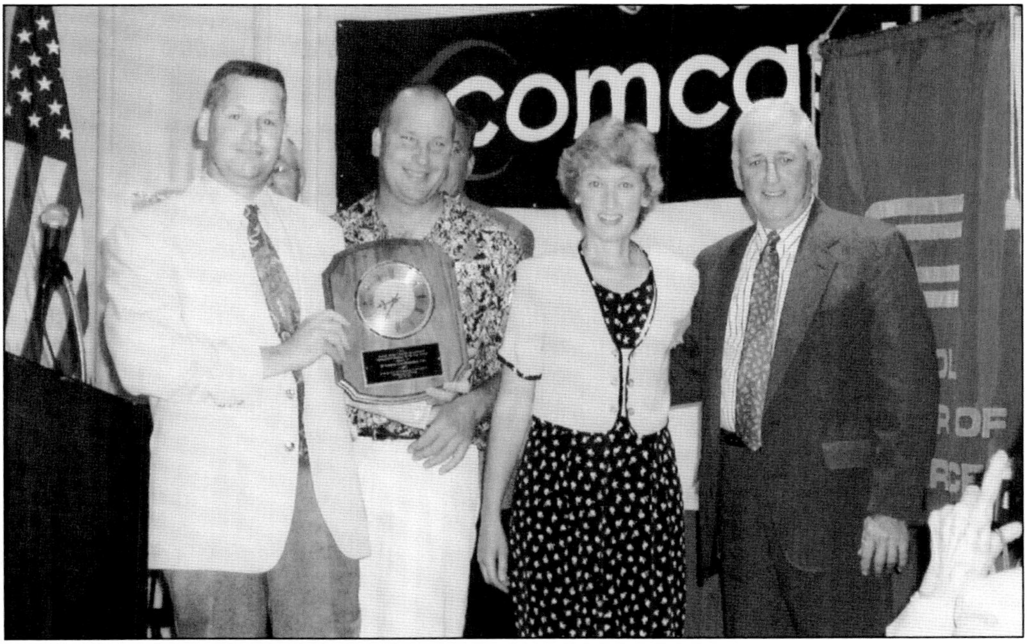

In 1961, Edward and Patricia D'Amato started their company, D'Amato Construction, on West Street. Their children, Eddie Jr., Tom, and Susan, joined the family business. In 1967, the business incorporated. Their building projects included Scarpelli's Drive-In, Abel Transmission, Baron and Young, Ingraham Manor, Northside Square, and construction work at Lake Compounce and local churches. The company's trademark is the color blue that is painted on all of their trucks and heavy equipment. The business is at 400 Middle Street with Ed Sr. as president and CEO, Eddie Jr. and Tom as vice presidents, and Susan as secretary. In this picture taken on June 13, 2003, at the annual dinner of the Bristol Chamber of Commerce, the company received the Distinguished Business of the Year Award. From the left to right are Eddie and Tom D'Amato, Susan D. Henne, and their father, Edward D'Amato Sr. (Courtesy of D'Amato Construction Company.)

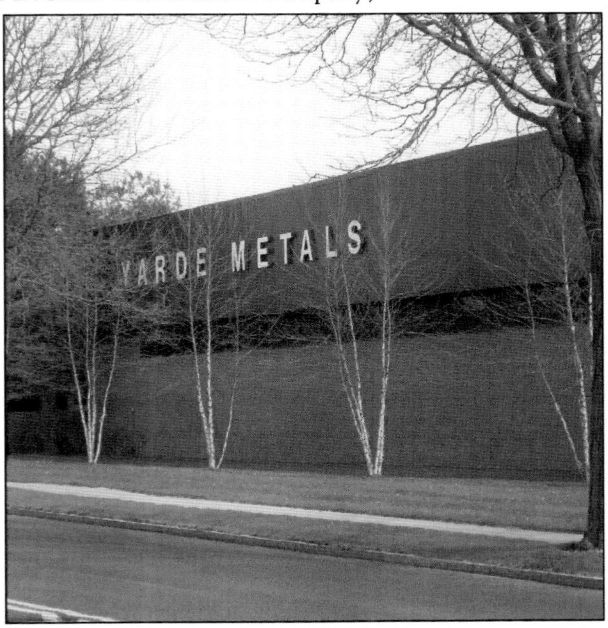

In 1976, Craig Yarde started his business, Yarde Metals, Inc., in his home in Bristol. He began brokering metal over the phone. Deliveries of metal orders were picked up and delivered by family members in Craig's station wagon. In 1977, Craig became partners with his brother, Bruce, and moved the business to a factory on 86 South Street in 1978. In 1986, Yarde Metals, Inc., moved into their 85,000-square-foot building on 71 Horizon Drive. They specialize in the processing and distribution of stainless steel and aluminum plate, rod, and bar products. The business is now located at 45 Newell Street, Southington. (Courtesy of Yarde Metals, Inc.)

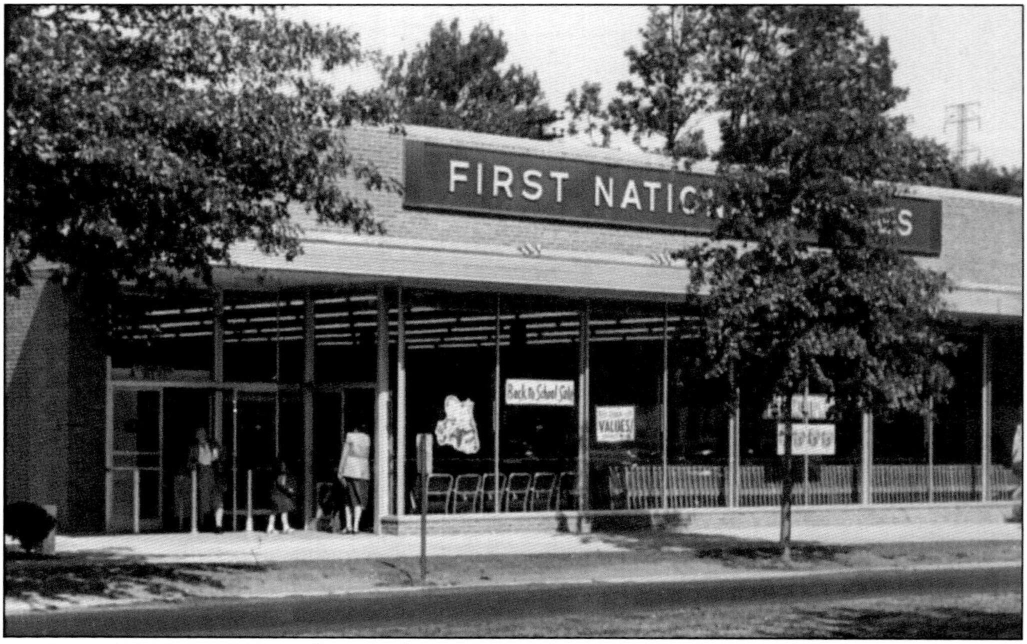

In March 1971, Lewis Volpicella owned a gas station located on U.S. Route 4 in Burlington. When he needed parts to repair cars, he bought them from the Bristol Auto Parts dealer. On an impulse, Lew ended up buying three NAPA-affiliated automobile parts stores, two in Bristol and one in Waterbury. He started on North Main Street. In 1972, Lew moved the business to 21 North Street in the former Rock Brothers Tire Company building. A giant Paul Bunyan was on the front lawn that customers could not miss. Later Bristol Auto Parts bought the old First National Store at 65 Memorial Boulevard, built in 1941 on the former site of the American Silver Company.

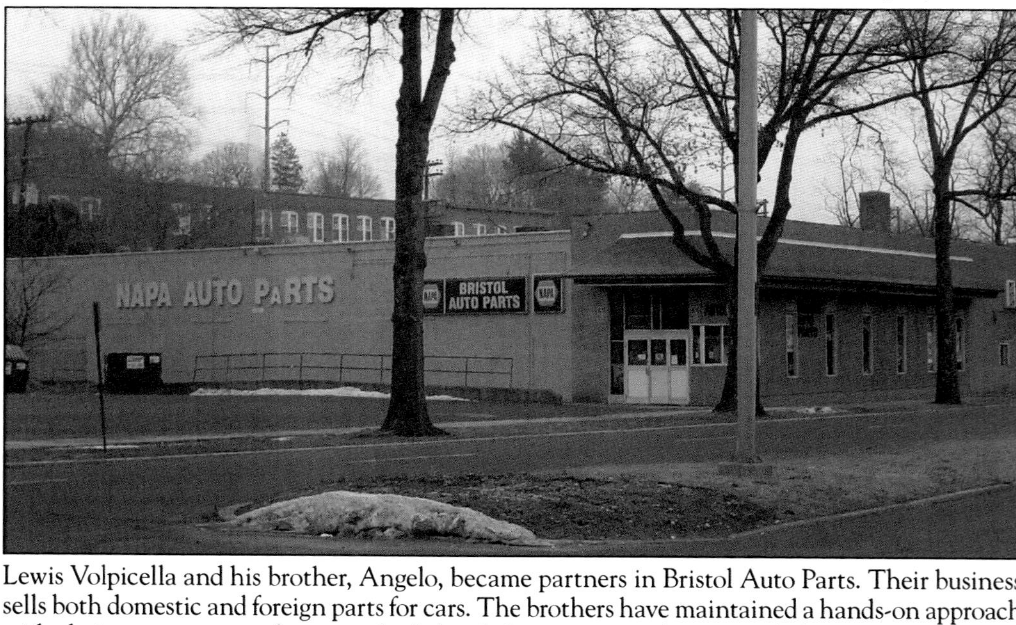

Lewis Volpicella and his brother, Angelo, became partners in Bristol Auto Parts. Their business sells both domestic and foreign parts for cars. The brothers have maintained a hands-on approach with their customers, preferring to be behind the counter and not at a desk. Bristol Auto Parts today continues with Lew and Angelo and Angelo's sons, Joey and John, as they look forward to 2011, when they celebrate 40 years in business. (Courtesy of Bristol Auto Parts.)

Five

The Merchants and Businesses

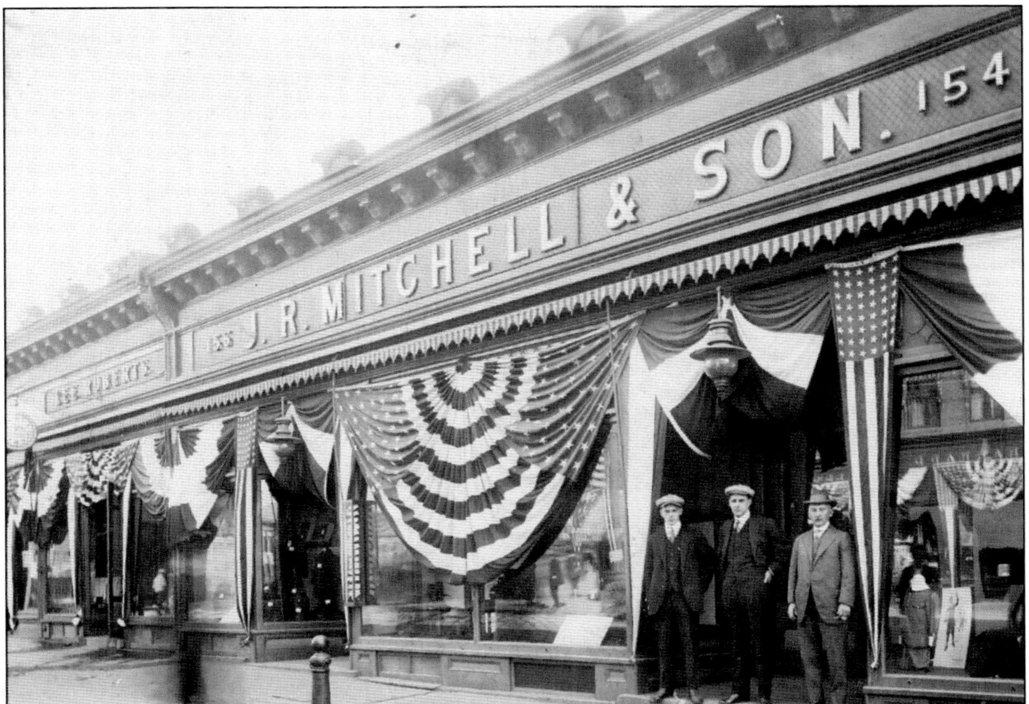

In 1776, George Mitchell and Thomas Barnes Jr. owned a general store on South Street. Mitchell went on to own his business on North and Pond Streets. When George died in 1852, his son, Julius R., continued his father's dry goods, clothing, and furnishings business. J. R. Mitchell moved to 154–156 Main Street. Pictured here in the late 1890s are the Lee Roberts store (left) and the J. R. Mitchell and Son store. Standing in front of J. R. Mitchell and Son are, from left to right, Paul Allaire, Harvey C. Russell, and William Theodore Smith. The building that J. R. Mitchell and Son business was in stands today on Main Street. (Courtesy of Bristol Historical Society.)

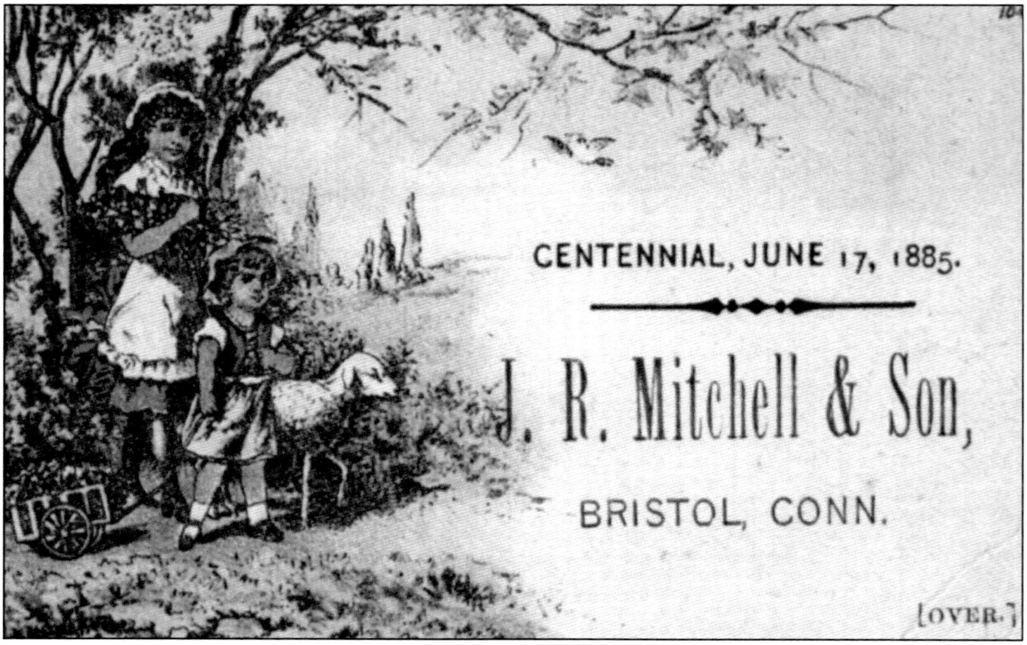

When Bristol celebrated their centennial on June 17, 1885, this card was made and handed out by J. R. Mitchell and Son, advertising the merchandise they sold at their store at 154–156 Main Street. (Courtesy of Gary Potter.)

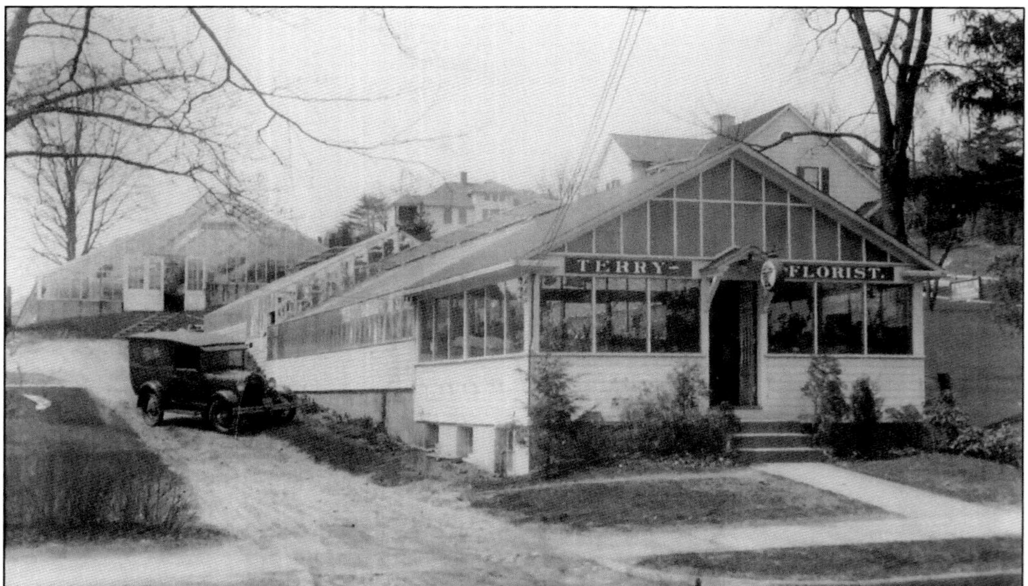

William Almeron Terry built this greenhouse in 1872 located at 287 West Street. The business was known as Terry's Florist. William was in business with his son-in-law, Judge Burdette A. Peck. Terry's two sons, William Bryant and Charles H., joined their father's business. Charles's son, Fowler, took over the business when his father died in 1938. Spartacus "Spark" Carpenter purchased the business in the 1940s. After World War II, Spark sold the business to his nephew, Dante Carpenter, who owned it until he died in 1966. Today the building is owned and operated by Bristol Pizza Restaurant.

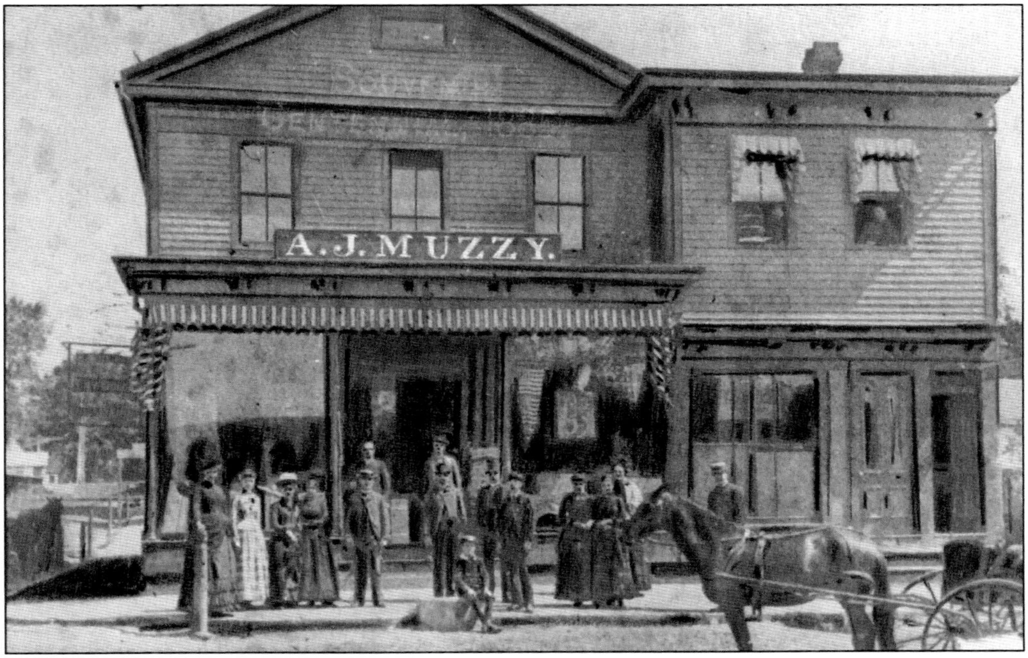

Adrian J. Muzzy, son of Henry and Mary Beach Muzzy, was born in Bristol in 1851. "A. J.," as he was known, had his first business at the age of 19 in flour and feed. With Thomas Barbour, they opened a men's clothing store called Barbour and Muzzy located in the Nott-Seymour building on upper Main Street. In 1876, A. J. bought the O. B. Ives dry goods business located on the corner of Main and Water Streets. A. J. Muzzy's stayed at this location until 1908 when the Bristol Trust Bank was built in its place. A. J. Muzzy's moved to the Masonic building on Main Street.

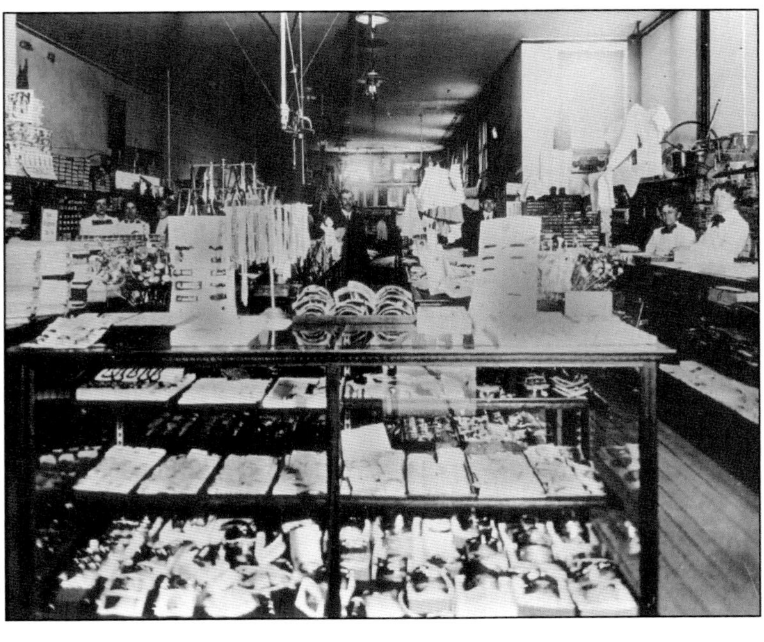

This interior view of A. J. Muzzy's store shows some of the merchandise they carried. On the left are employees Lillian Conchron and Mrs. Harold Beten. (The third woman is unidentified.) In the center is owner A. J. Muzzy, and on the right are employees Mrs. F. J. Weed and Mrs. Fanny Gowdy.

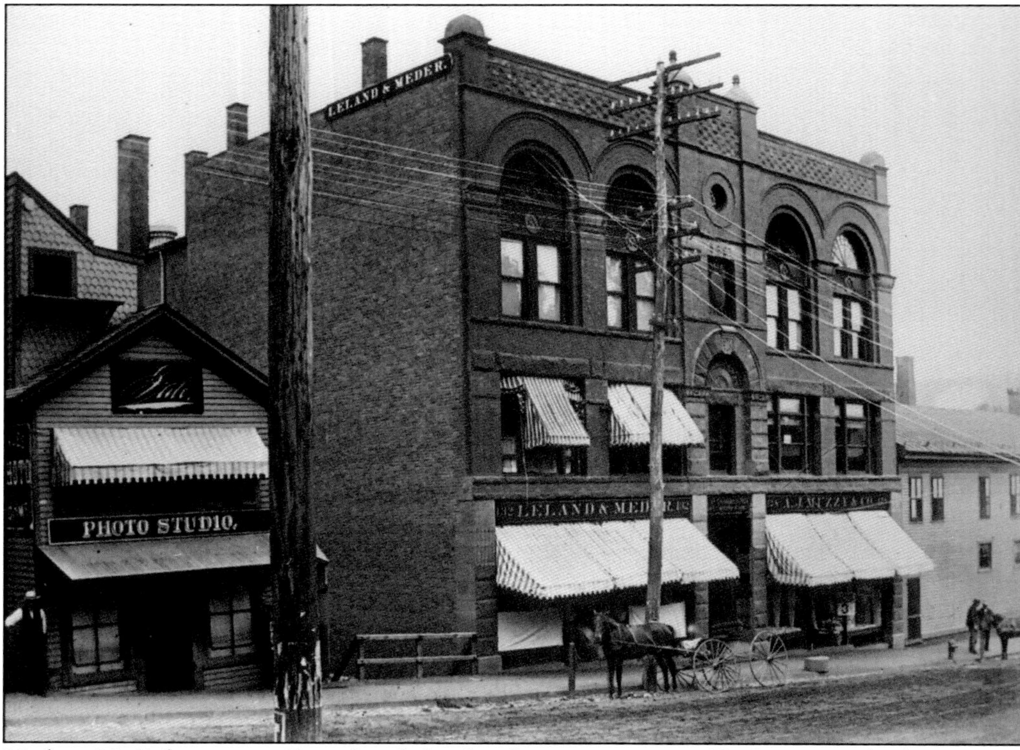

Herbert N. Gale came to Bristol with his family at a young age. He first started taking scenic pictures and then became partners with W. H. Wright making stereoscopic pictures. In 1878, Gale opened his photography studio at 136 Main Street. On September 30, 1902, while taking a flashlight picture of the employees at A. J. Muzzy's, the flash lamp he was holding exploded in his hand. From the force of the explosion, Gale died on October 21, 1902. In this picture, Gale's Studio is on the left and the Franklin Masonic building is on the right.

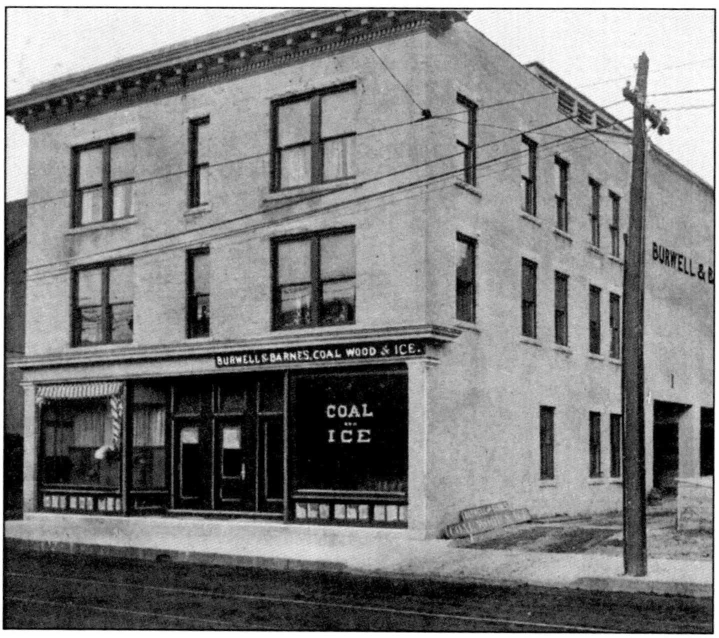

In 1893, Ernest A. Burwell and Joseph H. Ward started their coal and wood business called E. R. Burwell and Company, located at 21 North Main Street. In 1911, Burwell partnered with Clifford S. Barnes, changing the name to Burwell and Barnes, selling coal, wood, and ice. Barnes left the business in 1920 to become president of the Bristol Manufacturing Company on Riverside Avenue. (Courtesy of Gary Potter.)

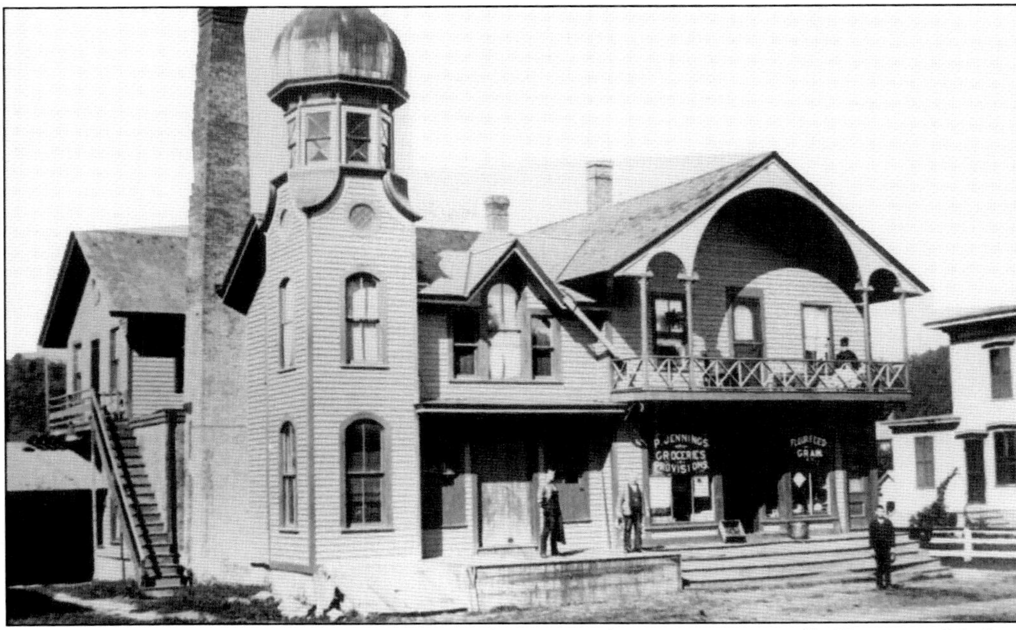

Peter Jennings, originally from Ireland, started his grocery business in 1882 called Jennings Market. The building was located at 225 North Main Street near the corner of Center Street. On the left of his store was the F. W. Giddings carriage shop. The Jennings owned the business until 1902. Later it would be torn down by New Departure Manufacturing to build Endee Inn.

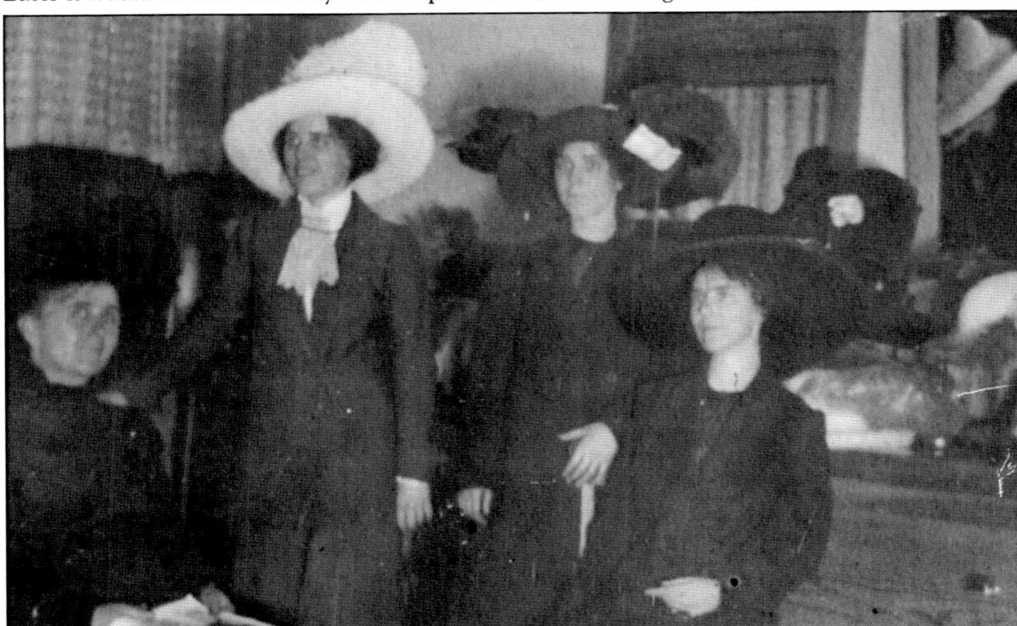

John Jennings was the son of Peter Jennings who owned Jennings market. John died in 1910 leaving his wife, Mary, to raise their 10 children. Mary's daughter, Catherine, worked in a millinery store in Hartford. In 1910, with the help of Mary's daughters, Catherine and Josephine, they opened a millinery store at 116 North Main Street called Jennings Millinery Store. The business closed in 1920. In this picture taken inside their store are, from left to right, Mary Jennings and her daughters, Catherine, Josephine, and Nellie. (Courtesy of Sheila Orefice.)

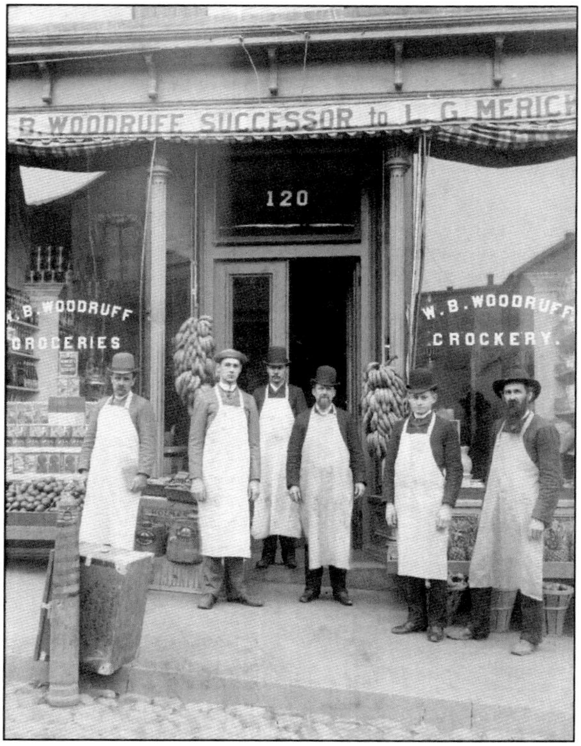

Leverett Griggs Merrick was the original owner of this grocery store at 182 Main Street. In 1886, the business was purchased by Walter B. Woodruff. It was renamed Woodruff's Grocery Store. When his business started making more baked goods, it became known as Woodruff's Bakery. In 1937, Walter's son, James, took over the business until 1948 when he retired. John Zawacki owned the business from 1949 to 1959. The current owner, Michael Triplett, is restoring the building and storefront back to its original look when it was constructed. (Courtesy of Bristol Historical Society.)

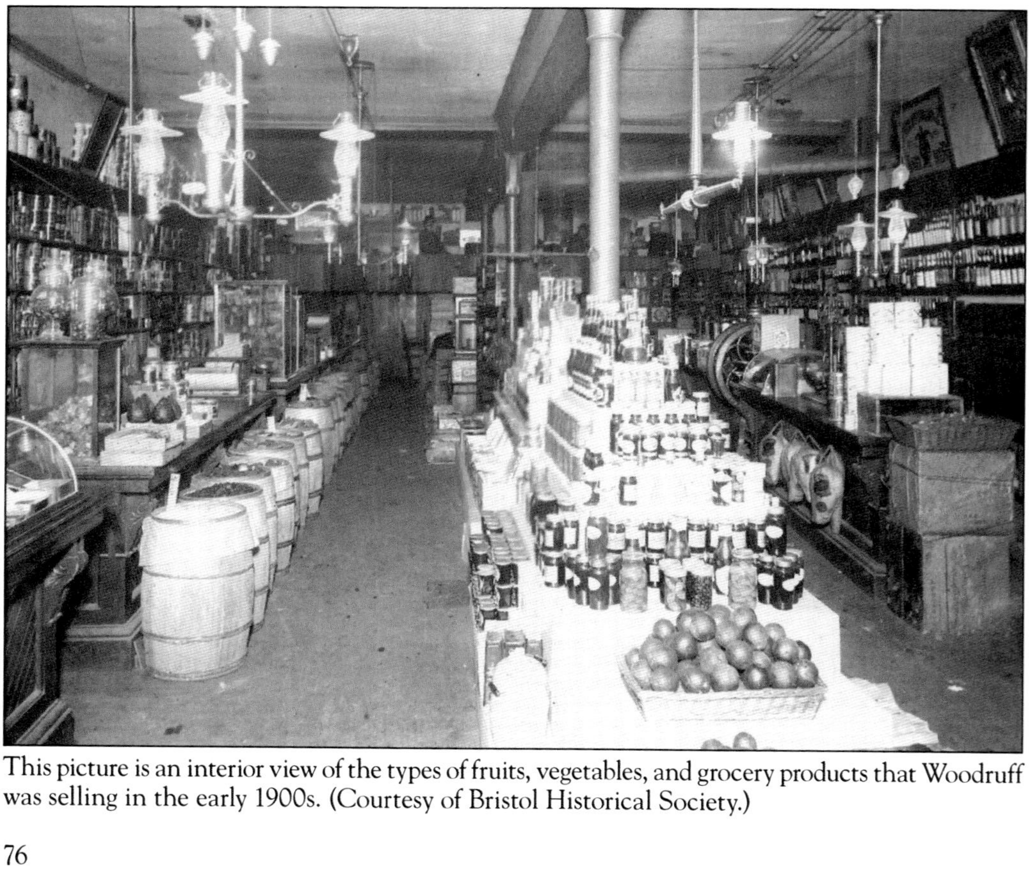

This picture is an interior view of the types of fruits, vegetables, and grocery products that Woodruff was selling in the early 1900s. (Courtesy of Bristol Historical Society.)

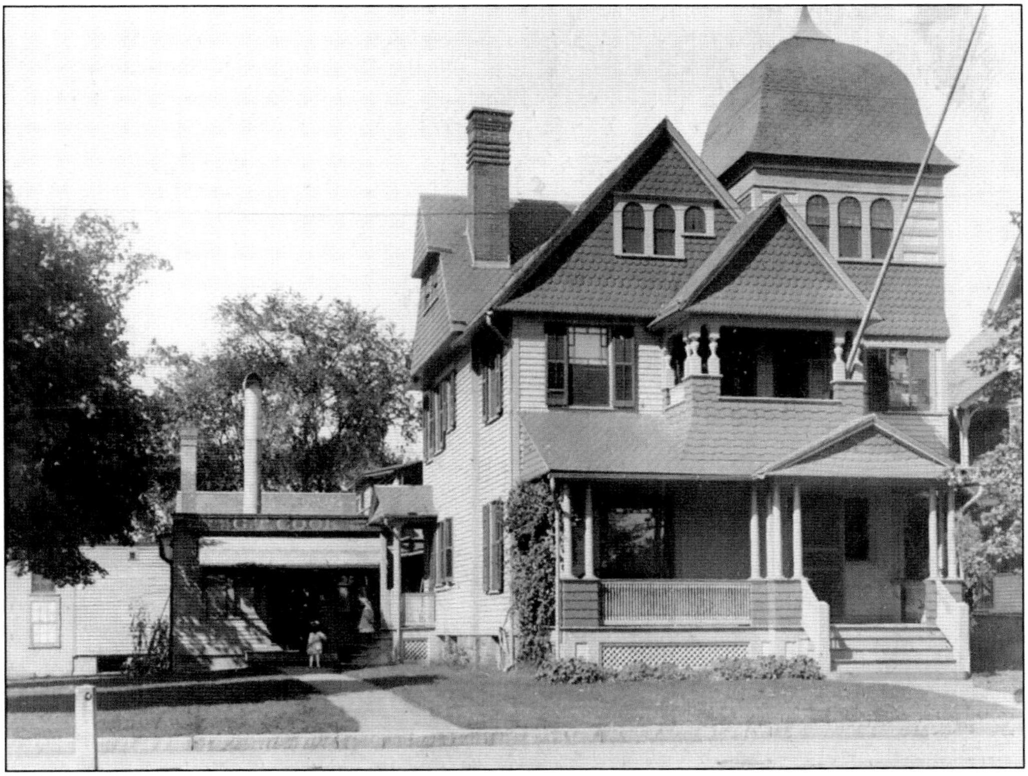

When George T. Cook first started his bakery business, it was located at 81 Main Street in a building next to his home. Besides the bakery, the business also advertised that they catered for weddings, private parties, and picnics. They also took orders by mail. (Courtesy of Gary Potter.)

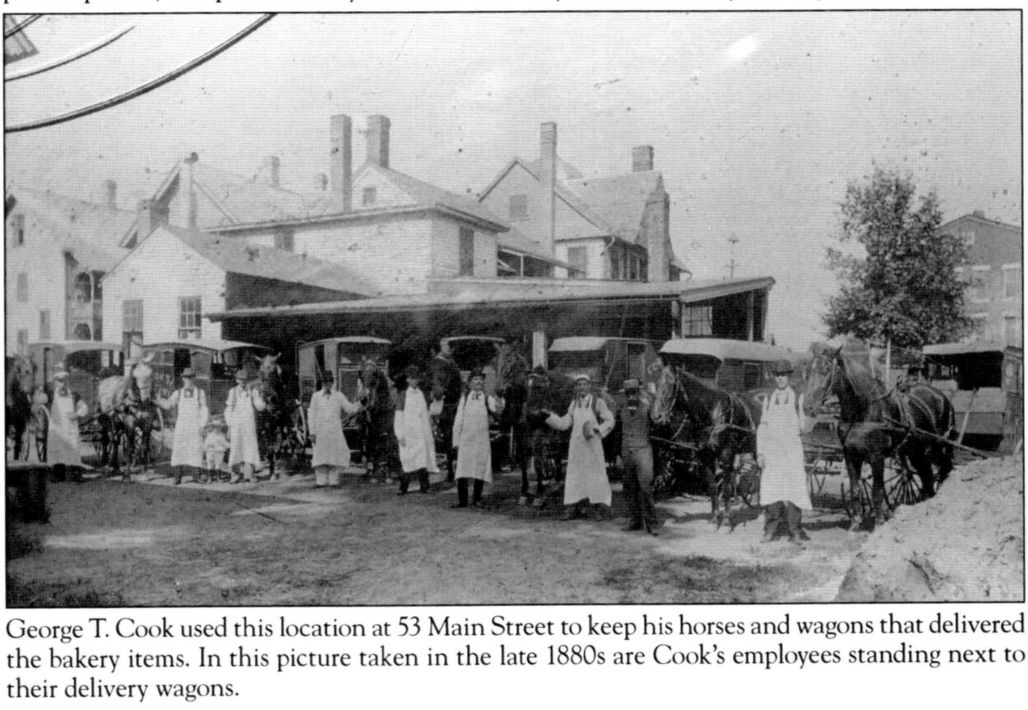

George T. Cook used this location at 53 Main Street to keep his horses and wagons that delivered the bakery items. In this picture taken in the late 1880s are Cook's employees standing next to their delivery wagons.

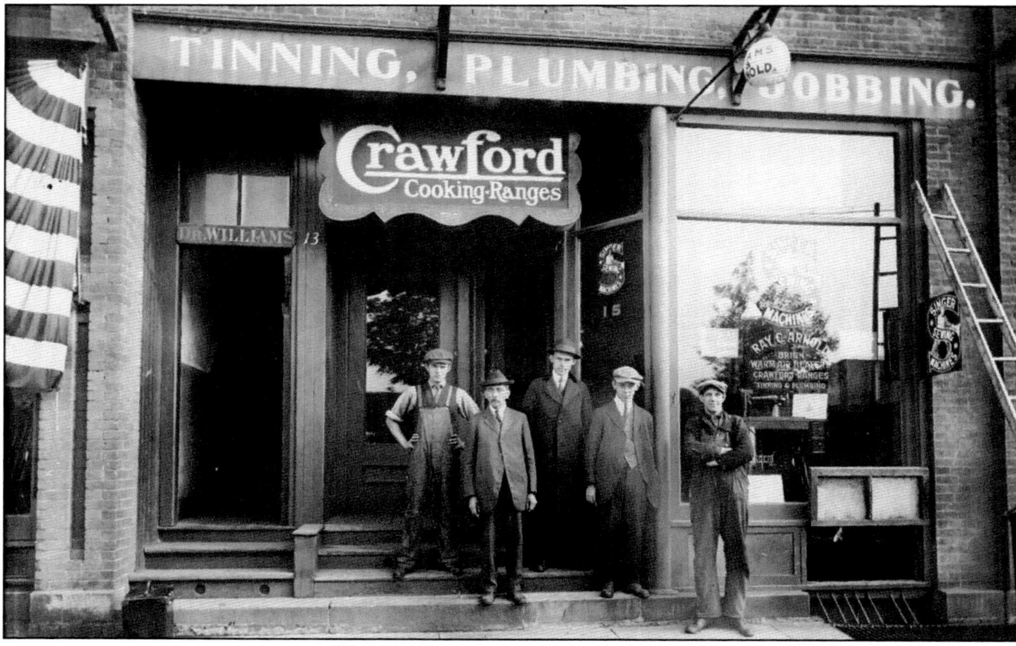

Frank A. Shaffer and Walter H. Blair started a plumbing business called Blair and Shaffer Company in 1890 at 34 Summer Street. When Blair died in 1901, Shaffer continued the business as F. A. Shaffer at 186 Main Street. In 1907, Shaffer became partners with Ray Marsh and called the business Shaffer-Marsh Company. That same year, Fred H. Herold Jr. became an employee of their business. In 1913, the business incorporated as F. A. Shaffer Company, Inc. In 1918, the company was bought by Fred H. Herold Jr. and his brothers, Charles and Harry. Members of the Herold family owned the company through the 1980s. This 1890s picture is of the Blair and Shaffer Company at 34 Summer Street. (Courtesy of the Shaffer Company.)

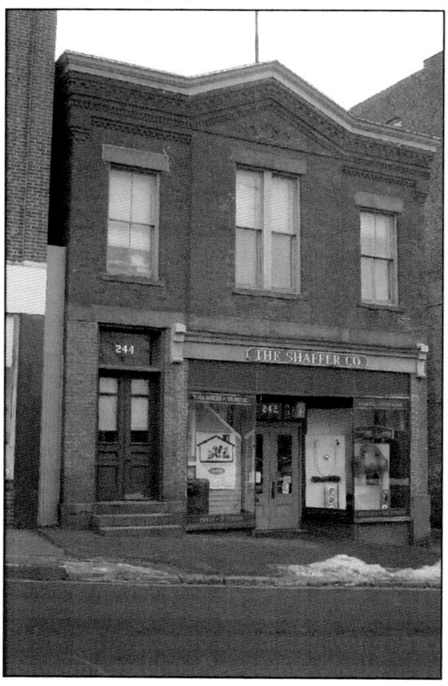

In 1924, the Shaffer Company moved into the former Bristol Savings Bank at 242 Main Street. In 1980, Bruce Hanson and Dominick "Nick" Ferro became junior partners with senior partners Harry A. Herold Jr., Russell L. Herold, Merton Baehr, and Robert Coleman. During the 1990s, all of the senior partners retired. Bruce Hanson is currently president of Shaffer Company, and Nick Ferro semiretired as an officer at the end of 2009. The Shaffer Company continues to provide full-service plumbing, heating, and air-conditioning. Their retail store is for residential, commercial, industrial, and municipal customers as it begins its 120th year in business in 2010. (Courtesy of Shaffer Company.)

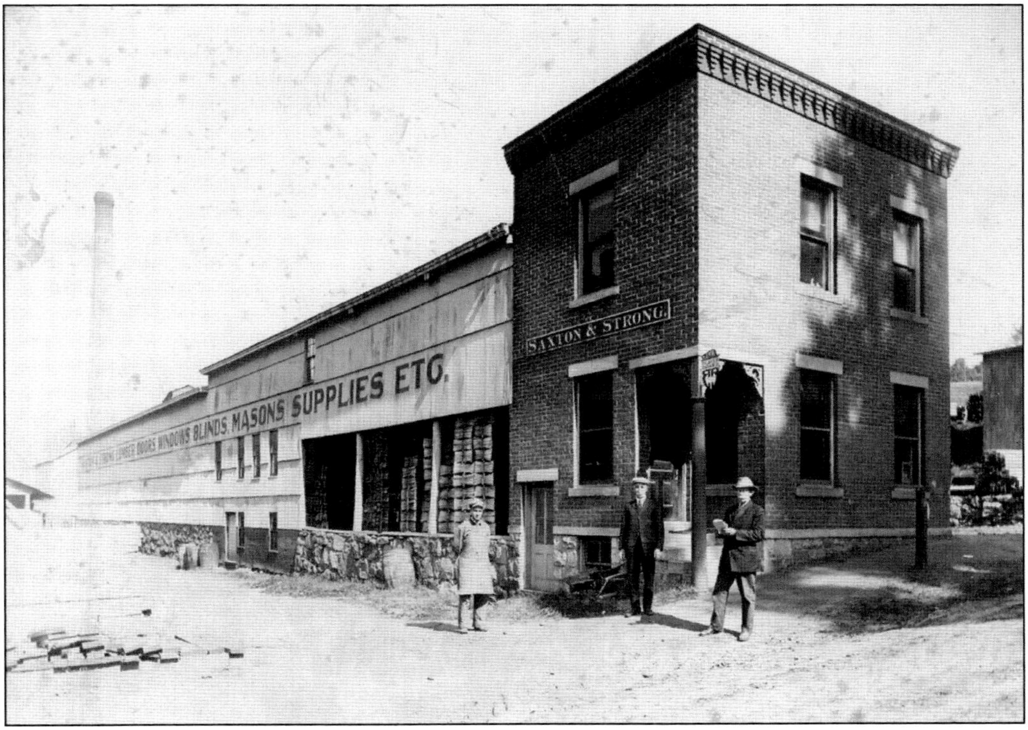

In 1879, Saxton and Strong lumber and timber business was on the corner of North Main and Center Streets. Besides wood, they sold mason supplies and a variety of glass, windows, and doors. In this picture taken in 1904 are, from left to right, Duane Beach and company owners William R. Strong and Frank Saxton. (Courtesy of Bristol Historical Society.)

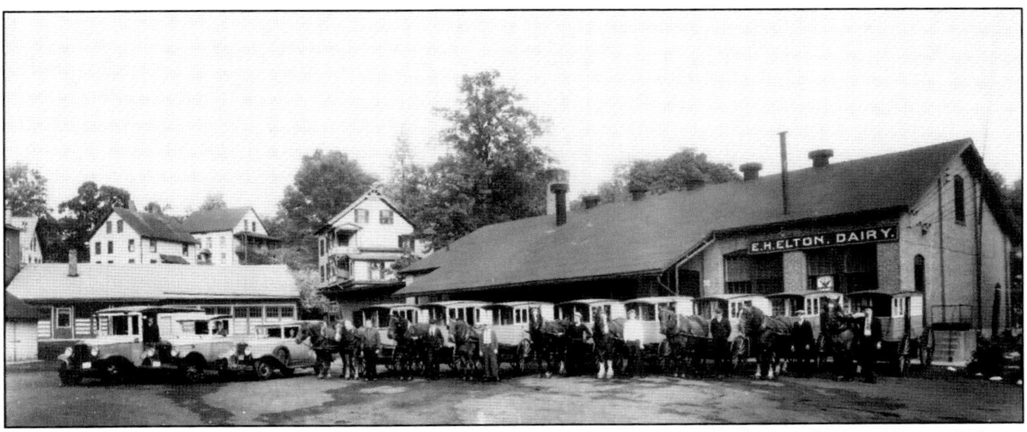

Edwin H. Elton was born in Bristol on November 5, 1882, the son of John and Mary Elton. Edwin started his dairy business in 1910 delivering to homes with one horse and wagon. As his business grew he moved to North Street near Federal Street. His staff grew to 25 men with 14 horses and wagons. Edwin became more efficient, replacing the horses with milk trucks and new machinery. In 1958, he sold the business to Guida-Sebert of New Britain. Edwin died on January 19, 1969. This picture shows Elton Dairy's building on North Street with employees standing next to the company's milk trucks. (Courtesy of Bristol Historical Society.)

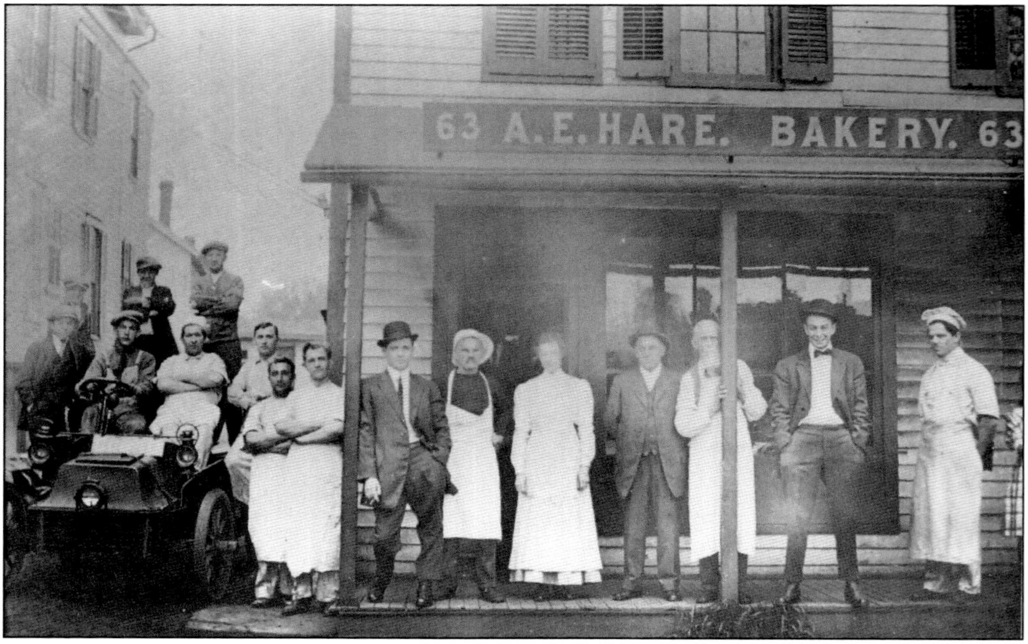

In 1897, Averitt E. Hare worked with George T. Cook under the name G. T. Cook and Hare Brothers. Averitt opened his own business called A. E. Hare Bakery located at 63 North Street. In this picture taken around 1905 are the employees of Hare's Bakery.

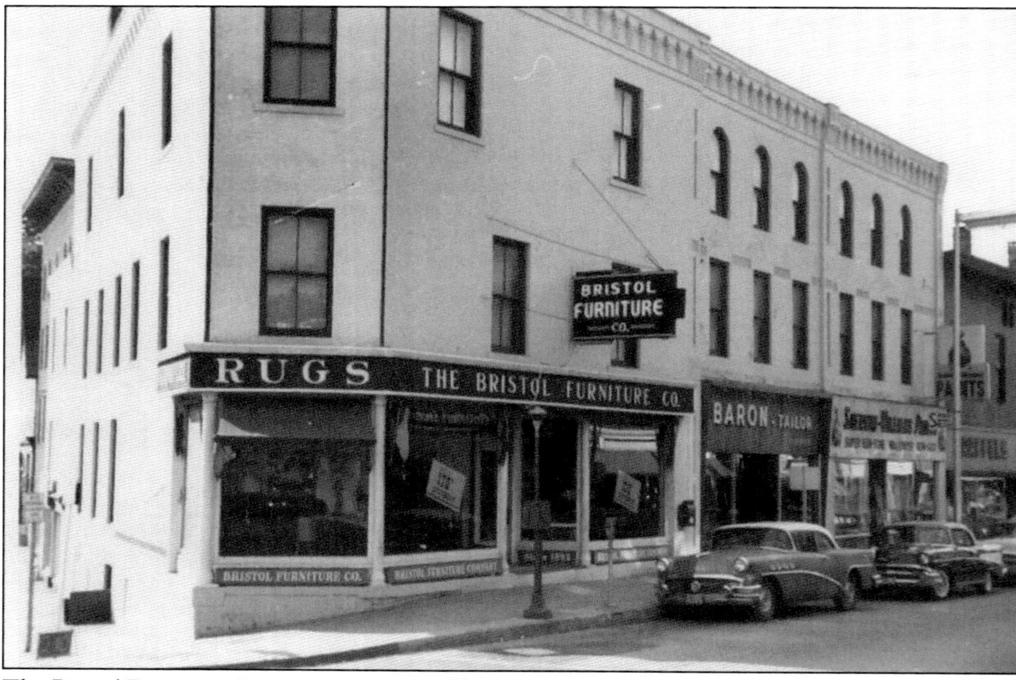

The Bristol Furniture Company was owned by James W. Skelly. In 1913, the business incorporated with James as president and Charles H. Hyde as secretary and treasurer. The business was located at 53 North Main Street with four floors that sold furniture, carpet, stoves, and ranges. In the 1960s, this building was torn down as part of the downtown redevelopment. (Courtesy of Bristol Town Clerk Office.)

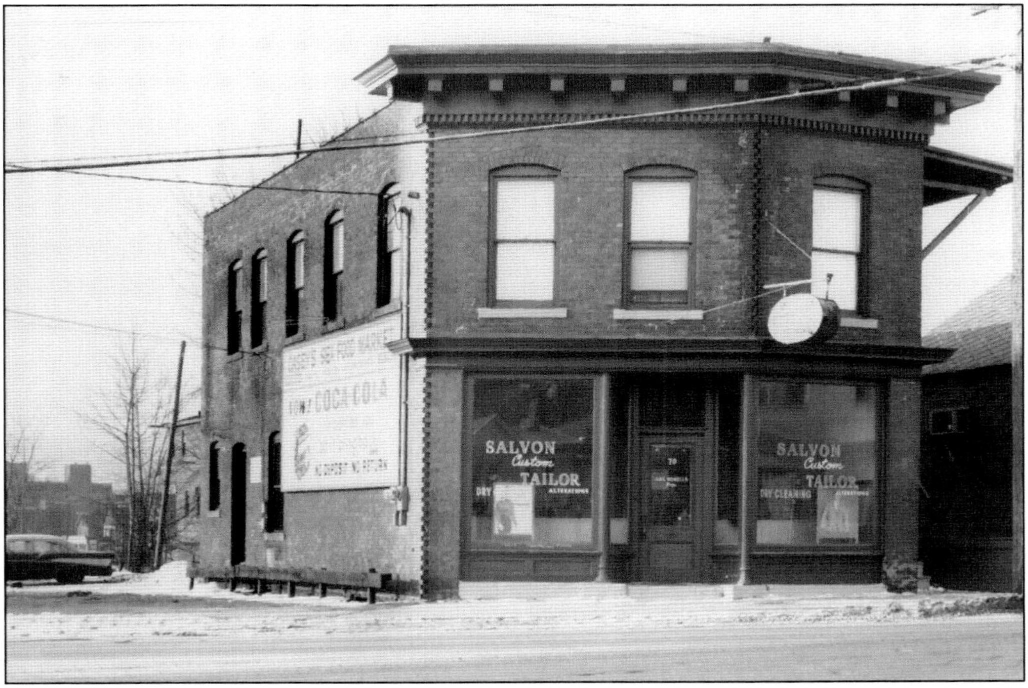

Casey Seafood Market was started by Daniel Casey in 1912 at 64 North Main Street. Daniel's three brothers, William, "Fluery," and Raymond, joined the business. Daniel's son, James P. Casey, worked for his father in 1933 and took over the business in 1955. James's brother, Bob, took over the business in 1968. When the building was torn down for redevelopment, Casey Seafood Market moved to 524 North Main Street across from the Bristol Polish Club. In this picture, Salvon Custom Tailoring business was in the building. The Casey Seafood Market sign is still on the left side of the building. (Courtesy of Bristol Town Clerk Office.)

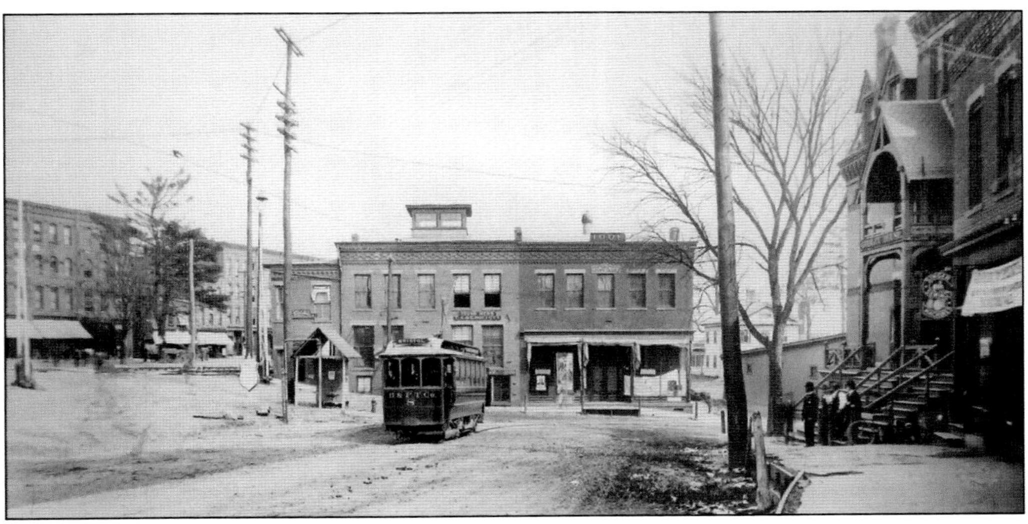

This 1890s picture was facing Main Street with Prospect Street on the left and the Nott-Seymour building and Gridley House on the corner.

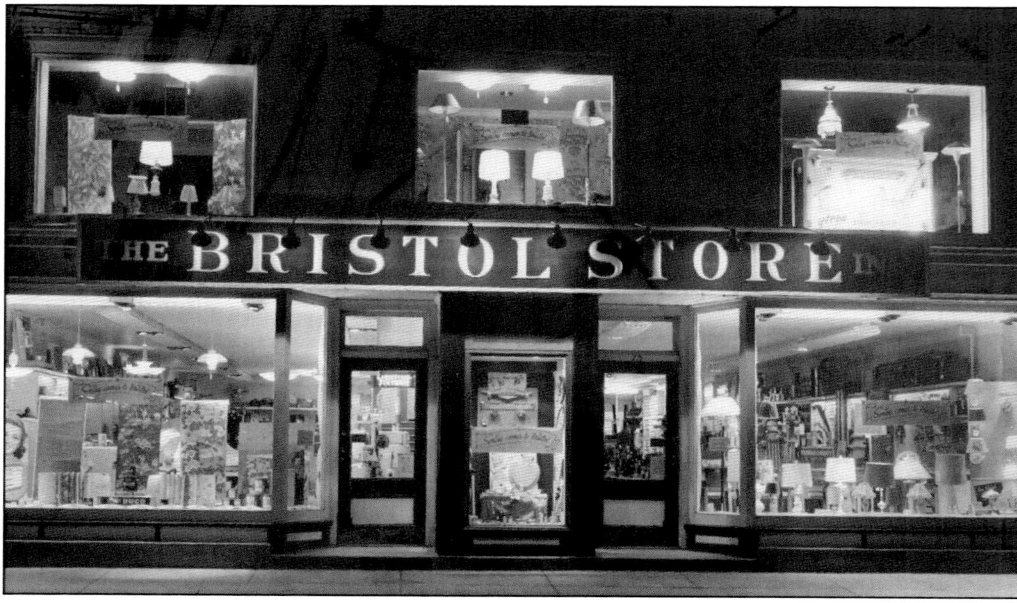

In 1919, Charles Kushlan started his business on North Main Street called the Bristol Under Price Store. As his business grew, Charles moved in 1941 to 71–75 Laurel Street and changed the name to the Bristol Store, Inc. In 1961, they bought the former Italian American Club next door so the business could expand. The Bristol Store sold major appliances, hardware, home decorations, contractor supplies, and lawn and garden supplies. When Charles died in 1965, his nephew, David Kushlan, took over the business. The business closed in 1986. (Courtesy of Bristol Chamber of Commerce.)

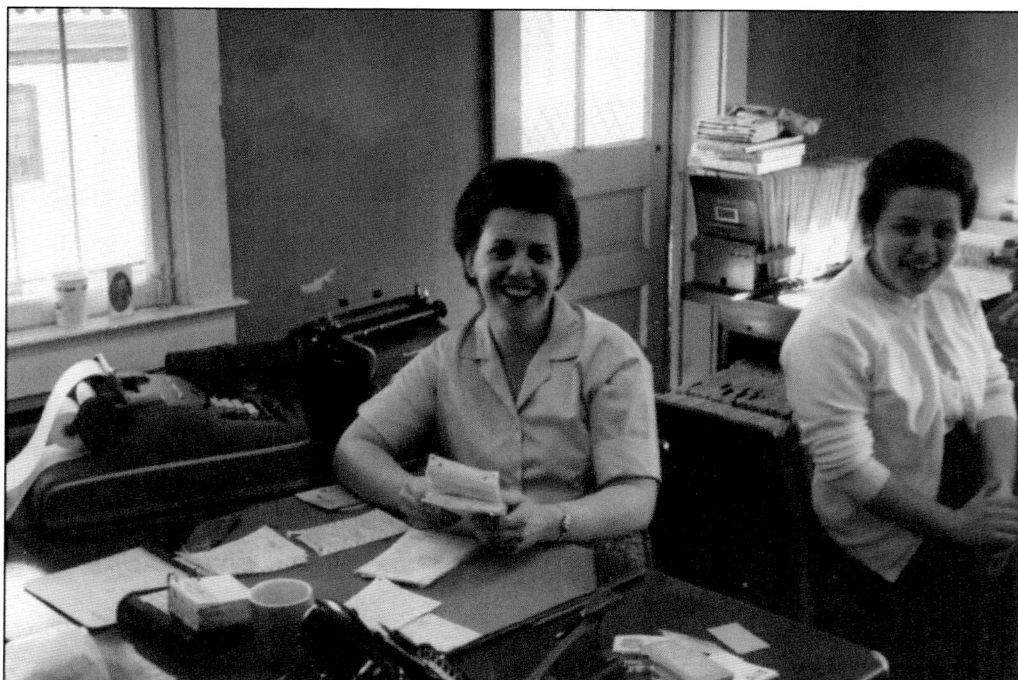

In this 1970s picture taken inside the office at the Bristol Store are employees, Gertrude Vasile and Theresa Shores, who were the bookkeepers for the company. (Courtesy of Sammy Vasile Jr.)

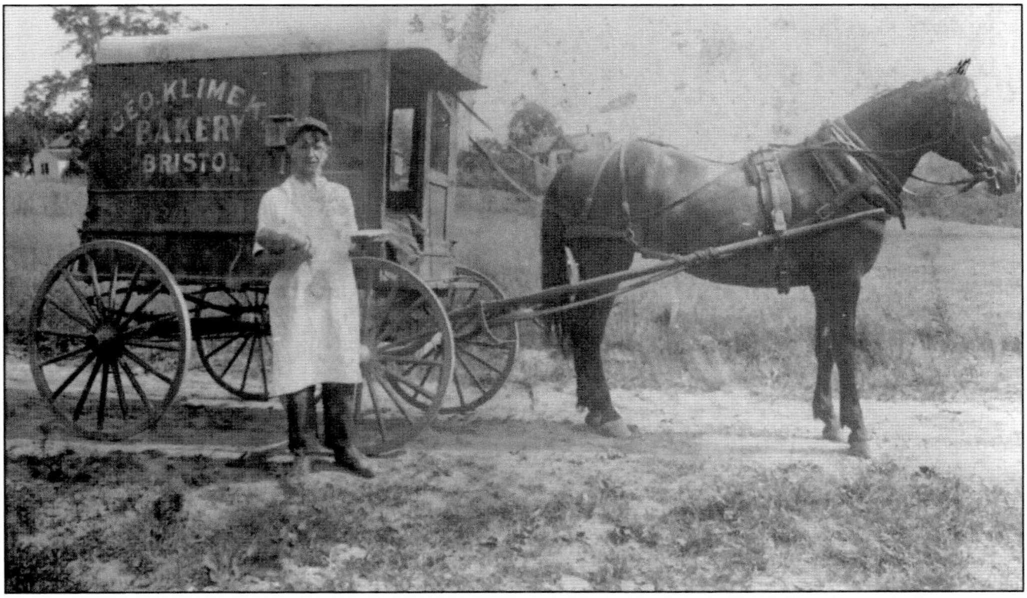

George Klimek was born in Touchow, Poland, in 1876. He arrived in the United States and came to Bristol in 1902. In 1907, George married Josephine Firlejowa, and they had six children. George had a bakery and grocery business located on Wolcott Street. In this picture, George is standing next to his delivery wagon holding his baked goods in the early 1920s. (Courtesy of Carol Deheny.)

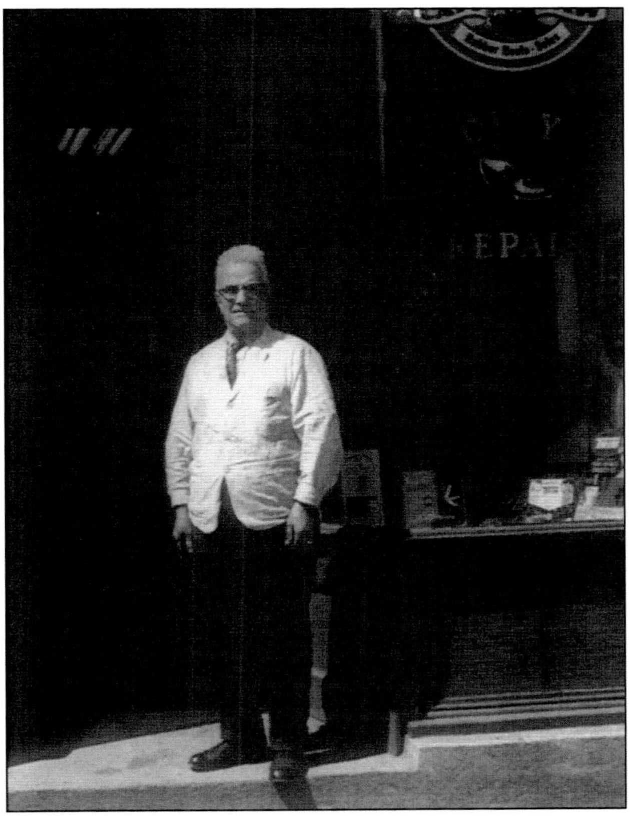

In the early 1920s, John Bettua worked at the New Departure Manufacturing Company on North Main Street. John left his job at the factory to start his own shoe repair business located at 92 Main Street called City Shoe Repairing. In 1942, John moved his business to 13 Main Street and would remain here through the 1950s. In this picture, John is standing outside of his store at 13 Main Street. (Courtesy of Bob Bettua.)

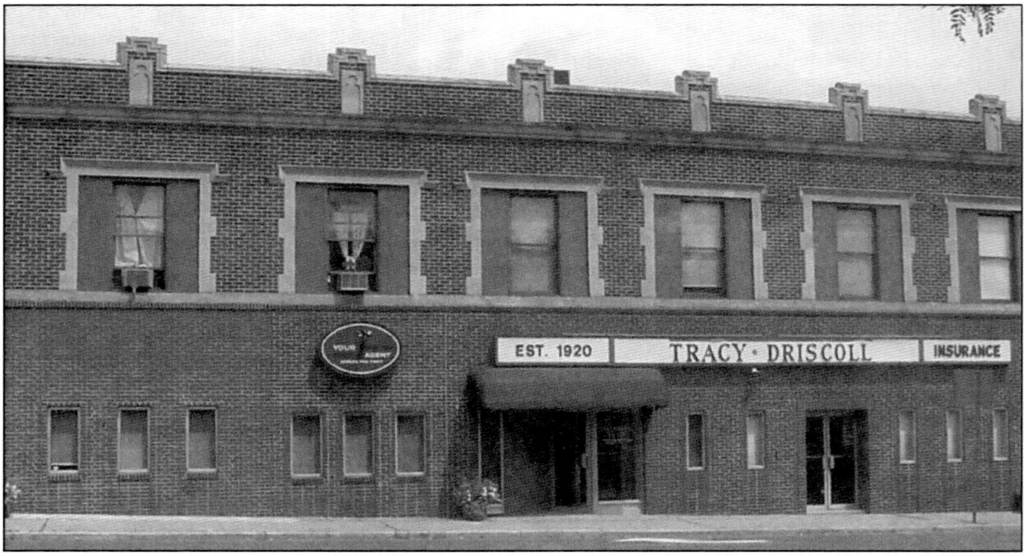

William J. Tracy and Hillary S. Driscoll started Tracy Driscoll Insurance on December 4, 1930, located at 2 Riverside Avenue. In 1924, the business moved to its present location at 126 Main Street. In 1927, the business became incorporated with its officers: William J. Tracy, president; William E. Tracy, secretary; and Hillary S. Driscoll, treasurer. Tracy Driscoll Insurance continued to grow, adding real estate to its personal, commercial, industrial, and group insurance. This picture was taken in 2000 of Tracy Driscoll after renovations to the building were done. (Courtesy of Tracy-Driscoll Company.)

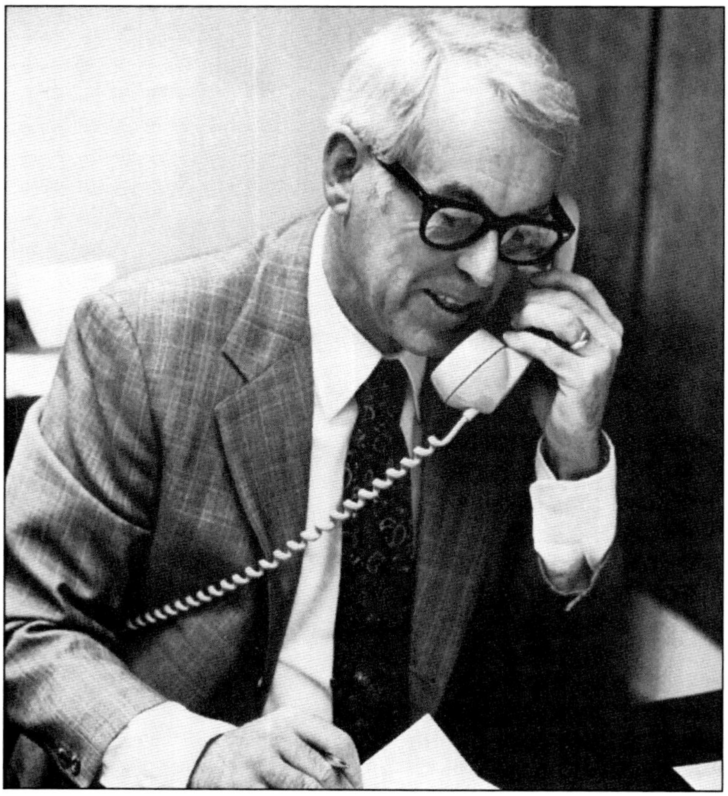

William J. Tracy's son, Bill, joined the company in 1951 after college. In 1980, the business was owned by Bill Tracy, Dick Bellemare, and Lyndon "Red" Ratcliff. Over the 90-year history, Tracy-Driscoll continues to provide insurance and financial services for their personal and commercial customers. Today the company is owned by five managing partners: Robert McFadden, Brian Dehm, Michael Rivers, Frederic DeNote, and Richard Caruso. In this picture taken in the 1980s, Bill Tracy is sitting at his desk talking to a client. (Courtesy of Tracy-Driscoll Company.)

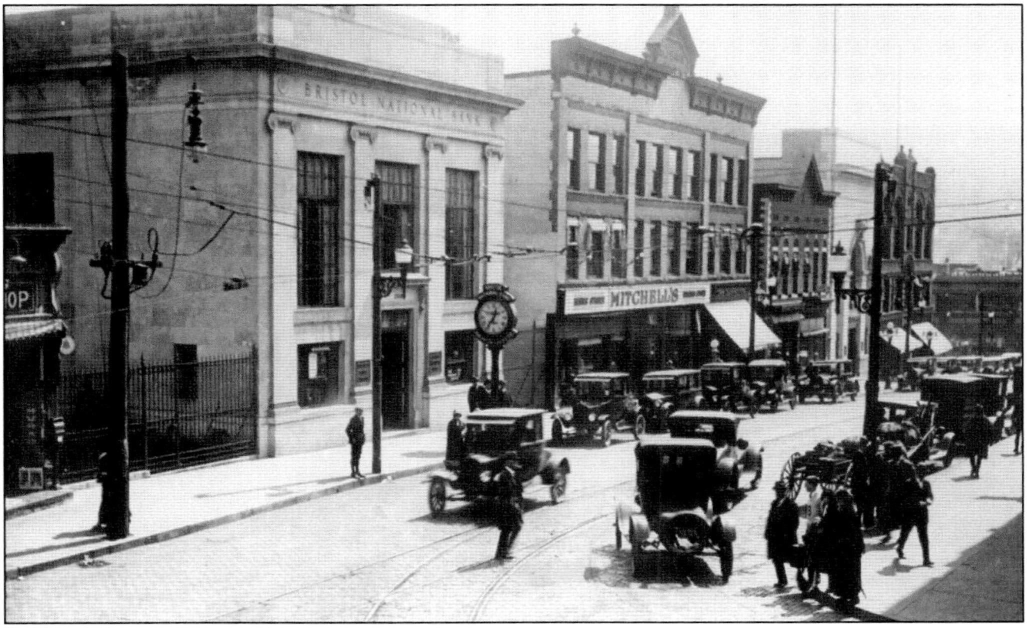

In this 1920s photograph of upper Main Street is the Bristol National Bank (at left) before they expanded on either side of the bank. Main Street at that time turned into North Main Street as seen in the picture along with the trolley tracks. Today the former bank is owned by United Way of Bristol, and the Greater Bristol Chamber of Commerce has their offices on the first floor.

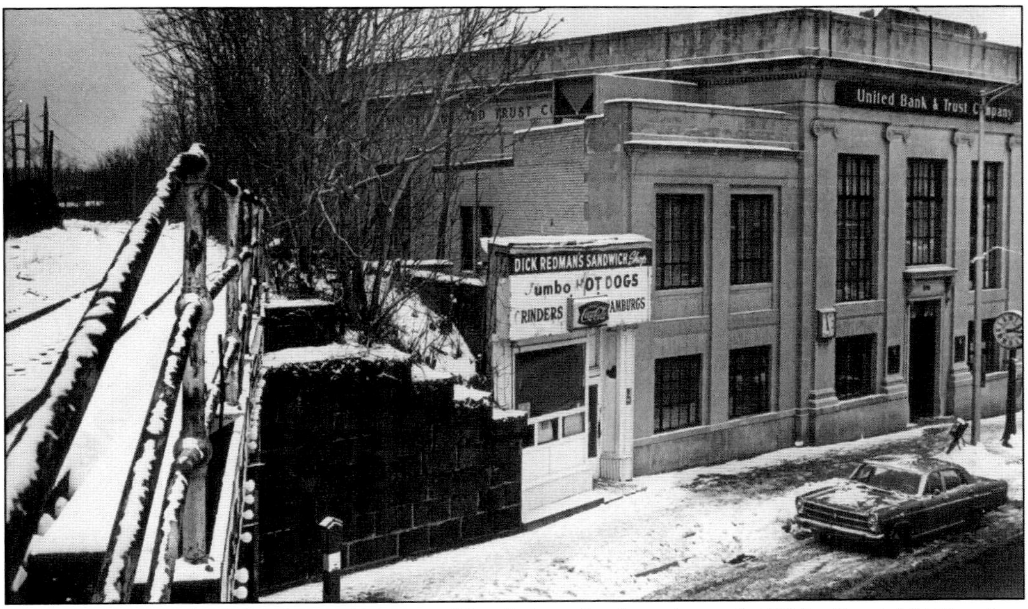

The building on the left of Bristol National Bank dates back to the early 1900s. Patrick F. Condon developed the land that was owned by the railroad. One of the early businesses was C. V. Mason Insurance. The Mohill Newsstand delivered magazines from here. Milt Schlossberg and Royden C. Barton operated their newsstand here. Joe Santaniello turned the place into a lunchroom followed by Doty's Restaurant. In 1976, when this picture was taken, Redman's Sandwich was in the building. When United Bank and Trust moved into the former Bristol National Bank, this building was torn down to make way for the expansion on either side of the bank.

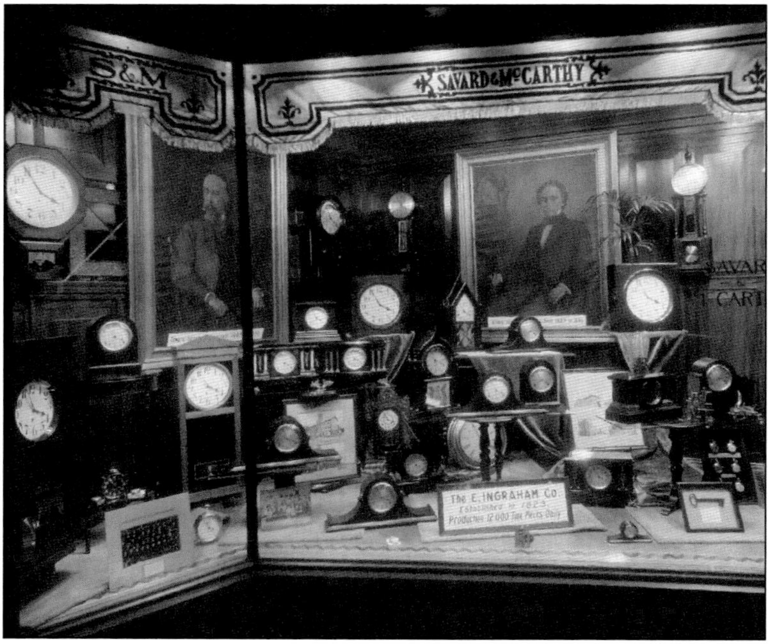

Savard and McCarthy was a men's clothing store owned by Joseph H. Savard and John E. McCarthy. Their business was located at 165 Main Street. In this 1924 picture, their storefront display shows the E. Ingraham clocks that Ingraham's was selling at the time. (Courtesy of American Clock and Watch Museum.)

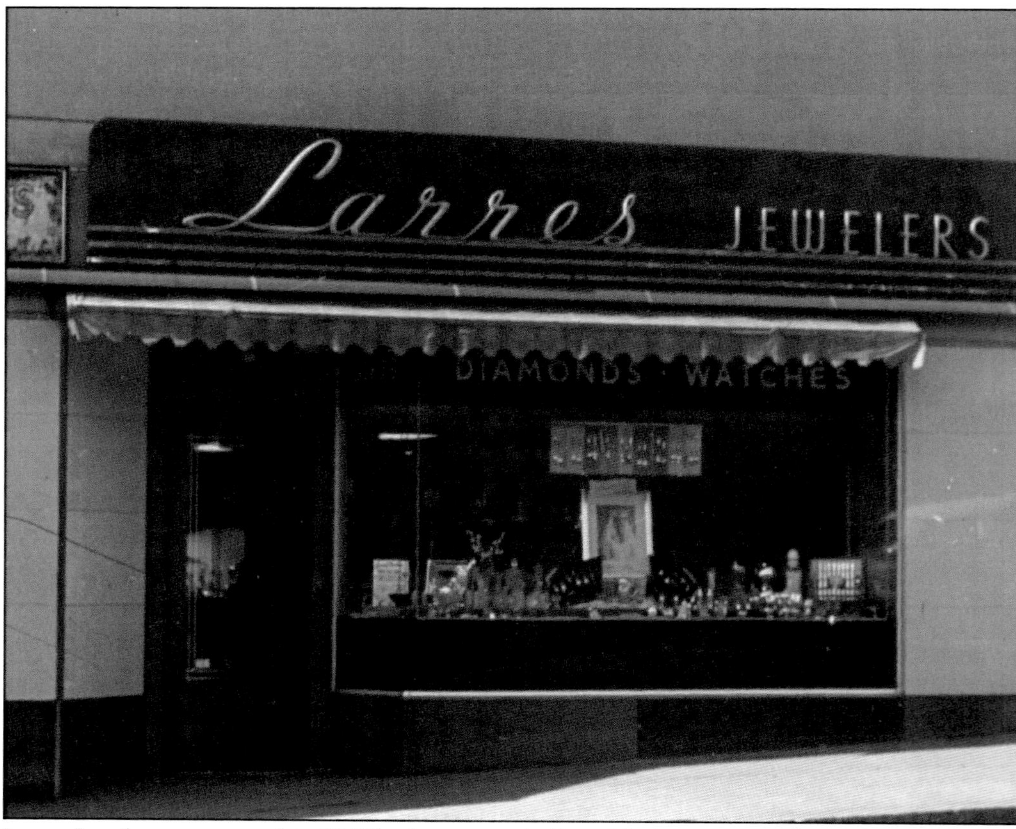

Larres Jewelers was started in 1947 by Lawrence A. Zipp. His business was located on the corner of North Main and Main Streets. During the 1960s, the business moved to its new location at 184 Main Street. (Courtesy of Bristol Chamber of Commerce.)

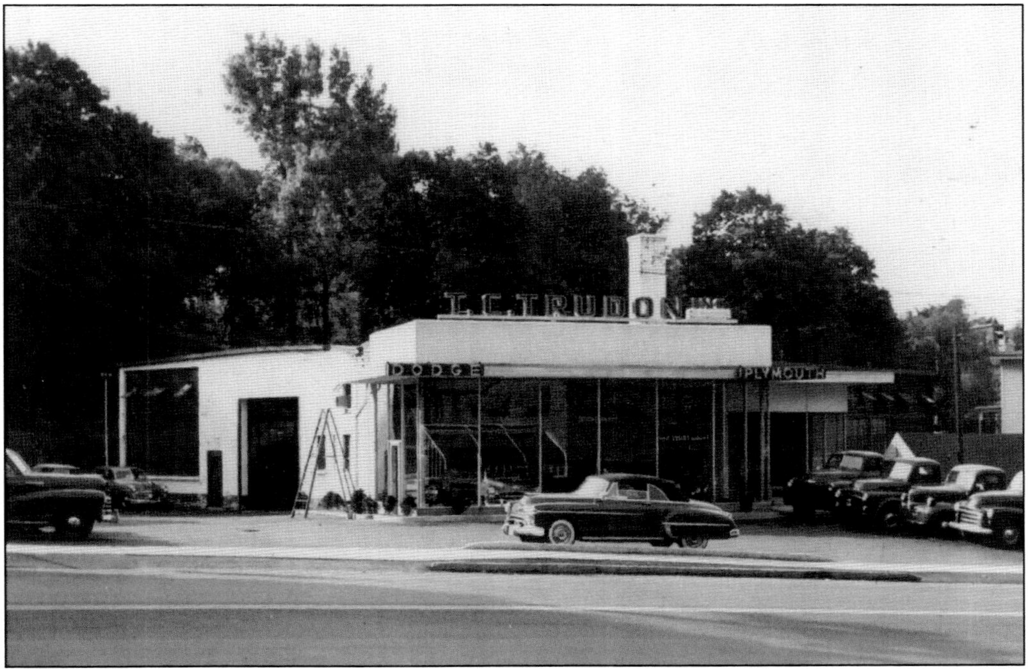

Theodore C. Trudon started his Ford automobile sales and service in 1936 at 142 North Street on U.S. Route 6. The company, T. C. Trudon, sold all Ford models, including LTD, Thunderbird, Torino, Pinto, Galaxie, Maverick, and Mustangs.

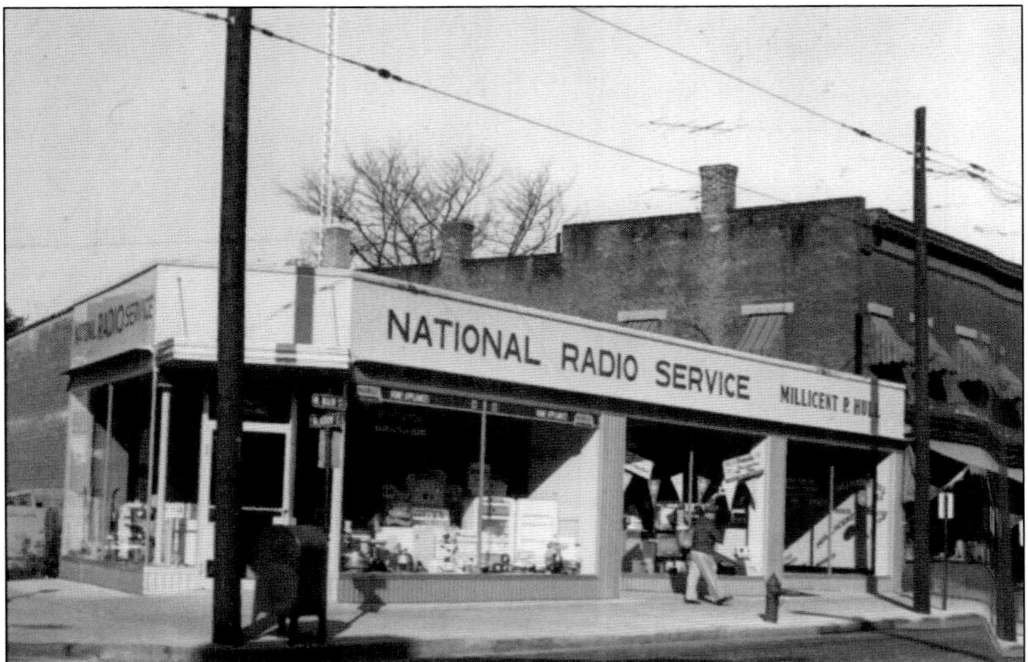

National Radio Service started in 1937 at 19 School Street selling and repairing all brands of radios and refrigerators and was owned by Leo F. LeFrancois. The business moved to 833 Farmington Avenue when downtown redevelopment tore down the building. (Courtesy of Bristol Chamber of Commerce.)

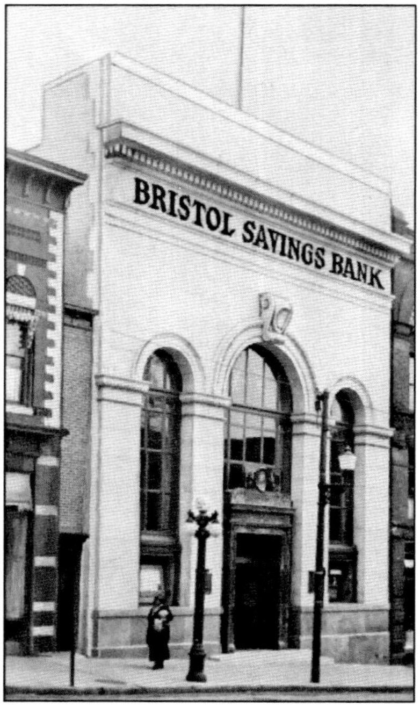

The Bristol Savings Bank constructed this building at 178 Main Street in 1923. This was the bank's third location since it opened in 1870. By 1937, Bristol Savings Bank needed more room and there was not sufficient land to expand this building. In 1937, the former Bristol Bank Trust building was for sale on 150 Main Street. The Bristol Savings Bank bought the building and moved there in 1938.

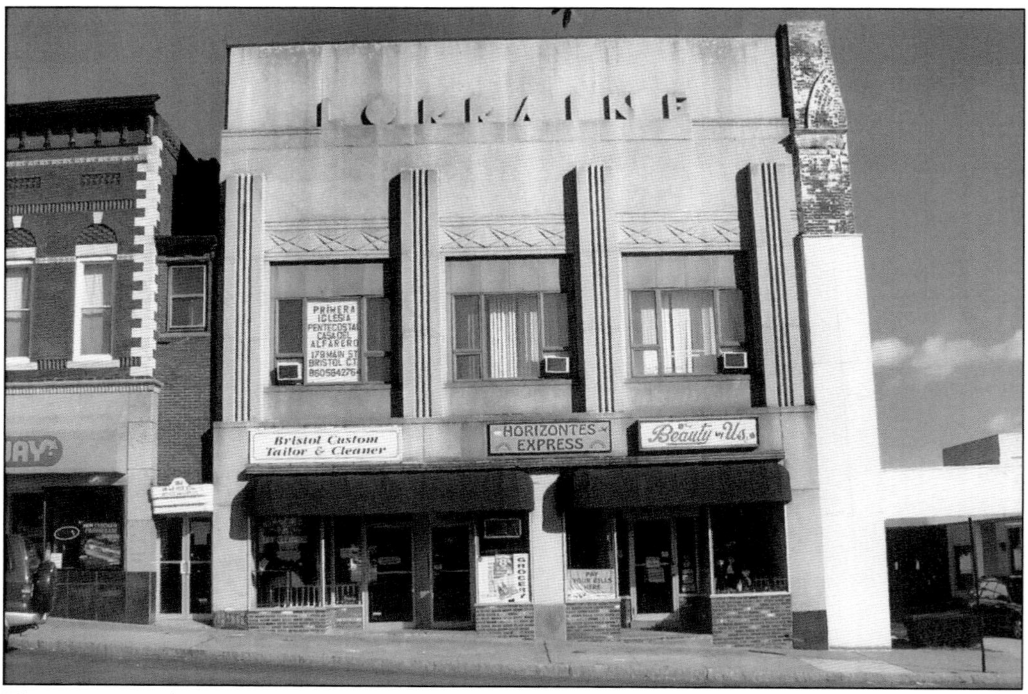

The Lorraine Shoe Company, Inc., was started in 1930 at 193 Main Street by David A. Lipman and his wife, Esther. In 1940, Lipman bought the building from Bristol Savings Bank for their business. In the 1960s, Loreto and Sharon Nicoletti bought the building. Nicoletti opened Bristol Custom Tailor and Cleaner store. On March 28, 2006, Mark Policki purchased the building from Nicoletti and started Bristol Cleaners and Custom Tailoring. Mark rents out the rest of his building to Beauty by Us, the Family Store, and upstairs to the church Primera Iglesia Pentecostal Casa Del Alfarero, Inc. (Courtesy of Mark Policki.)

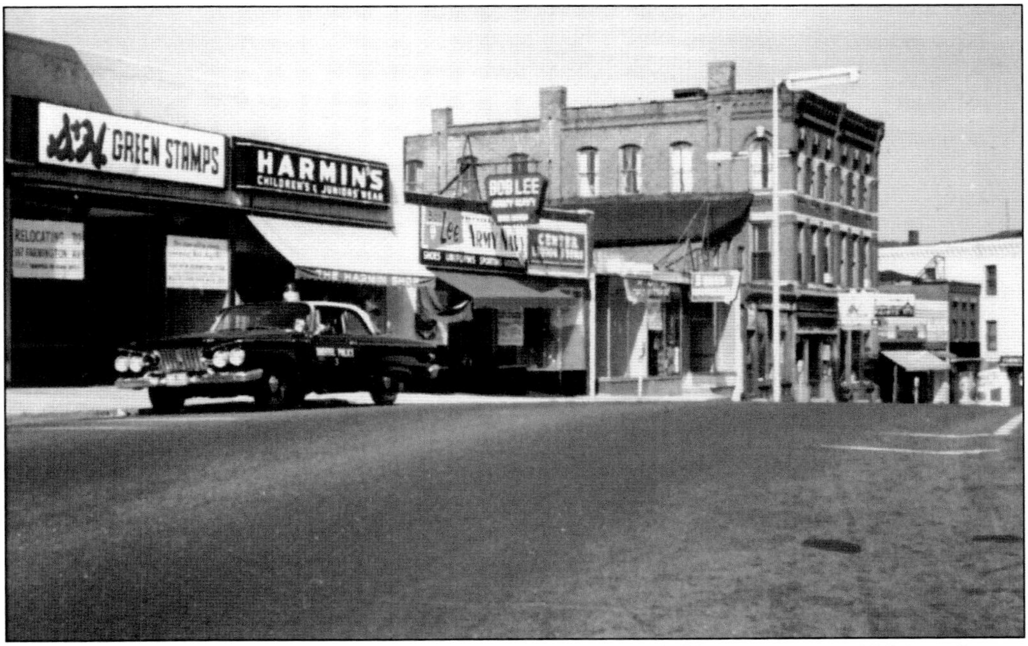

In 1941, John and Mina Laurit opened Harmin's, their first children's store at 193 Main Street. In 1949, Harmin's moved to 35 North Main Street. In this picture was their North Main Street location that was later torn down for redevelopment in the 1960s.

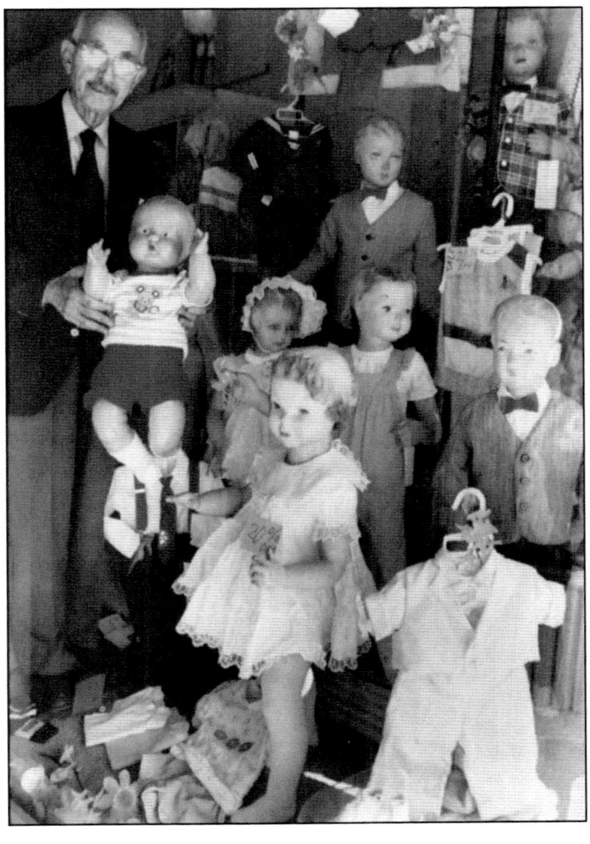

In this picture, owner John Laurit is finishing a children's display in the window of his store, Harmin's. The dolls were used as mannequins to display the clothes the store sold. (Courtesy of Bristol Historical Society.)

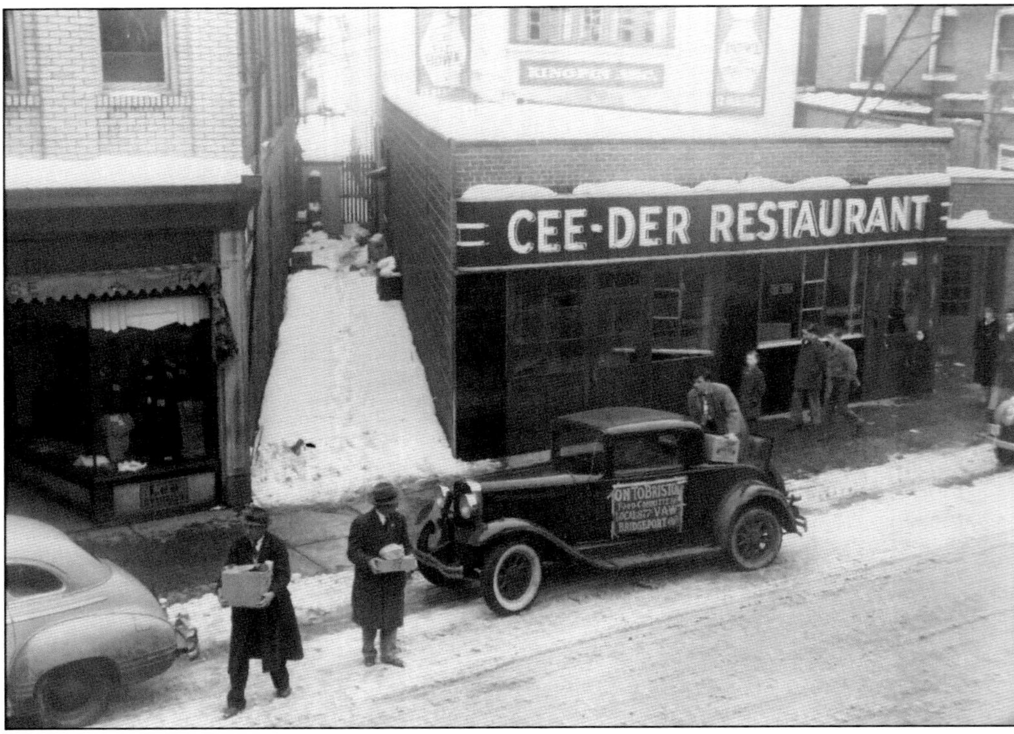

In 1942, Domenico A. and Camillo T. Sinisgalli started their business, Cee-Der Restaurant, located at 147 North Main Street. In this picture taken in 1945 in front of the restaurant were workers from around the state that were supporting the General Motors employees that were on strike in Bristol.

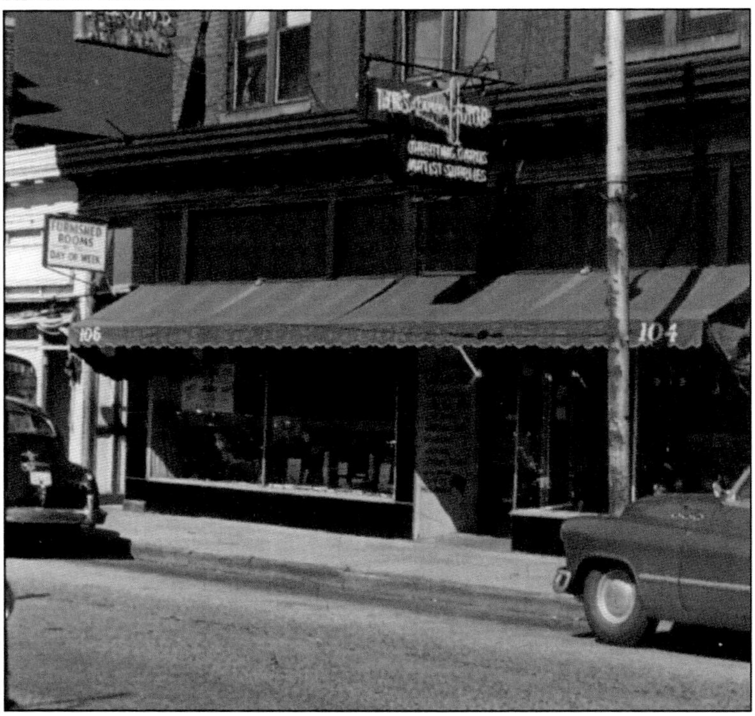

Tab's Camera Shop owned by Nicolas Tabellione was located at 104 North Main Street. The business sold cameras and projectors, photograph supplies, and serviced cameras. Tab's also did professional photography. When the Bristol Plaza was built in 1960 by Carpenter Construction, Tab's opened a second store there. (Courtesy of Bristol Chamber of Commerce.)

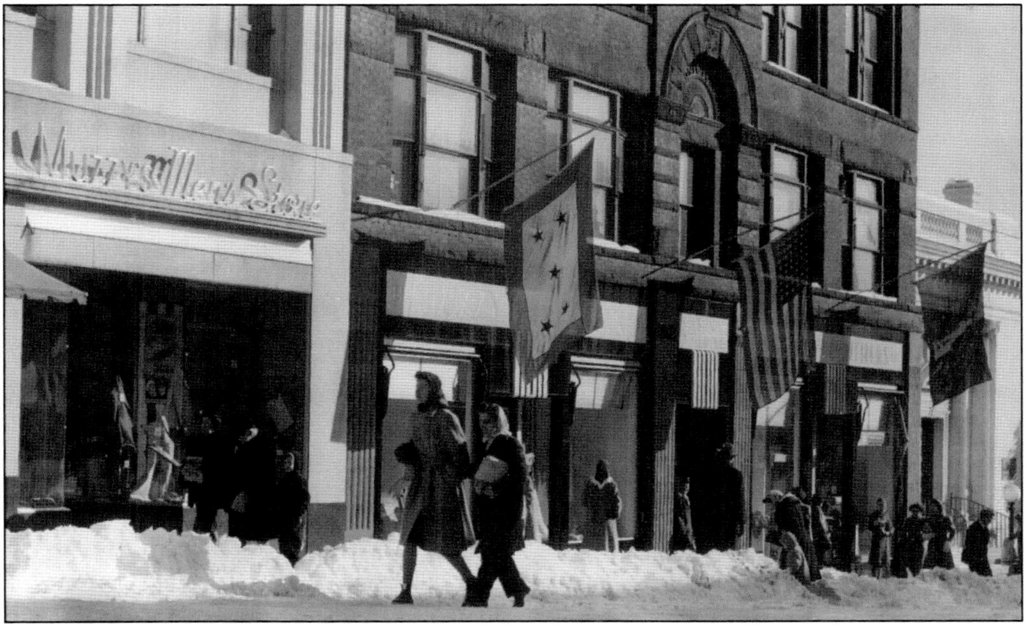

In the 1950s, A. J. Muzzy's business name was changed to Muzzy Brothers Department Store. The store was three levels and now carried everything from clothing and housewares to appliances, accessories, and gifts. On October 4, 1961, the building was destroyed by fire and was torn down.

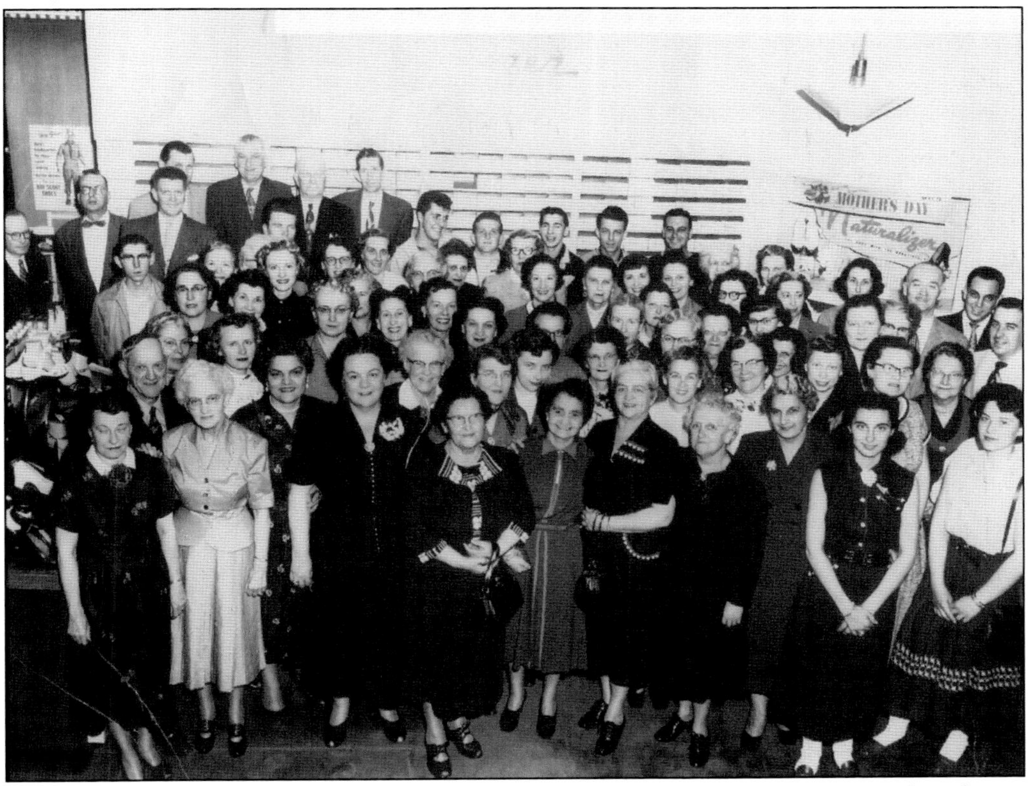

This 1955 picture, taken by photographer Gene Marchand of Bristol, shows a group of employees who worked at Muzzy Brothers Department Store.

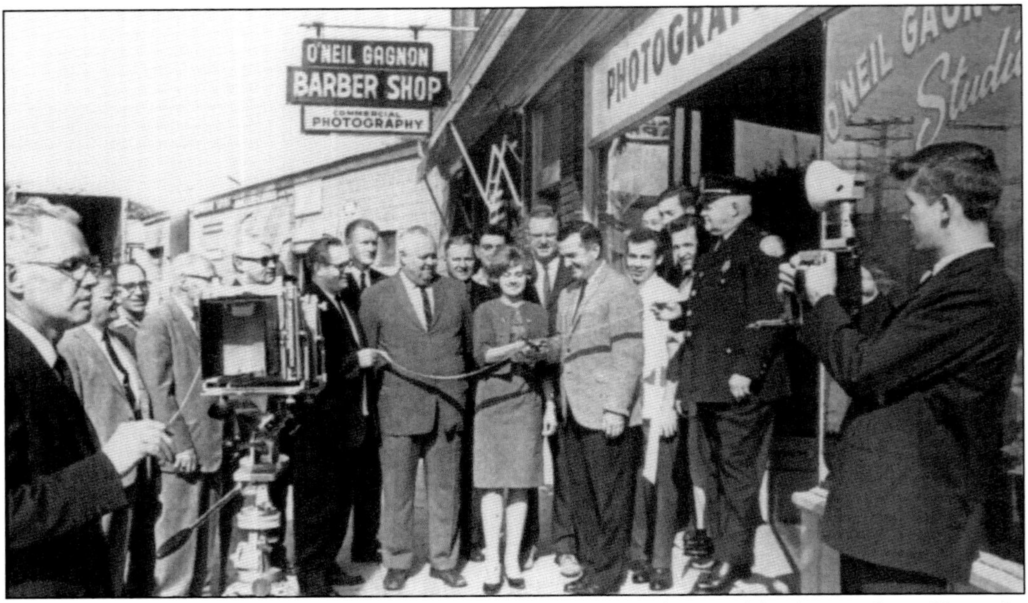

In 1944, O'Neil Gagnon Sr. came to Bristol. He was a professional barber and a self-taught photographer. O'Neil worked at various shops, including Tony's Barbershop at 6 Divinity Street. He also worked as a photographer for the *Bristol Press* for 20 years. In 1961, Gagnon opened his barbershop and photography studio on 160 School Street. At left taking the picture is O'Neil Gagnon Sr. From left to right holding the ribbon are fire commissioner Robert T. Adams; copublisher of the *Bristol Press*, Clarkson S. Barnes; Gagnon's secretary, Linda Suchodolski; Mayor Walter J. Murphy Jr.; and police chief Thomas V. McCarthy. On the right is Gagnon's son, Raymond, holding the camera. (Courtesy of Neil Gagnon.)

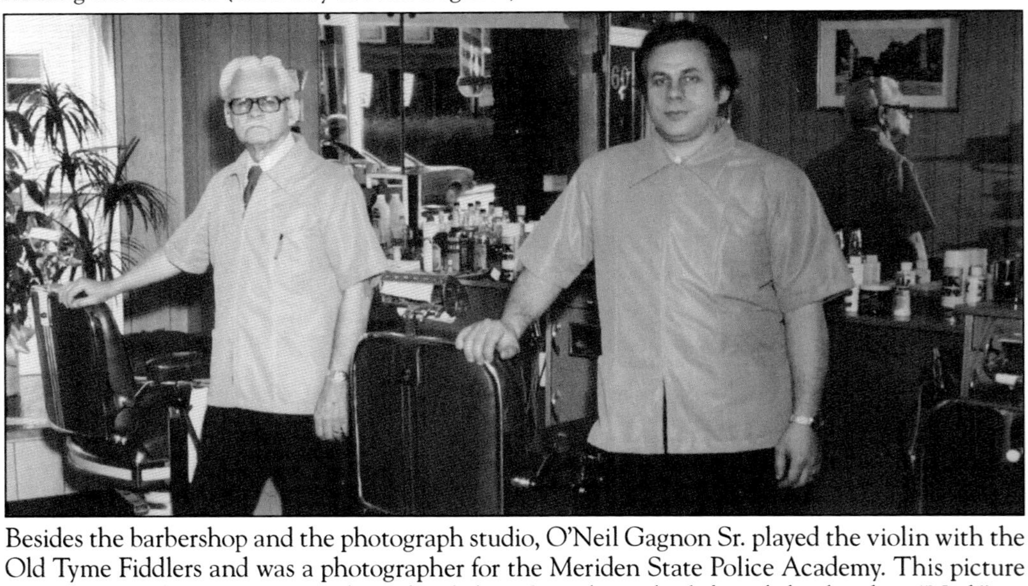

Besides the barbershop and the photograph studio, O'Neil Gagnon Sr. played the violin with the Old Tyme Fiddlers and was a photographer for the Meriden State Police Academy. This picture taken in 1982 by Ray Gagnon shows his father, O'Neil, on the left with his brother, "Neil," on the right, standing next to the chairs where they cut hair on 160 School Street. Neil worked with his father for 20 years in their barbershop. In 1999, Neil bought the business and the building from his father. In 2004, O'Neil Gagnon Sr. died, and in 2009, Neil sold the building. (Courtesy of Neil Gagnon.)

Six

Around the Town

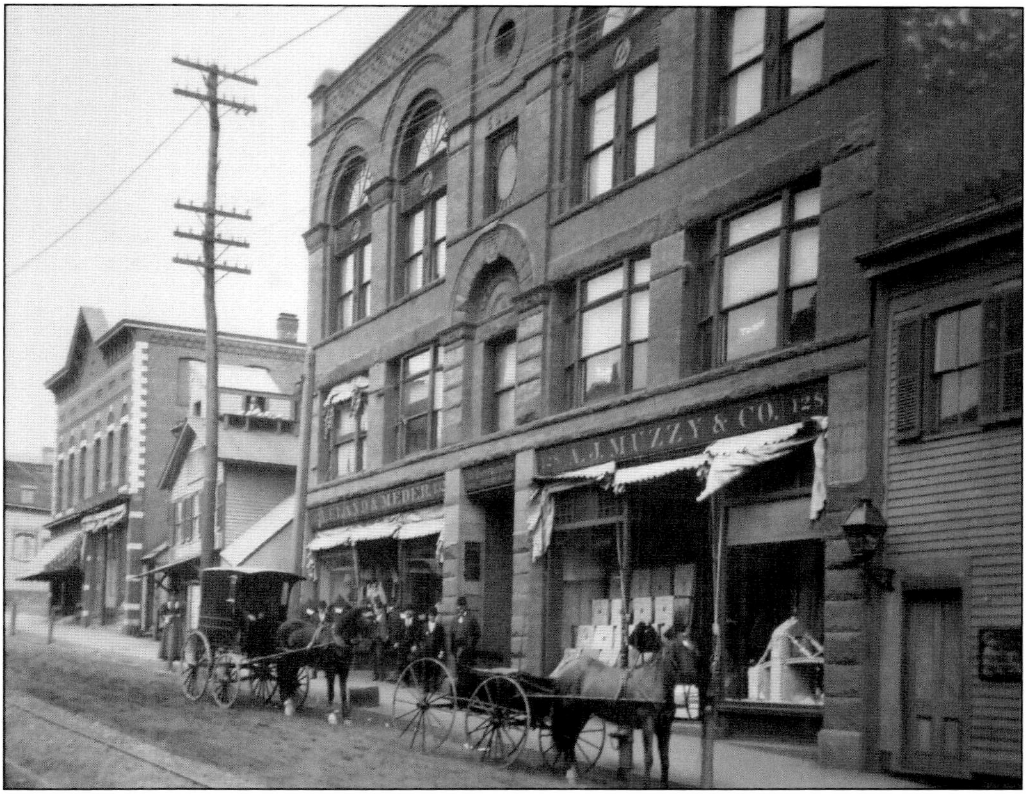

By 1910, this group of businessmen on upper Main Street was already established. The first building on the left was Woodruff's Bakery. The next building was Gale Photography Studio, which was later torn down when the Bristol Savings Bank constructed their building. On the right was the Franklin Masonic building constructed in 1891. In their building on the first floor were the Leland and Meder business (left) and the A. J. Muzzy and Company (right). The Masonic building was torn down after a fire destroyed the construction on October 4, 1961. Today Webster Bank has their drive-through service where the building stood.

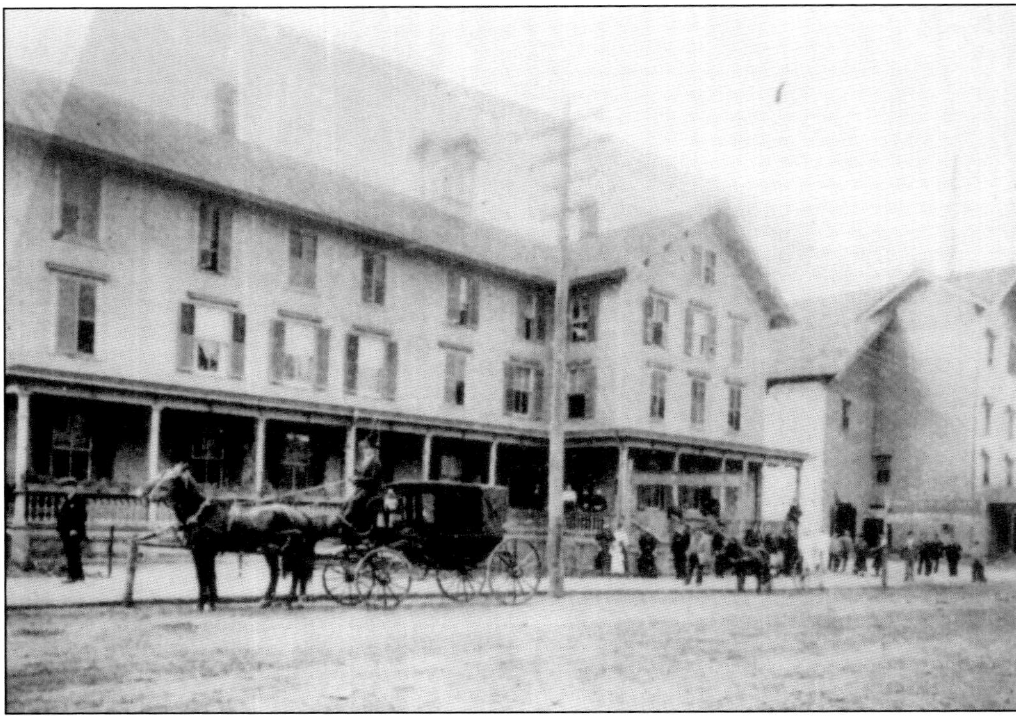

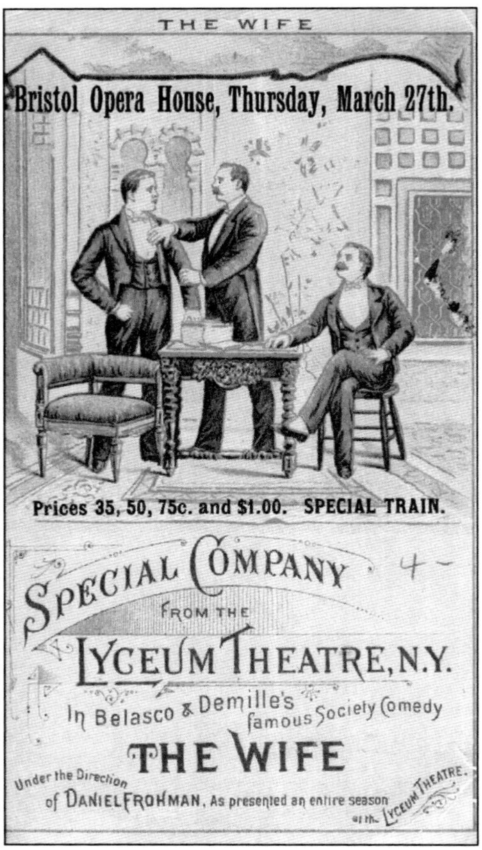

By 1883, both the Commercial House and the Bristol Opera House were established at 17–19 Laurel Street. Charles F. Michael, proprietor, offered lodging at $2 per day with livery stables behind the buildings. The opera house next door showed plays and hosted other events. On December 5, 1912, the Bristol Opera House was destroyed by fire and was torn down.

This was an advertisement for one of the plays called *The Wife* that performed at the Bristol Opera House. (Courtesy of Gary Potter.)

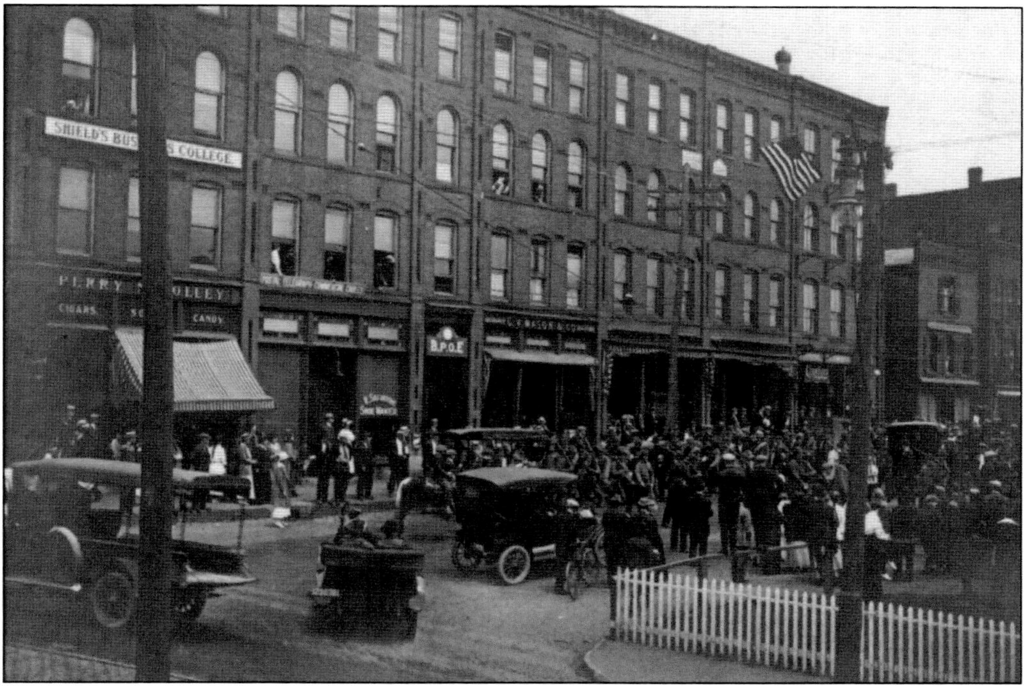

This picture was taken in 1919 on the corner of Main and Prospect Streets and shows the Funk building with a variety of businesses. The Shield's Business College was on the second floor. On the first floor, C. V. Mason Insurance Company occupied space, and next to them, Funk's had their furniture and carpet store along with their undertaking business. Opposite the Funk building was Railroad Park and the train depot. (Courtesy of Tom Dickau.)

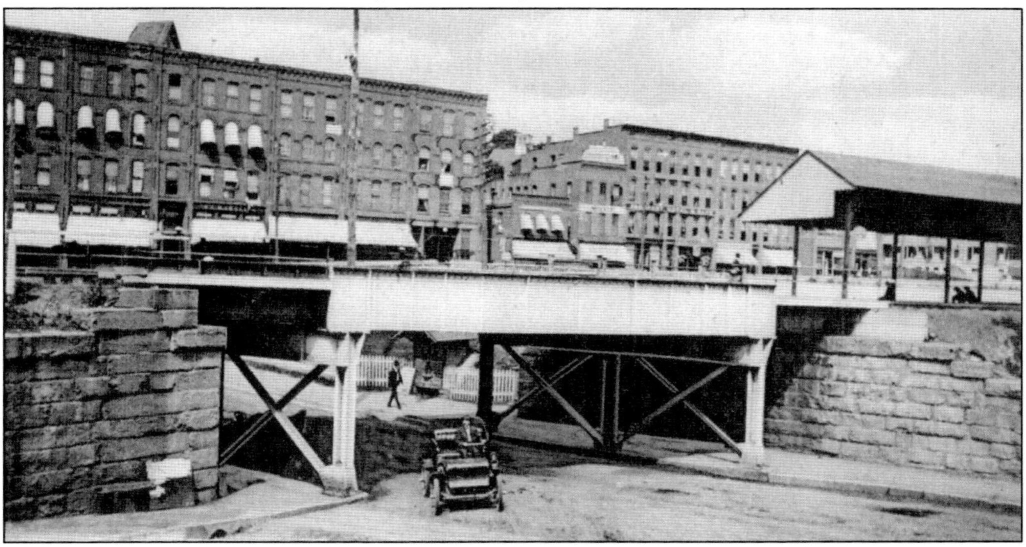

Before the Main Street trestle was built, the railroad tracks were at street level, causing many accidents. On June 19, 1890, a petition was sent from the town selectmen to the New York and New England Railroad Company to consider lowering the grade of Main Street, to remove tracks, and to stop switching over that crossing. In 1901, the railroad trestle was built. In this picture taken at the intersection of Main and North Main Streets, a car is going under the trestle showing Prospect Street on the left in back. (Courtesy of Gary Potter.)

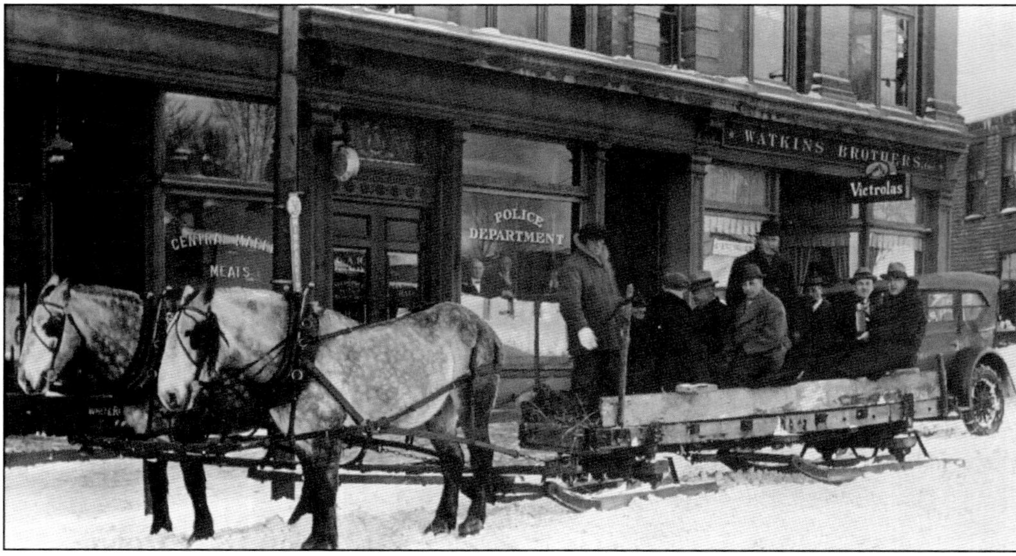

Bristol's first town hall building was constructed in 1901 and was located on North Main Street. The building had three floors. The first floor had retail stores, and the second and third floors were the town offices. From left to right in this 1920s picture are Central Market, the police department, and Watkin Brothers.

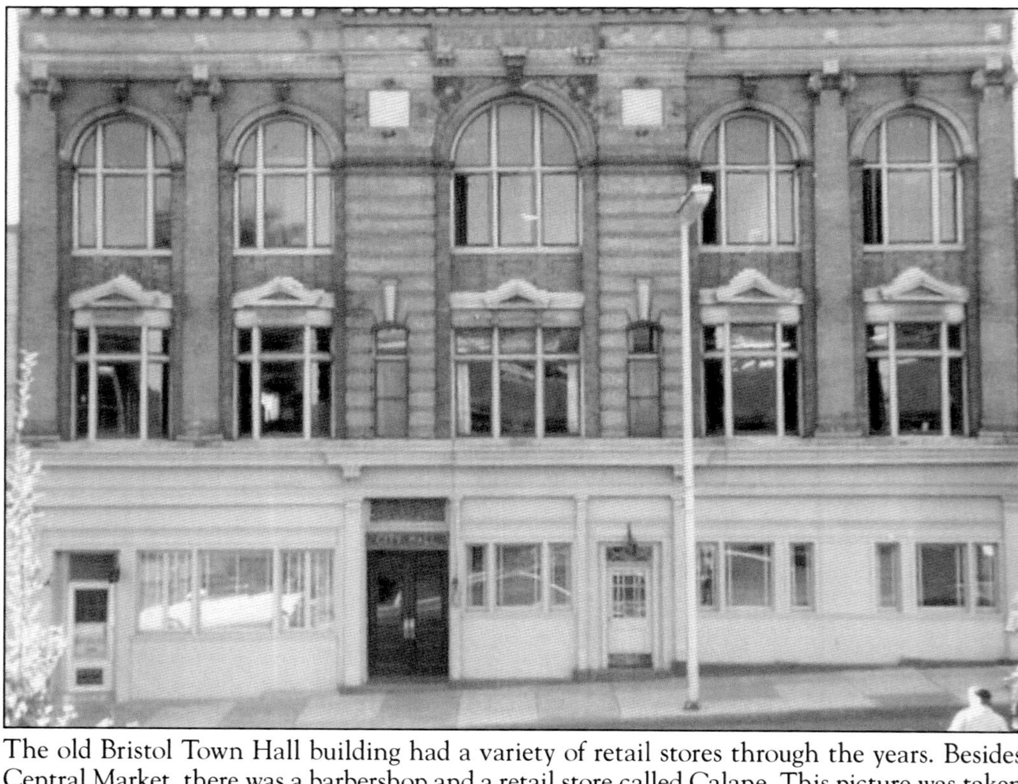

The old Bristol Town Hall building had a variety of retail stores through the years. Besides Central Market, there was a barbershop and a retail store called Calane. This picture was taken in 1961 before it was demolished as part of the downtown redevelopment. (Courtesy of Bristol Town Clerk Office.)

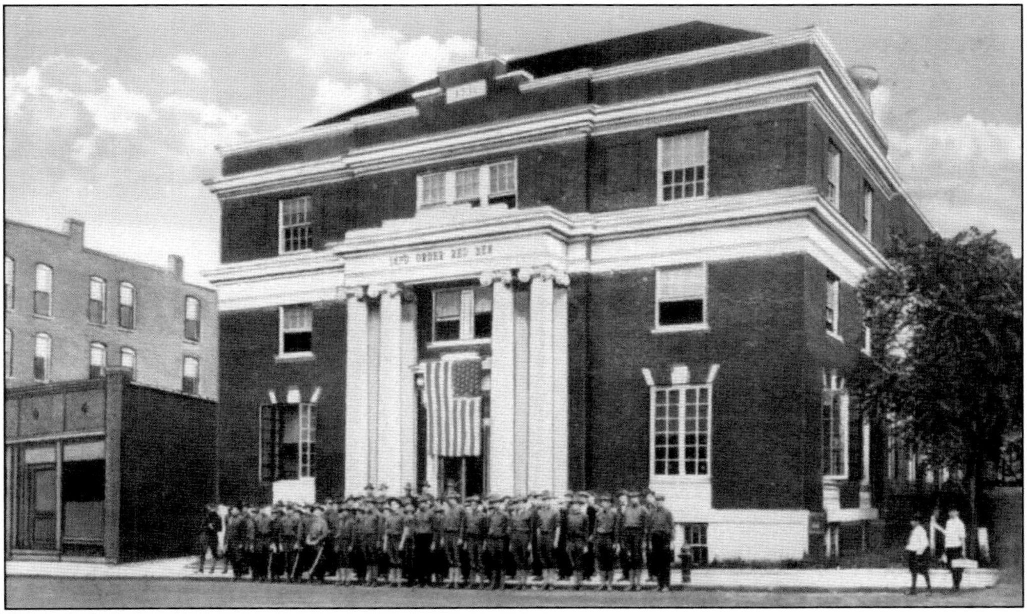

The organization Improved Order of Redmen in Bristol was formed on December 11, 1890. In 1910, the organization became the Redmen Building Company, Inc., when they constructed this building on 43 Prospect Street. Known as Redman's Hall, it was used as the Bristol State Armory until they constructed their building on 61 Center Street around World War I. Later the building became a movie theater called the Carberry Theater. The building now belongs to the Christian Fellowship Center. In this picture are World War I soldiers standing outside when the state armory was in the building.

On the left in this picture was the Rowe Coal and Oil Company started by William H. Rowe in 1910 and located at 184 North Main Street. The Bristol Grain and Supply Company became a business in 1930, selling flour, feed, and poultry supplies. The Bristol Theater in the late 1940s was built to the right of the Bristol Grain and Supply Company. This picture of the two businesses was taken on February 21, 1934, during a blizzard.

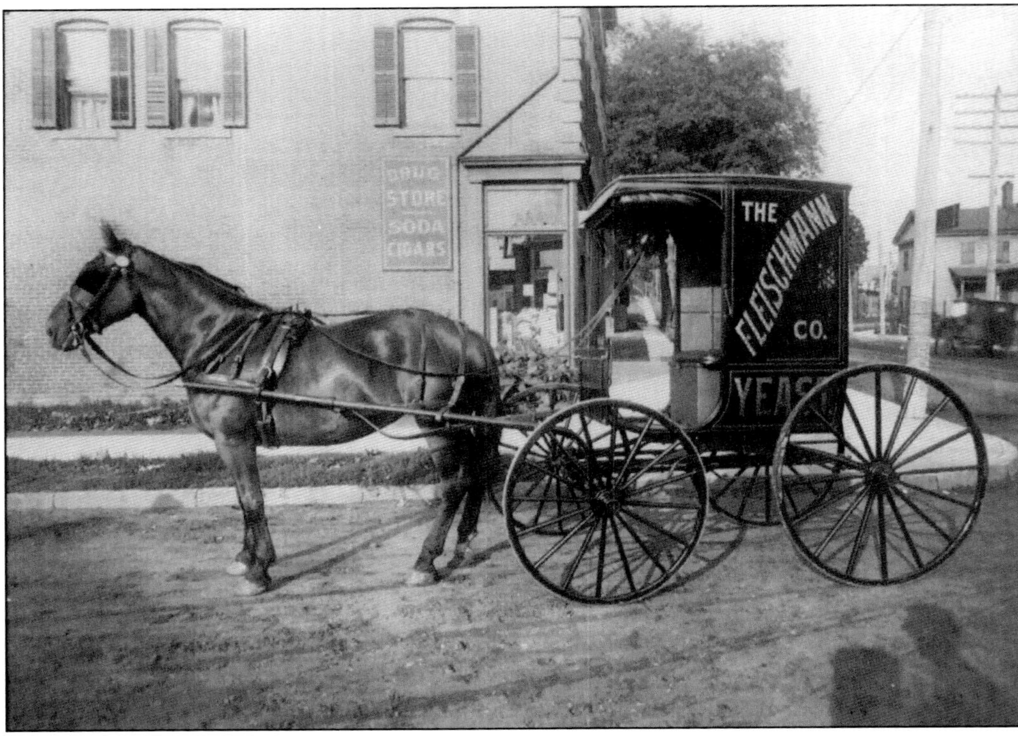

Before automobiles, horse and wagons were used to deliver businesses merchandise. In this *c.* 1914 picture, the Fleishmann Yeast Company is making a delivery to a drugstore on the corner of West and Divinity Streets.

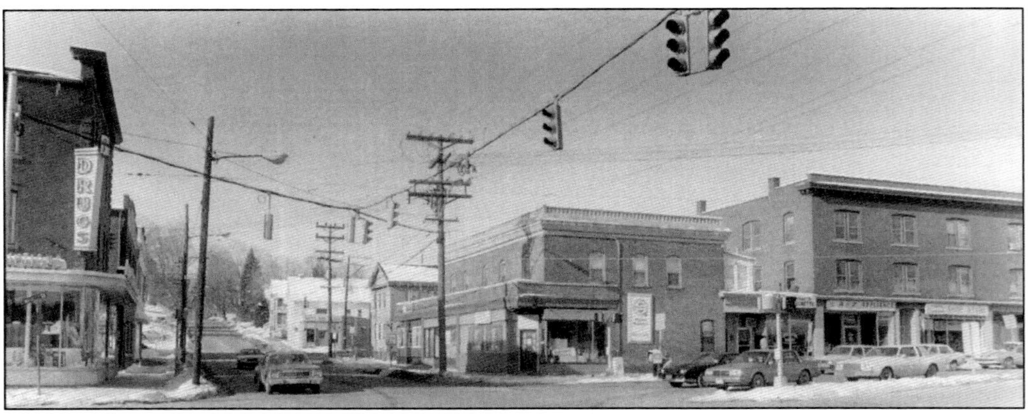

Seventy years later, in 1984, at the intersection of West and Divinity Streets, was another drugstore, Noveck's Pharmacy, owned by Nathan and Irving Noveck. Their business was located on 1 Divinity Street.

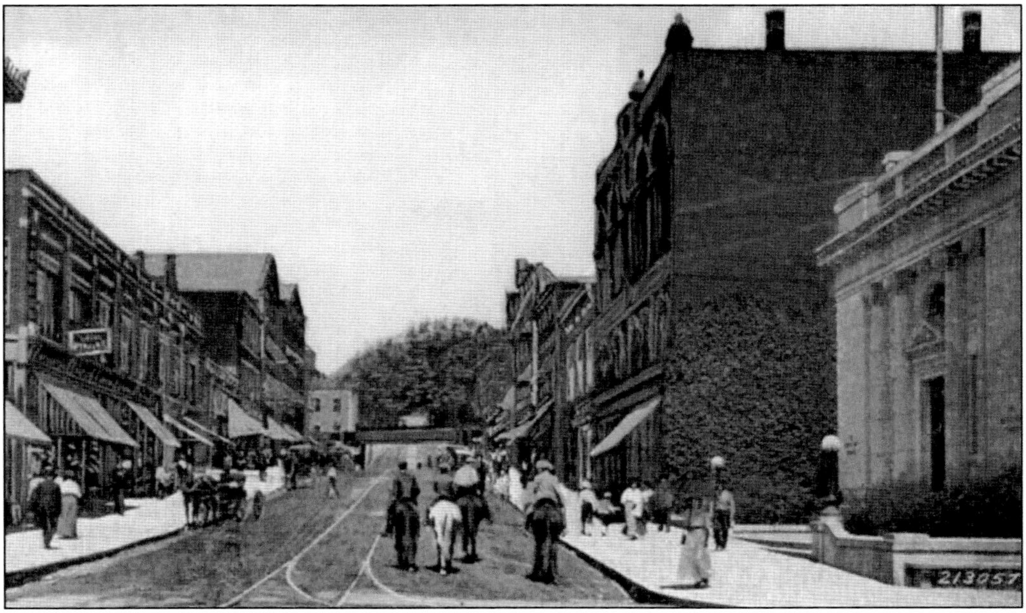

In this postcard view of lower Main Street taken around 1911, on the right is the Bristol Trust Company bank located on the corner of Main Street and Riverside Avenue. The street was not paved yet making it easy to ride horses. Note in the center are the trolley tracks that went up Main Street.

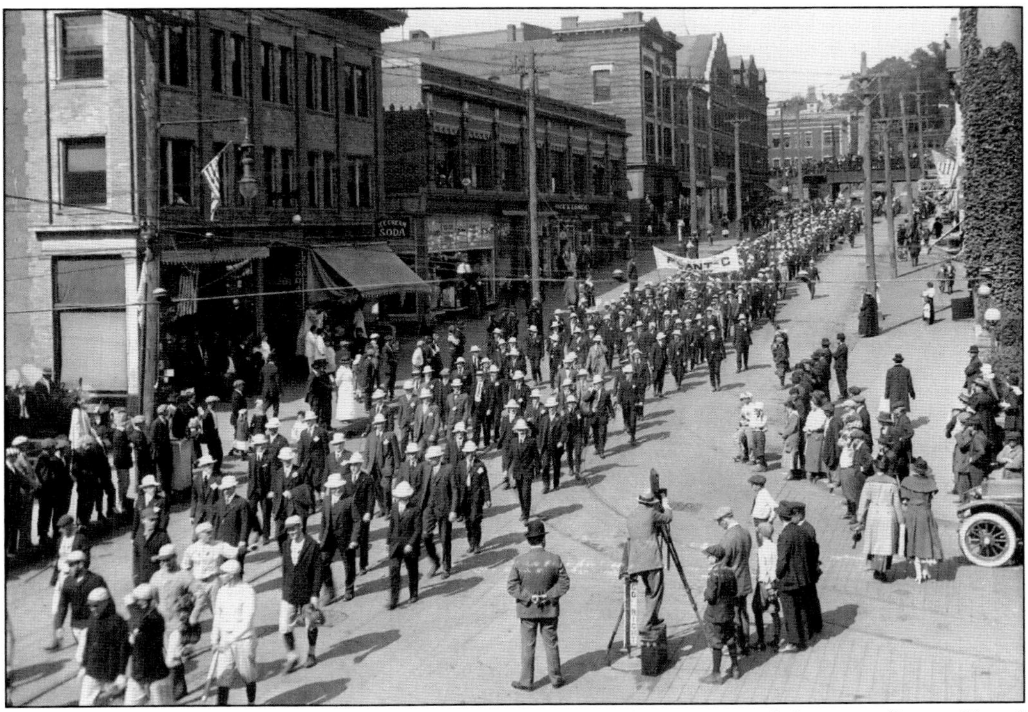

New Departure Manufacturers was one of the companies that supported the war efforts of local citizens. In this picture taken on September 29, 1917, New Departure held this parade with 3,000 employees marching down Main Street to their company's annual picnic. (Courtesy of Bristol Chamber of Commerce.)

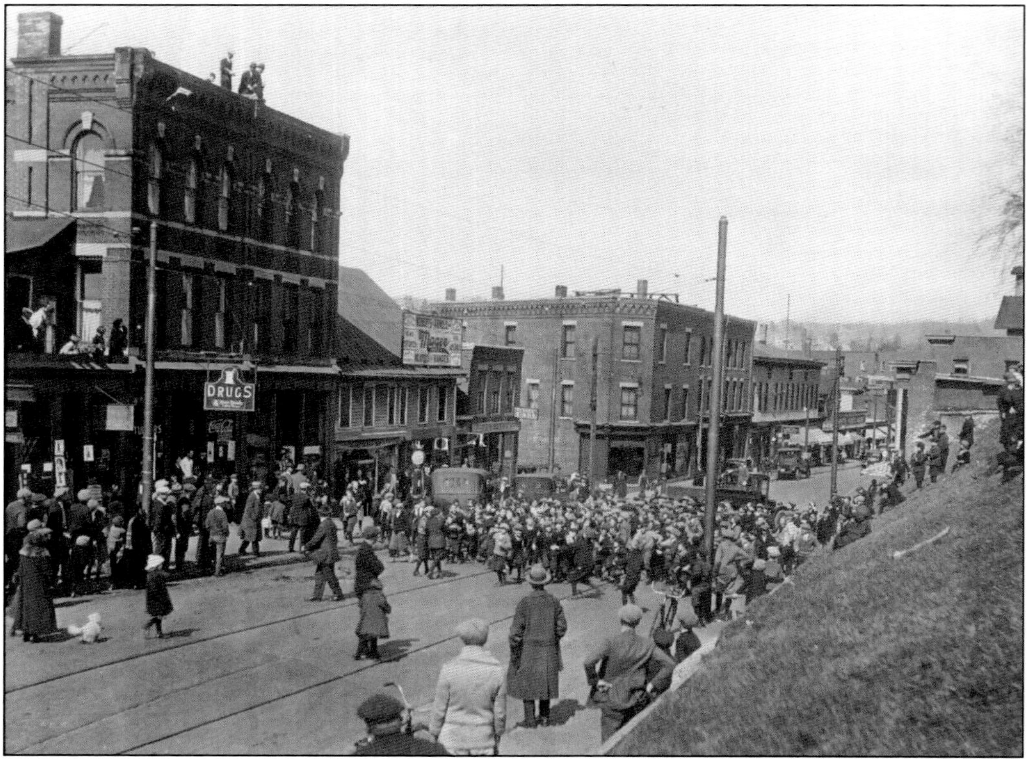

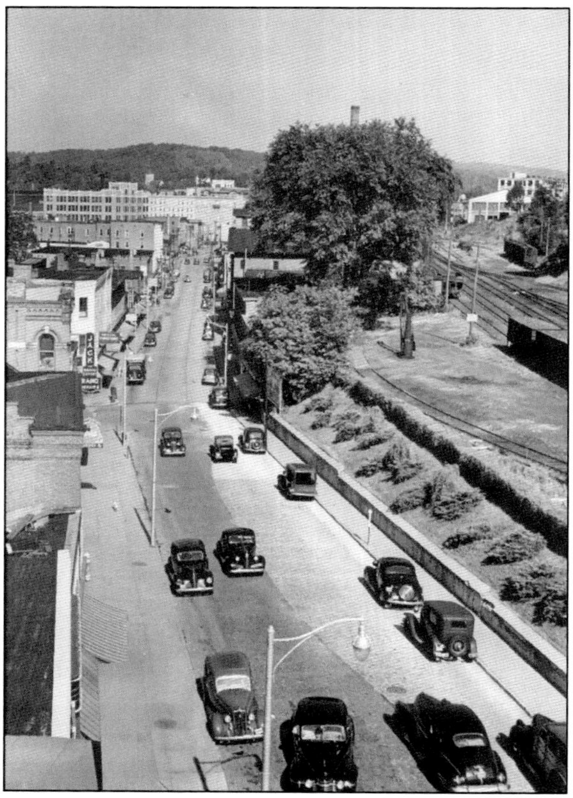

In this scene on North Main Street taken in the 1920s, employees of the Bristol Hardware Store are throwing free hardballs from the roof to a crowd of children below. The Bristol Hardware Store was located in the Skelly Block building. Tucker's Drug was another business in the building. On the right in this picture, there were no buildings, just grass.

This view was taken from the town hall building looking at North Main Street in the 1940s. This was the old North Main Street with the freight office on the right that was part of the New York and New England Railroad Company. In the 1960s when the downtown redevelopment was starting to rebuild, the Centre Mall would be located on the right.

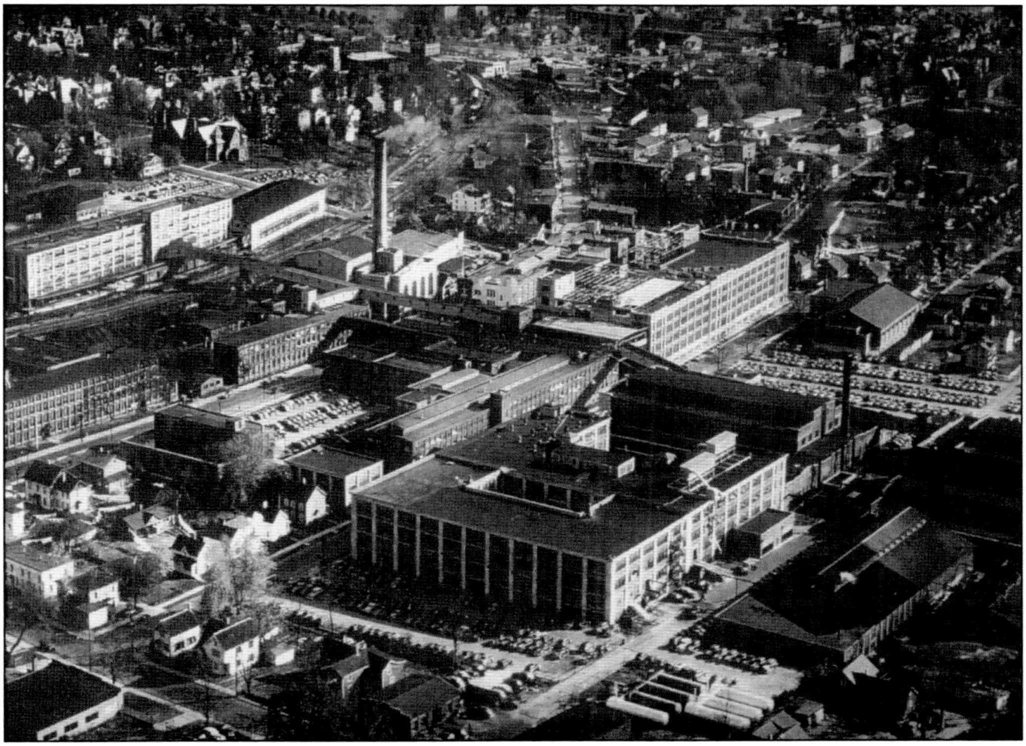

This is a 1940s view of North Main Street when both the E. Ingraham Company and New Departure Manufacturing factories were still here. (Courtesy of Carpenter Construction Company.)

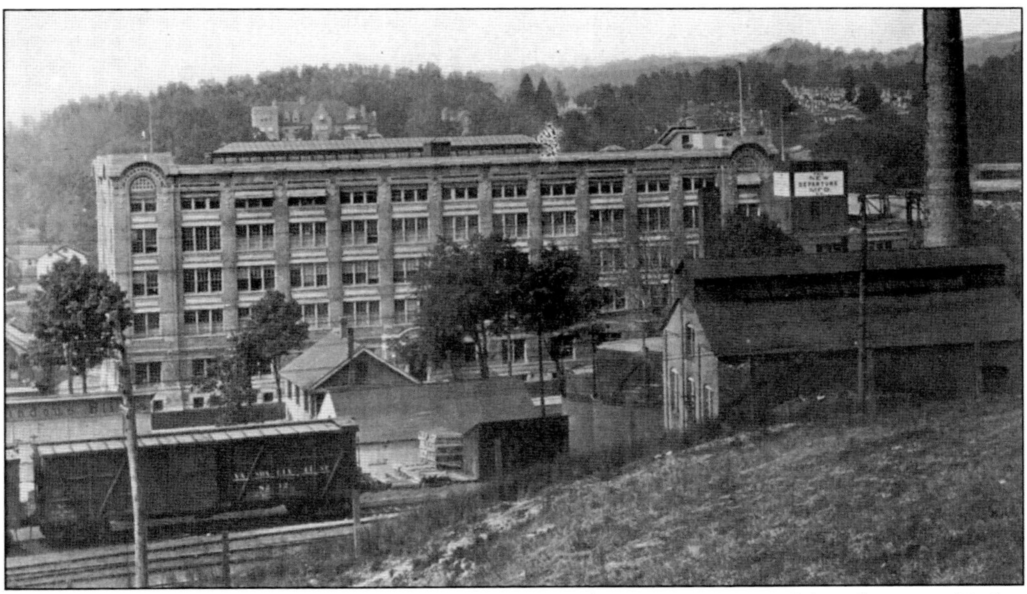

In the center of this picture on North Main Street was the New Departure Manufacturing Endee building where employees and their families could stay. The Bristol Lumber Company was in front of the train tracks that were located on the corner of Center and North Main Streets. On the hill behind New Departure Manufacturing was Brightwood Hall owned by Albert and Nettie Rockwell and located on West Street.

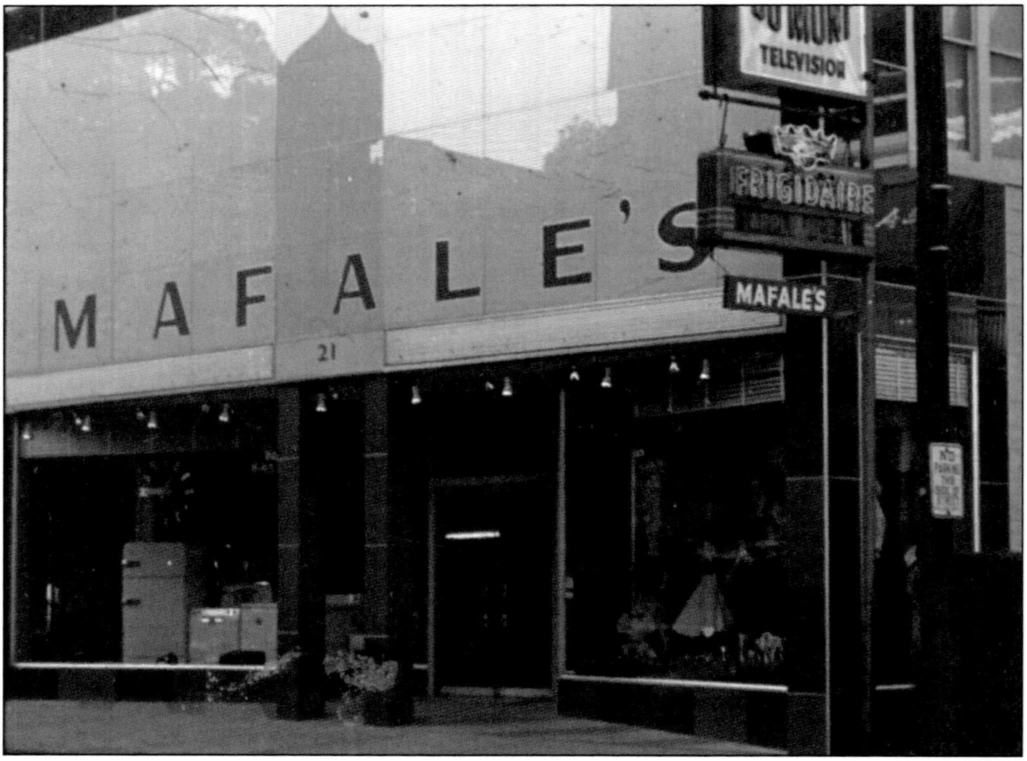

In 1940, Nathan J. Mafale opened up his business at 21 Main Street called Mafale's Radio and Television Company. The business sold electrical appliances, including Philco, Crosley, and Admiral Refrigerators. Philco, RCA, Emerson, Zenith, and Admiral were the brands of radios they sold and serviced. (Courtesy of Bristol Chamber of Commerce.)

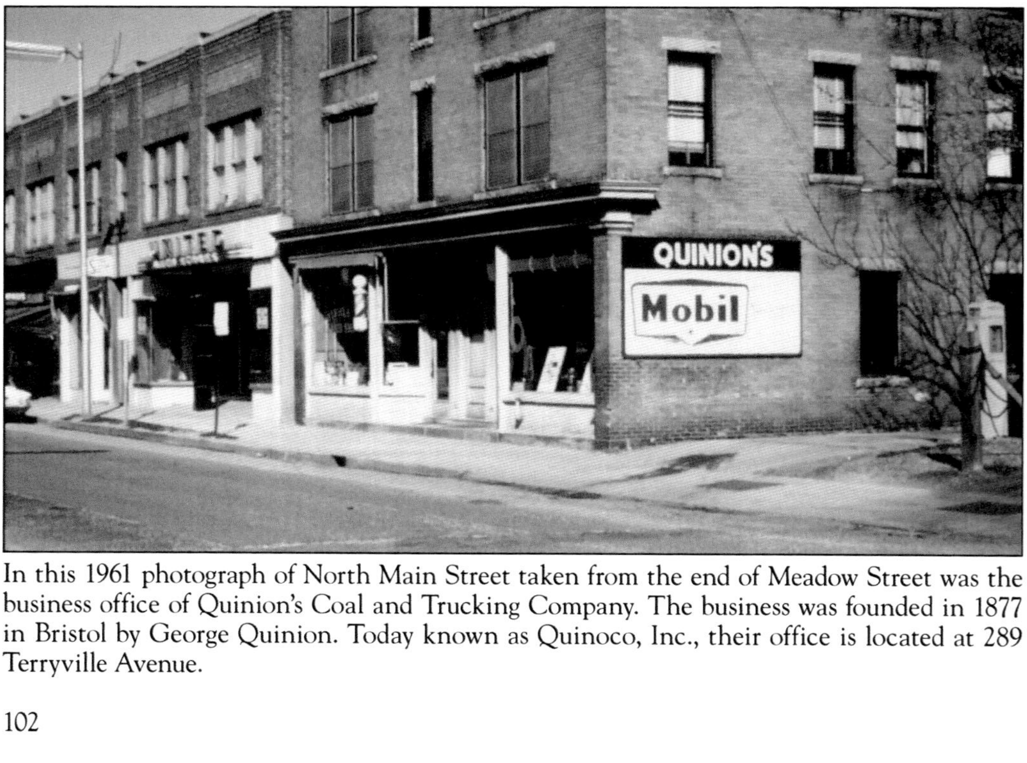

In this 1961 photograph of North Main Street taken from the end of Meadow Street was the business office of Quinion's Coal and Trucking Company. The business was founded in 1877 in Bristol by George Quinion. Today known as Quinoco, Inc., their office is located at 289 Terryville Avenue.

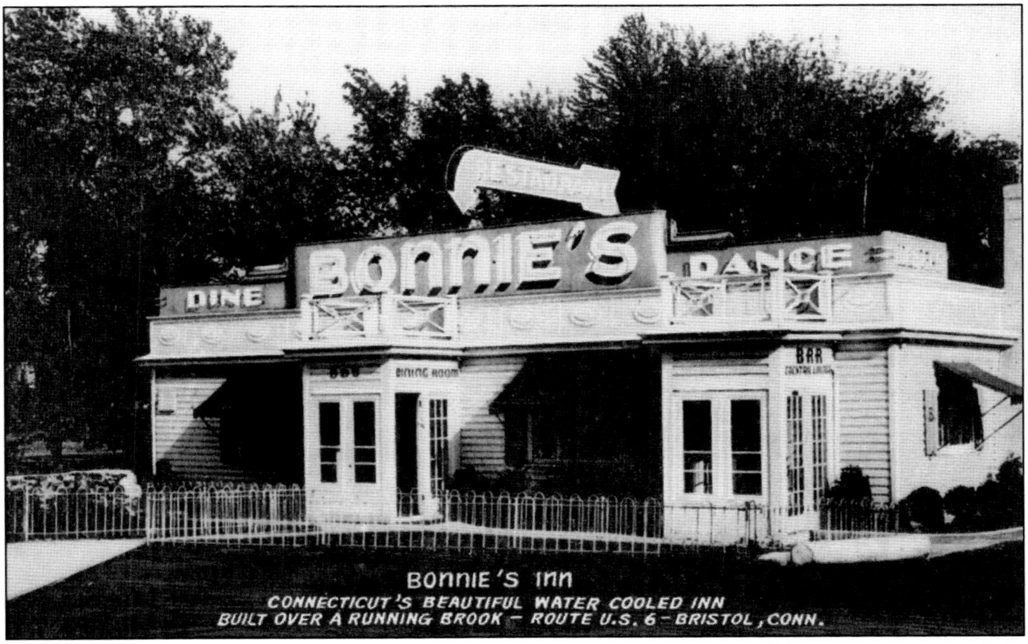

Bonnie's Grill first opened for business by Carmen Bonachis, owner of the restaurant in 1948. Located on 868 Farmington Avenue next to Brook Street, the name was changed to Bonnie's Inn and advertised that the inn was built over a running brook. When the building was torn down, a group of stores were developed with the parking lot where the inn stood. (Courtesy of Gary Potter.)

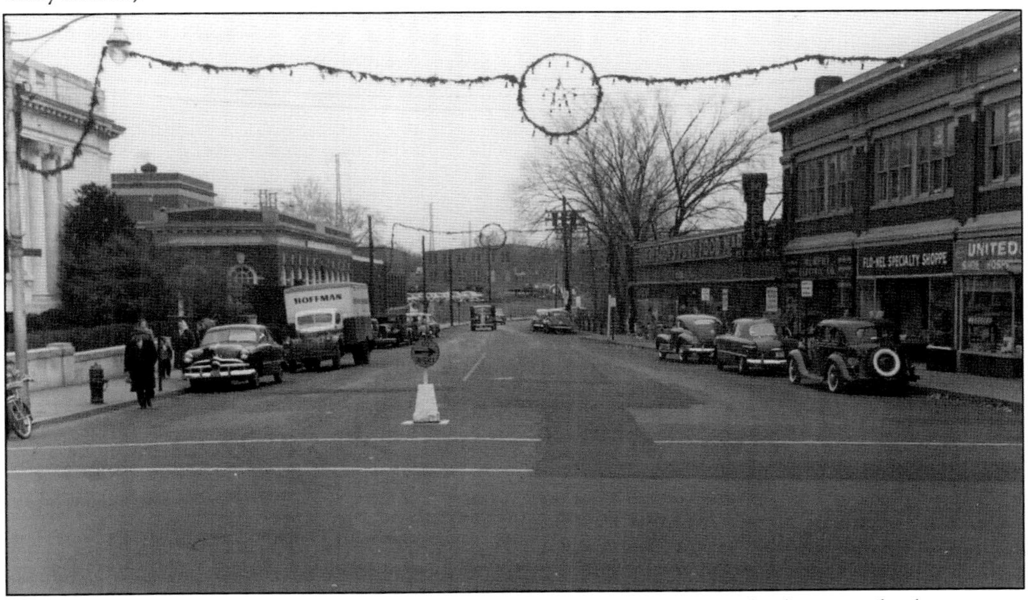

This is a 1949 view taken during Christmastime from Main Street looking at the beginning of Riverside Avenue. On the left is Bristol Savings Bank. On the right side was United Shoe Hospital, Flo-Nel Specialty Shoppe, Murphy's Electric Company, and Everybody's Pure Food Market. On June 2, 1973, there was a major fire that destroyed stores on the right side of the street, including Jon Marie, United Shoe Hospital, and W. T. Grant Company. The second floor was never replaced after the fire.

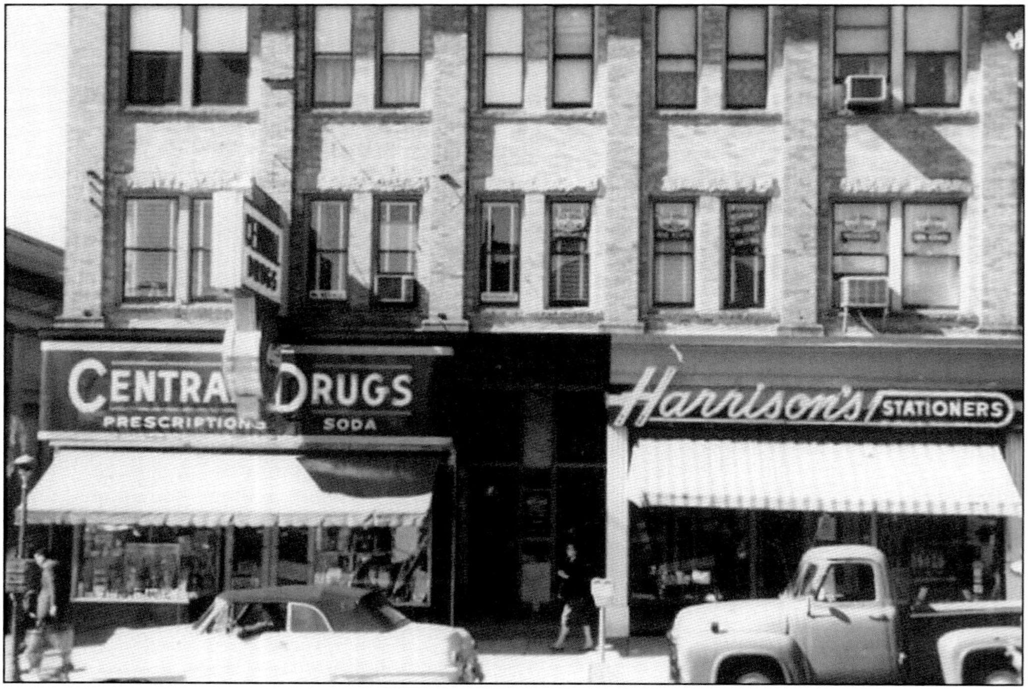

This 1961 photograph shows Central Drugs and Harrison Stationers, located at 155 Main Street in the former location of where Ernest Podesta had his fruit and confectioners store. To the left of Central Drugs was the post office. When these buildings were torn down in the 1960s to make way for the Centre Mall, Harrison's moved to the Bristol Plaza on Farmington Avenue. (Courtesy of Bristol Town Clerk Office.)

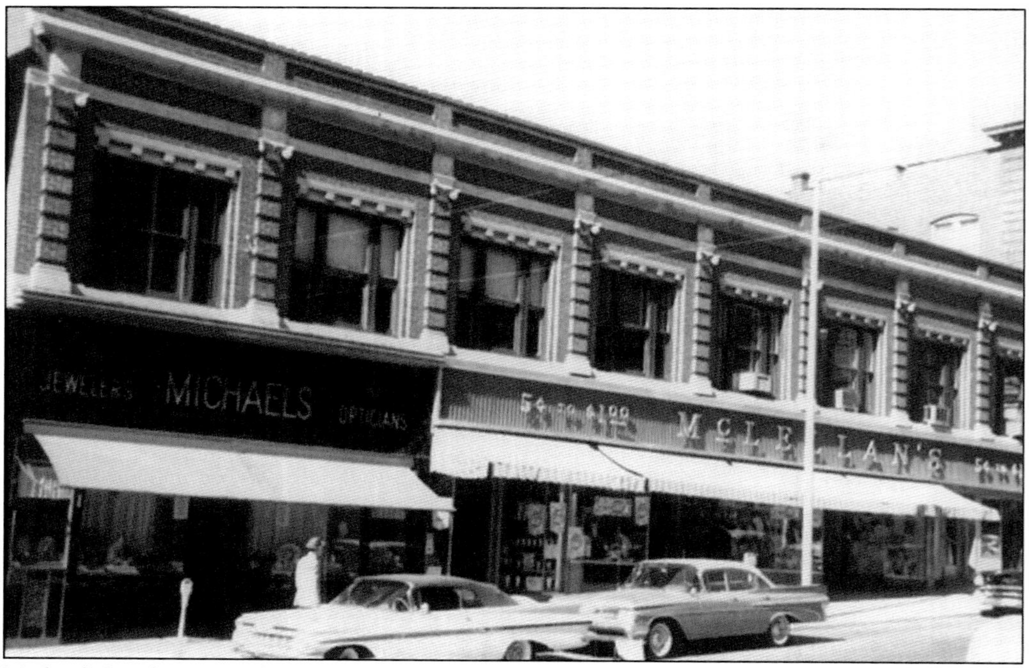

Michael's Jewelers, owned by Max Rubin, was located at 165 Main Street. When these buildings were torn down, Michael's moved into the Centre Mall. (Courtesy of Bristol Town Clerk Office.)

Seven

INFORMING THE PUBLIC

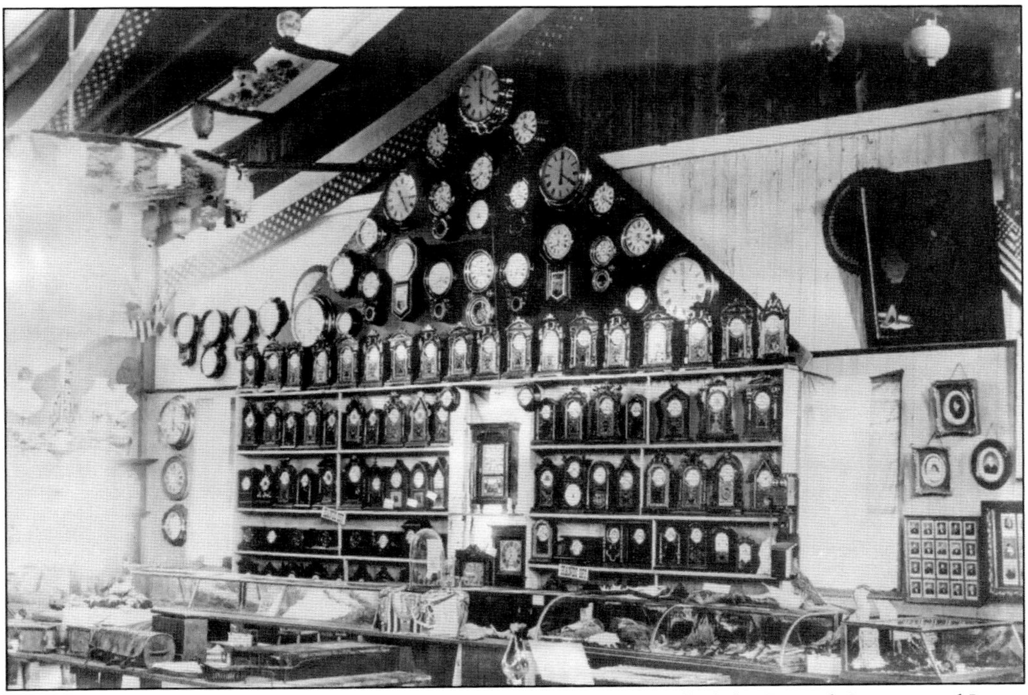

The City of Bristol's centennial committee planned an event called the Bristol Centennial Loan Exhibit to celebrate the 100th anniversary of Bristol becoming a town. The event started on Saturday, June 13, 1885, and ended on June 20, 1885. It was held at the coliseum skating rink on Laurel Street. This picture was a display from the Ingraham clock factory that was done by Elias Ingraham, founder of the company, showing the clocks his business made at that time. (Courtesy of American Clock and Watch Museum.)

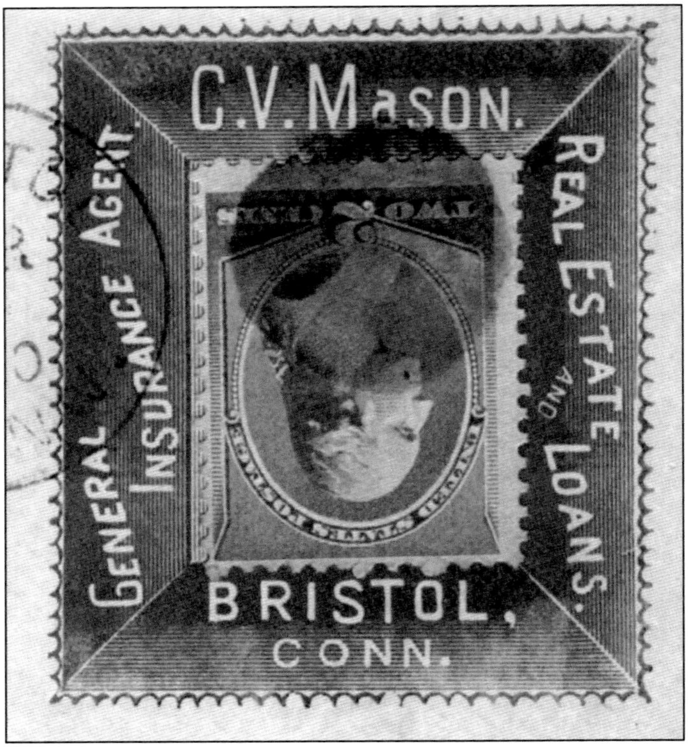

In the late 1800s, one way a business could advertise was the advertising collar. A collar was placed around the postage stamp. This advertising collar for C. V. Mason was on an envelope dated 1890. Note the stamp is upside down so the name C. V. Mason shows up first and not the stamp. (Courtesy of Tom Dickau.)

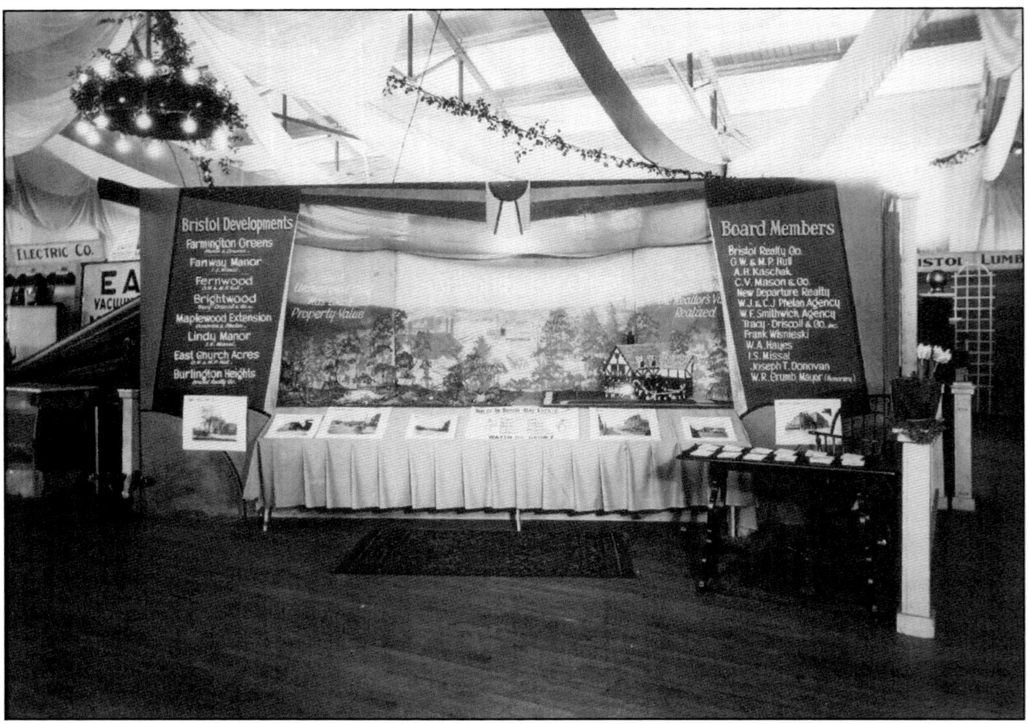

This is one of the displays from the Bristol Chamber of Commerce "Progress Shows" held at the Bristol Armory, April 25–27, 1929. This display by Bristol Developments showcased a variety of properties and a list of its board members.

At the Bristol Chamber of Commerce Home Show held October 4–6, 1974, the Shaffer Company displayed the types of plumbing and heating products they sold for both commercial and residential customers. (Courtesy of Bristol Chamber of Commerce.)

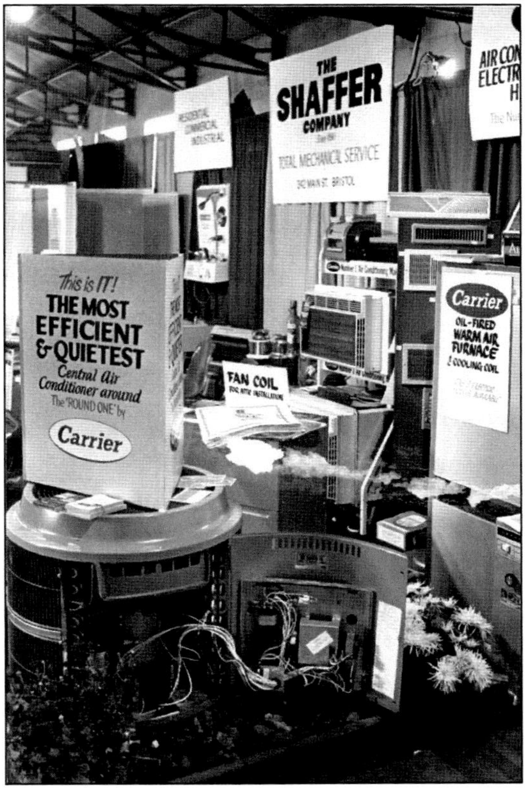

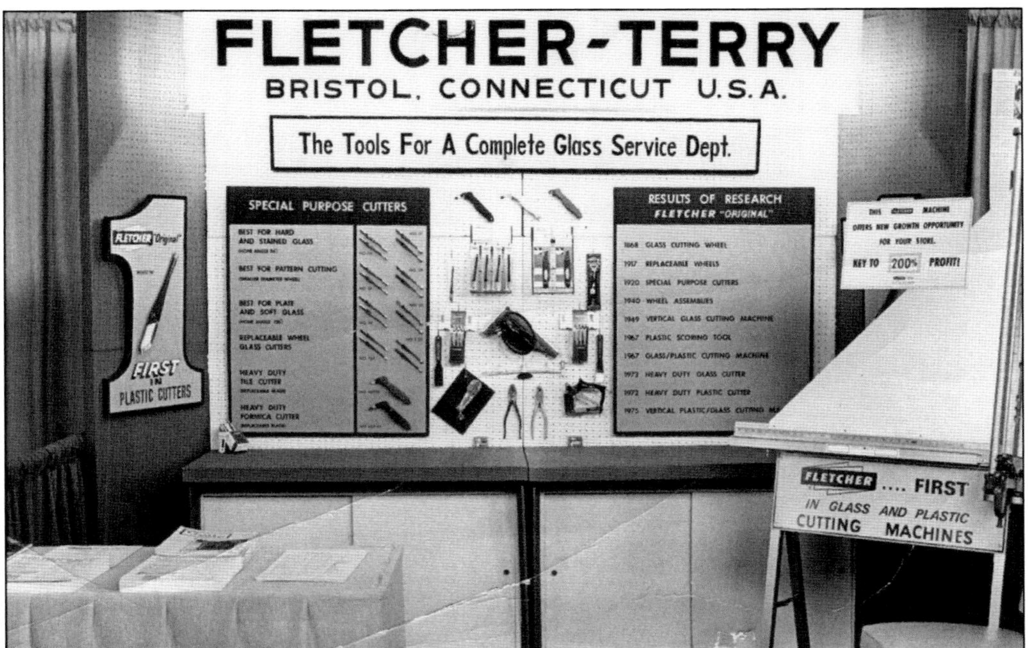

At the chamber-in-action show, part of the first Connecticut Trade Show held June 11–13, 1975, in Hartford, the Fletcher-Terry Company, manufacturer of glass tools, was one of the companies from Bristol displaying their products. (Courtesy of Bristol Chamber of Commerce.)

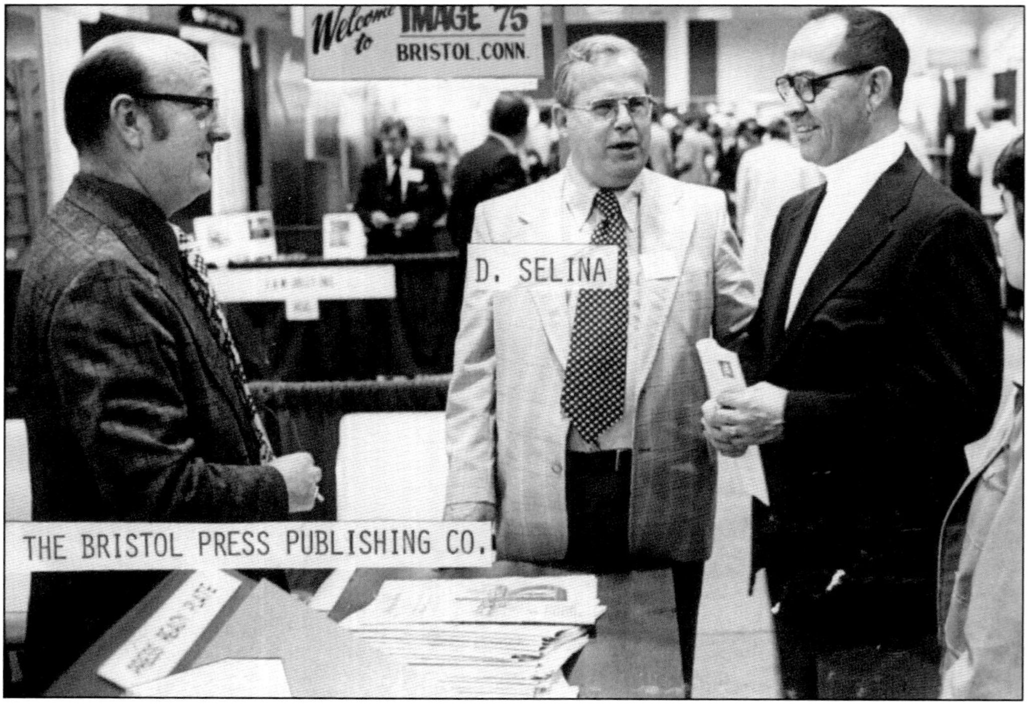

Donald Selina became assistant general manager and purchasing agent of the *Bristol Press* in the 1960s. At the chamber-in-action first Connecticut Trade Show in Hartford, June 11–13, 1975, Donald was general manager and was there representing the *Bristol Press*. (Courtesy of Bristol Chamber of Commerce.)

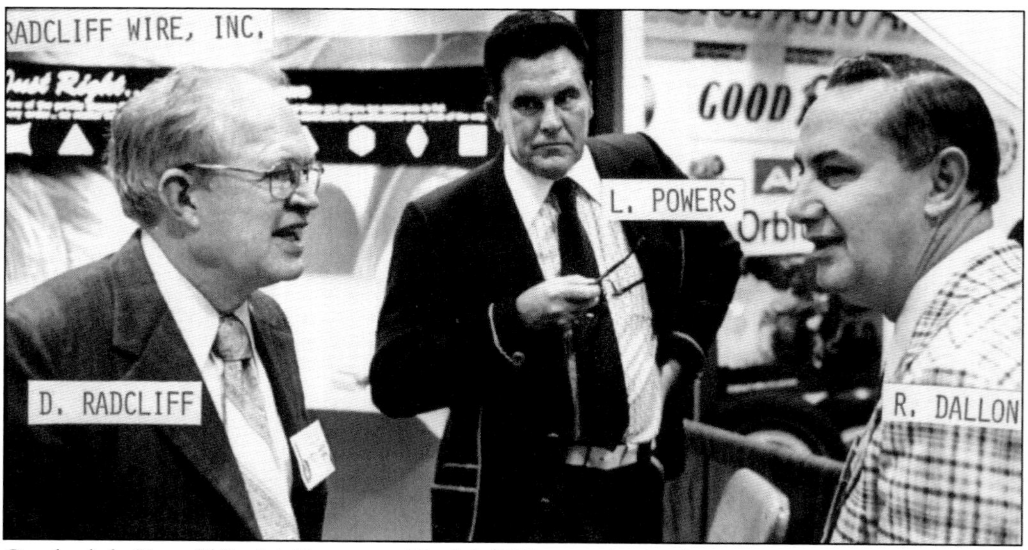

On the left, Donald Radcliff, owner of Radcliff Wire, with Lloyd Powers, a salesman for Radcliff Wire, and Robert Dalton, vice president of sales from the Arthur G. Russell Company, are at the first Connecticut Trade Show in Hartford in 1975. (Courtesy of Bristol Chamber of Commerce.)

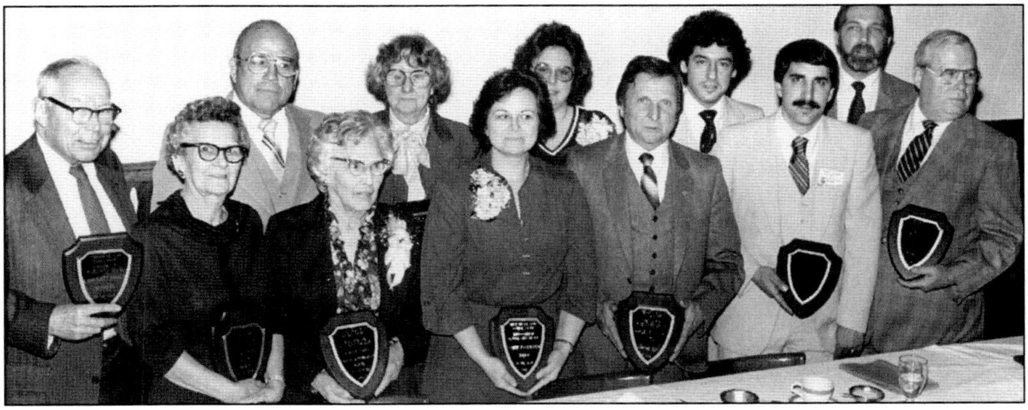

The Bristol Chamber of Commerce hosts the Interservice Club annual dinner each year. The Bristol organizations each chose someone in their clubs for outstanding service or commitment they make on behalf of their club. At the March 16, 1982, dinner, the following received plaques from their clubs. From left to right are (first row) E. Bartlett Barnes—Rotary Club, Helen Pease—Quota Club, Alma M. Trail—Woman's Club, Connie Rosengren—Junior Woman Club, Charles E. Maynard—Civitan Club, and Thomas Ragaini—Jaycees; (second row) Ernest Brandt—Exchange Club, Melba H. Leary—Altrusa Club, Linda Henry—Junior Woman Club, Dr. Sidney L. Shafran—Lions Club, and Paul J. Fanelli Jr.—Unico Club. (Courtesy of Bristol Chamber of Commerce.)

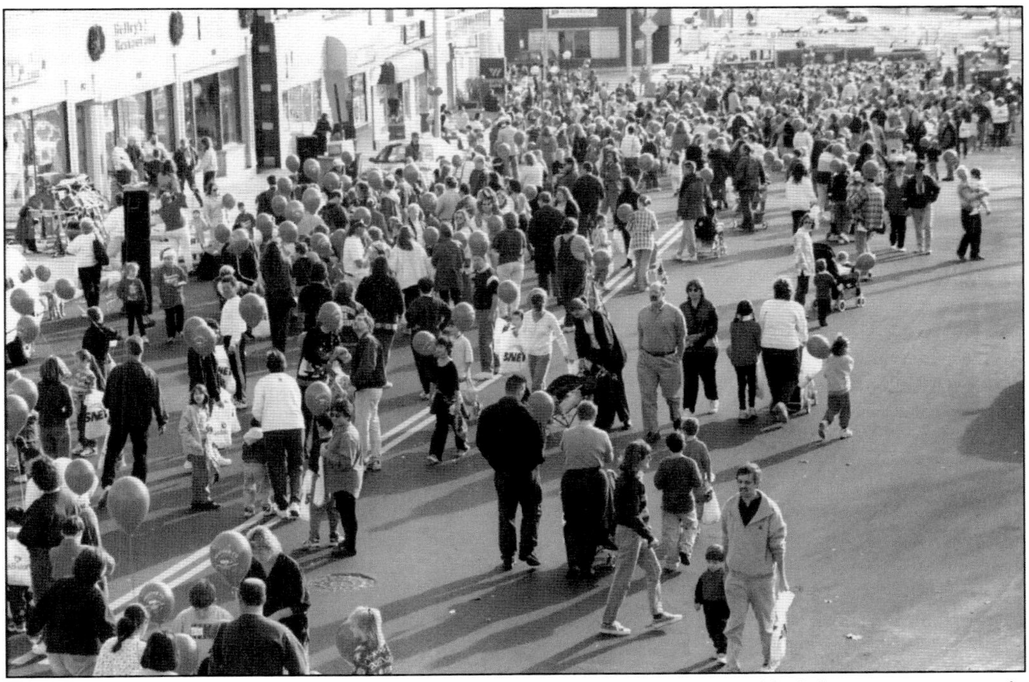

In 1991, the Bristol Chamber's Art and Tourism Council started a special holiday event—a parade in reverse that would be held in the downtown area called the Children's Holiday Parade. The parade participants would remain stationary on the sides, and the viewers would stroll along the parade route from Federal Hill Green to the center of downtown. Along the way, the parade goers are entertained by singing, dancers, mimes, gymnasts, and cheerleaders; children receive gifts from area merchants and organizations. This picture shows one of the children's parades on Main Street. (Courtesy of Bristol Chamber of Commerce.)

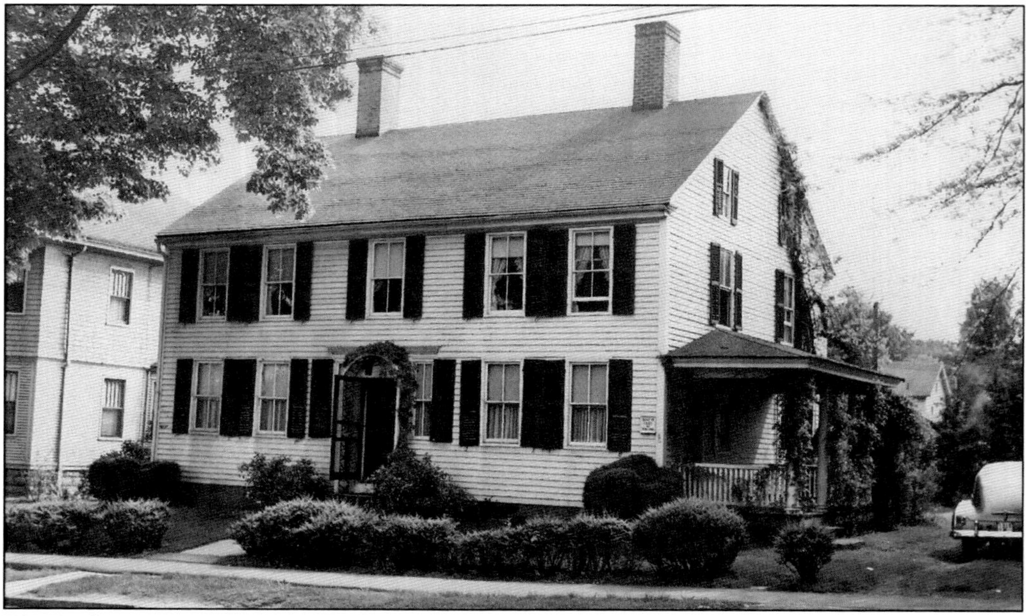

The Miles Lewis House at 100 Maple Street was built in 1802. The Bristol Clock Museum purchased the home in 1953. The building was restored to how it looked in Colonial days. On April 10, 1954, the museum opened with about 300 clocks on display and historic artifacts from the clock manufacturing industry that were vital pieces of Bristol's history. In 1958, Bristol Clock Museum changed their name to the American Clock and Watch Museum, Inc. The above picture is from the museum in 1953 before restoration was done. (Courtesy of American Clock and Watch Museum.)

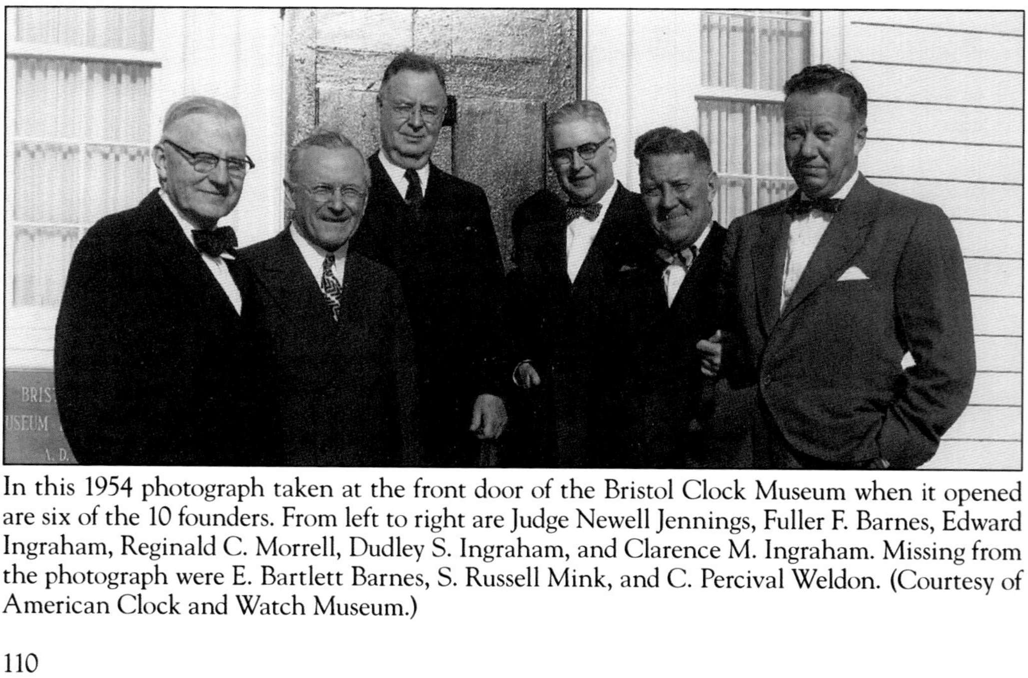

In this 1954 photograph taken at the front door of the Bristol Clock Museum when it opened are six of the 10 founders. From left to right are Judge Newell Jennings, Fuller F. Barnes, Edward Ingraham, Reginald C. Morrell, Dudley S. Ingraham, and Clarence M. Ingraham. Missing from the photograph were E. Bartlett Barnes, S. Russell Mink, and C. Percival Weldon. (Courtesy of American Clock and Watch Museum.)

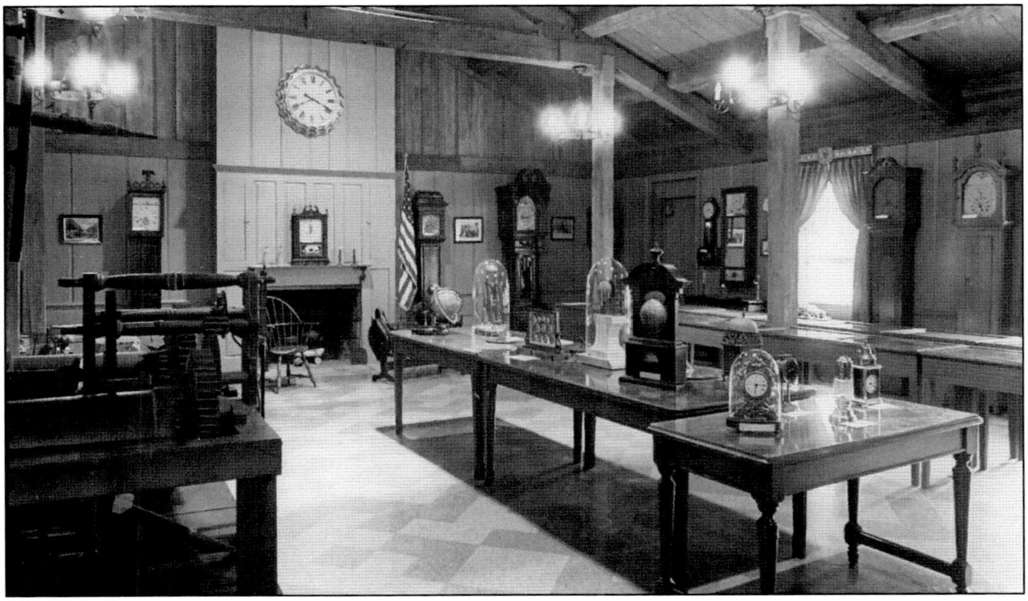

In 1956, through the generosity of Fuller F. Barnes of Wallace Barnes Company, the Ebenezer Barnes Memorial Wing opened. This room was constructed with wood paneling taken from the 1728 Ebenezer Barnes homestead, and the beams were taken from the Lewis Lock Company factory in Terryville. This wing allowed the museum to add to their collection. In 1987, the Ingraham Memorial Wing was added. This 1966 photograph was taken of the Ebenezer Barnes Wing with a variety of clocks on display. (Courtesy of American Clock and Watch Museum.)

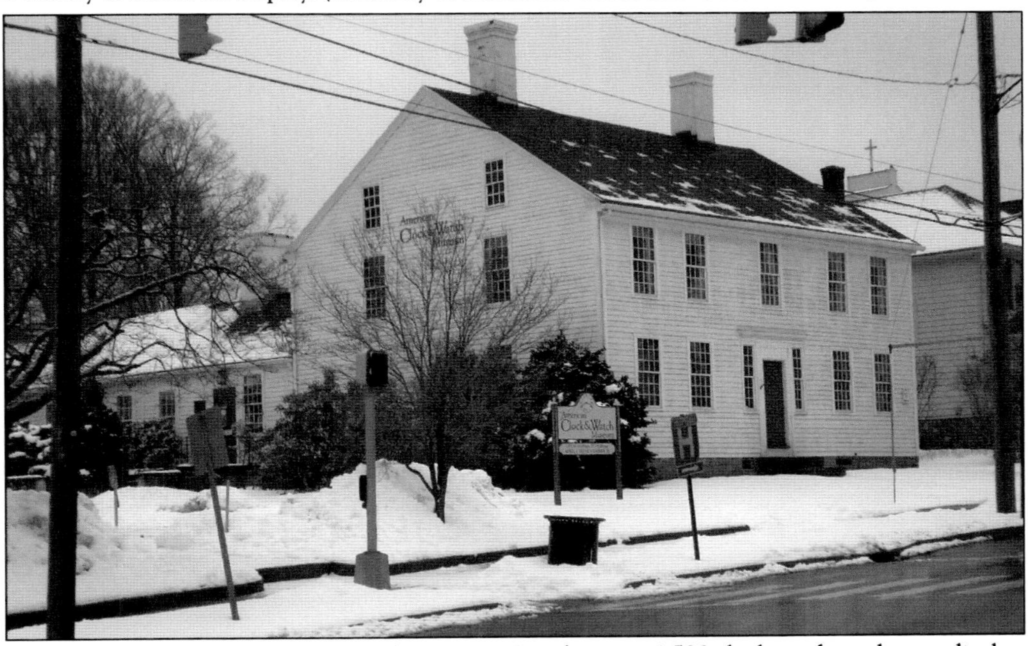

Today the American Clock and Watch Museum, Inc., has over 1,500 clocks and watches on display. Their collection includes grandfather clocks, old advertising clocks, railroad clocks, punch clocks, and blinking-eye clocks, along with many more that can be seen at the museum. The museum offers visitors a chance to see how important clocks were to the growth of Bristol through local manufacturers. (Courtesy of American Clock and Watch Museum.)

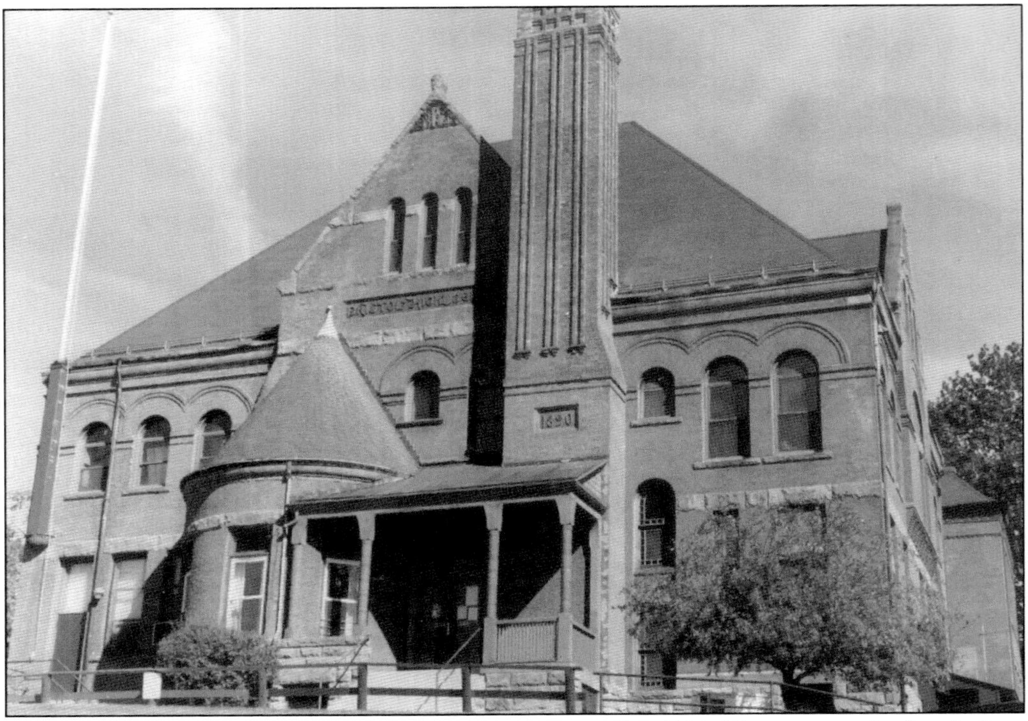

The Bristol Historical and Scientific Society was organized in 1890. They met on the fourth floor in the Linstead Building on Prospect Street. The collection from this organization became part of the Bristol Historical Society founded in 1971. In 1973, the Bristol Historical Society used the former Terry Home on Middle Street. In 2002, they purchased the former Bristol High School built in 1890 and located at 98 Summer Street. Both the Memorial Military Museum and the Bristol Sports Hall of Fame now reside in the building with the Bristol Historical Society. (Courtesy of Bristol Historical Society.)

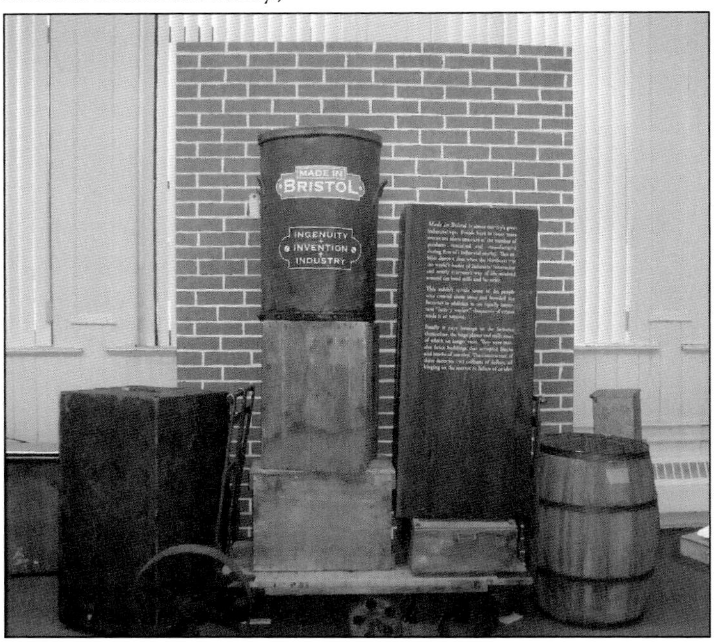

In 2006, the Bristol Historical Society contracted Richard Rich, owner of Rich Learning Experience from Bristol, to create a new exhibit of the industrial history in Bristol. Rich created exhibits from some of the artifacts in the historical society's inventory and contacted other businesses in Bristol for display items. In 2007, the new Made in Bristol exhibit was opened. The exhibit remains as a permanent display at the museum. (Courtesy of Bristol Historical Society.)

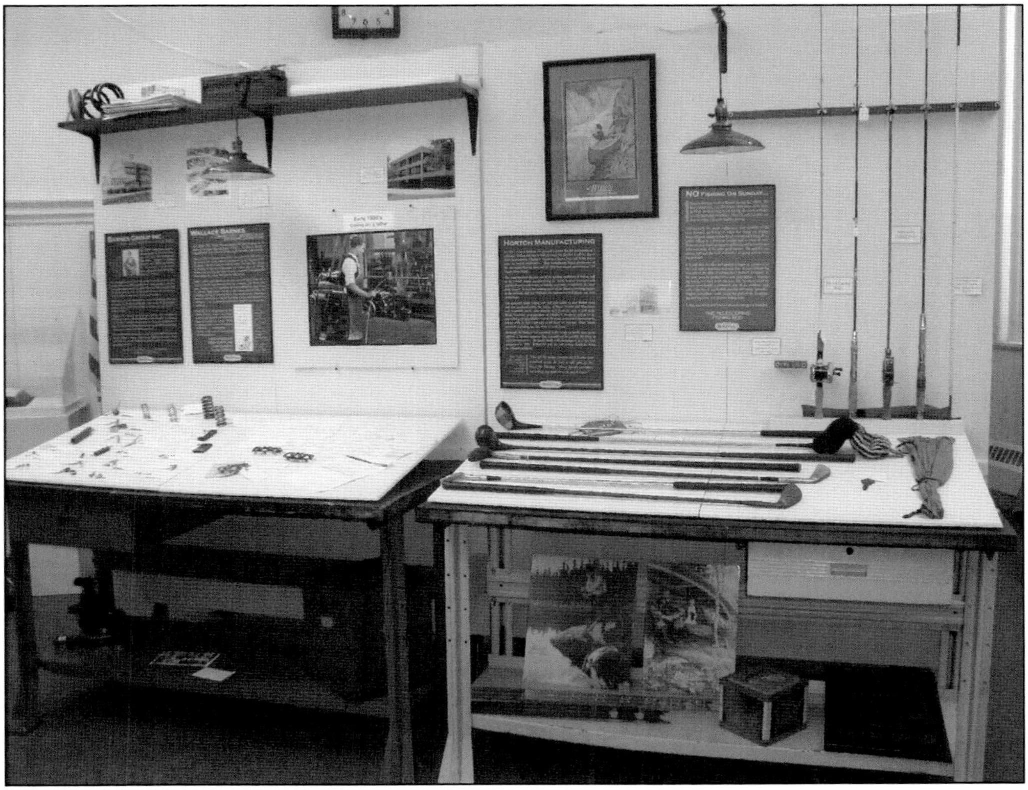

In this display from the Made in Bristol exhibit are manufactured products from the Barnes Group, Inc., and Wallace Barnes, a division of Associated Spring (at left). On the right are fishing rod, reels, and golf clubs that were made by the Horton Manufacturing Company. (Courtesy of Bristol Historical Society.)

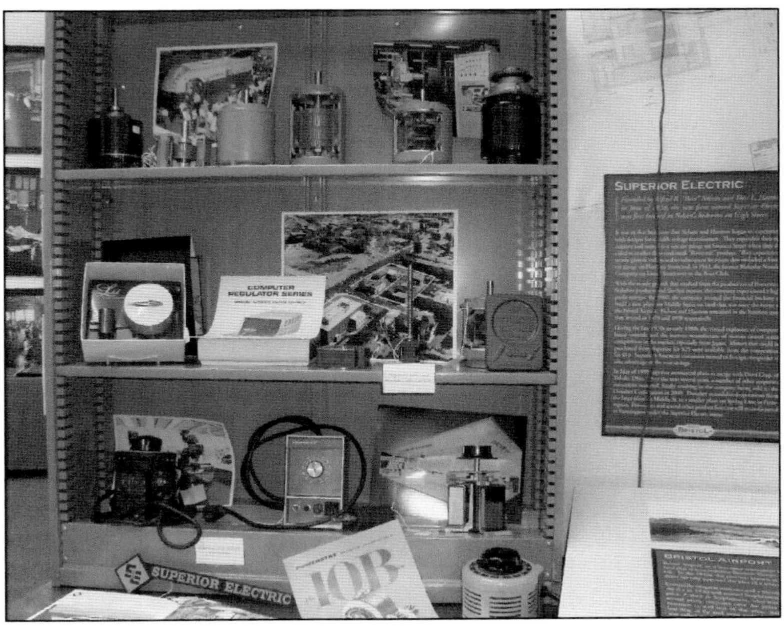

In this display from the Made in Bristol exhibit are the products made by the Superior Electric Company. (Courtesy of Bristol Historical Society.)

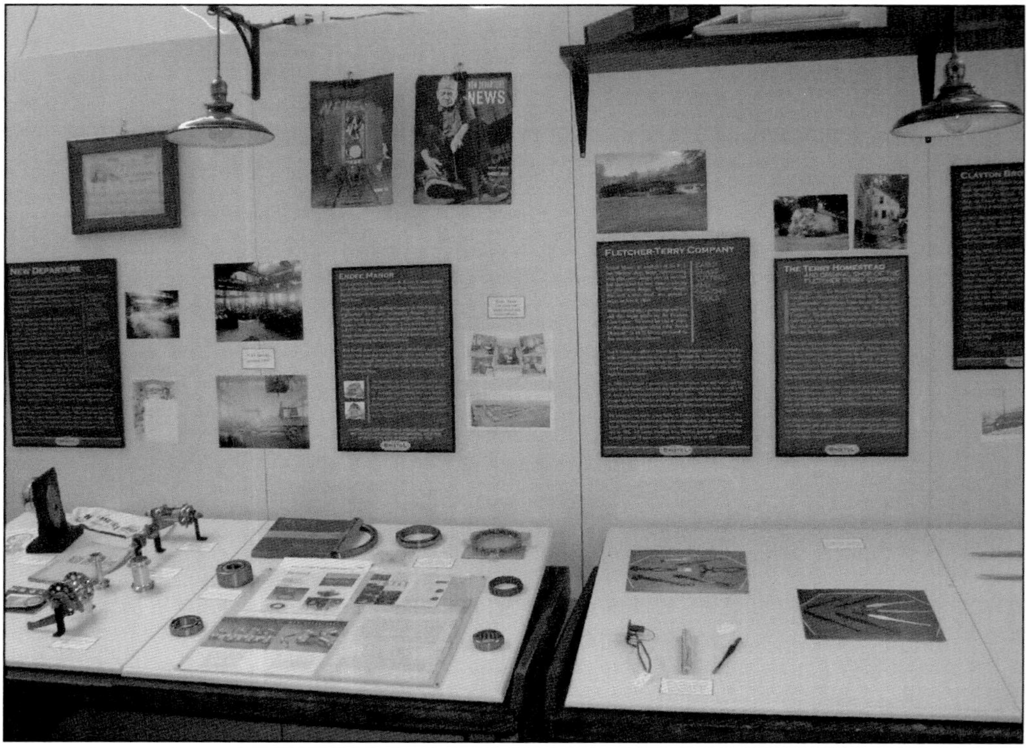

From left to right in the Made in Bristol exhibit are the following displays: New Departure Manufacturing Company products; Fletcher-Terry Company, manufacturer of glass products; and Clayton Brothers, manufacturers of shears and scissors, located on Union Street in the former Dunbar Factory. (Courtesy of Bristol Historical Society.)

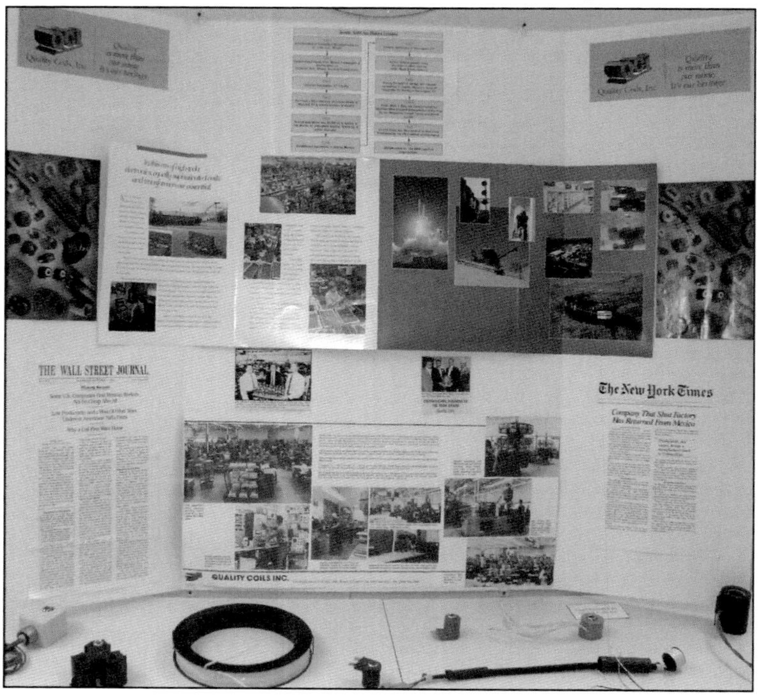

Quality Coils, Inc., was started by Archibald A. Gibson, John Comerford, and W. B. Crumb in 1965. When "Archie" Gibson died in 1989, his three sons, Keith, Mark, and Gary, managed the company until 1991 when they took over the business. The company is located at 748 Middle Street. In this Made in Bristol exhibit are the products that Quality Coils, Inc., manufactures here in Bristol. (Courtesy of Bristol Historical Society.)

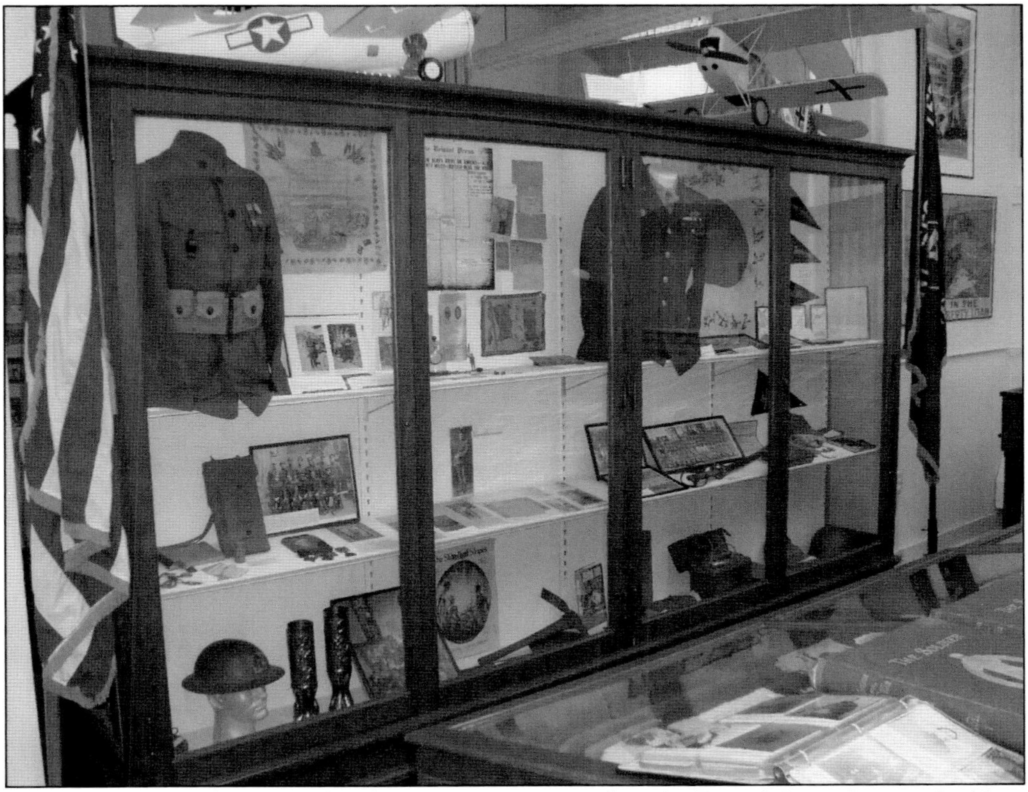

In 1978, the Bristol Memorial Military Museum opened in the Bristol State Armory building located on 61 Center Street. In April 2008, the museum moved into the Bristol Historical Society building. In this exhibit on display are artifacts from World War I and World War II. (Courtesy of Bristol Historical Society.)

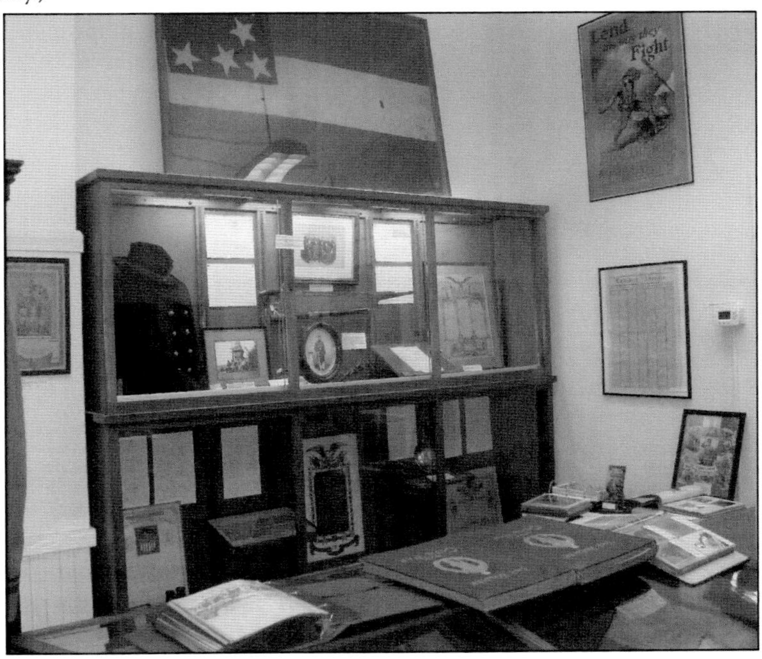

Parts of the permanent display in the Memorial Military Museum are Civil War memorabilia as shown in this picture. (Courtesy of Bristol Historical Society.)

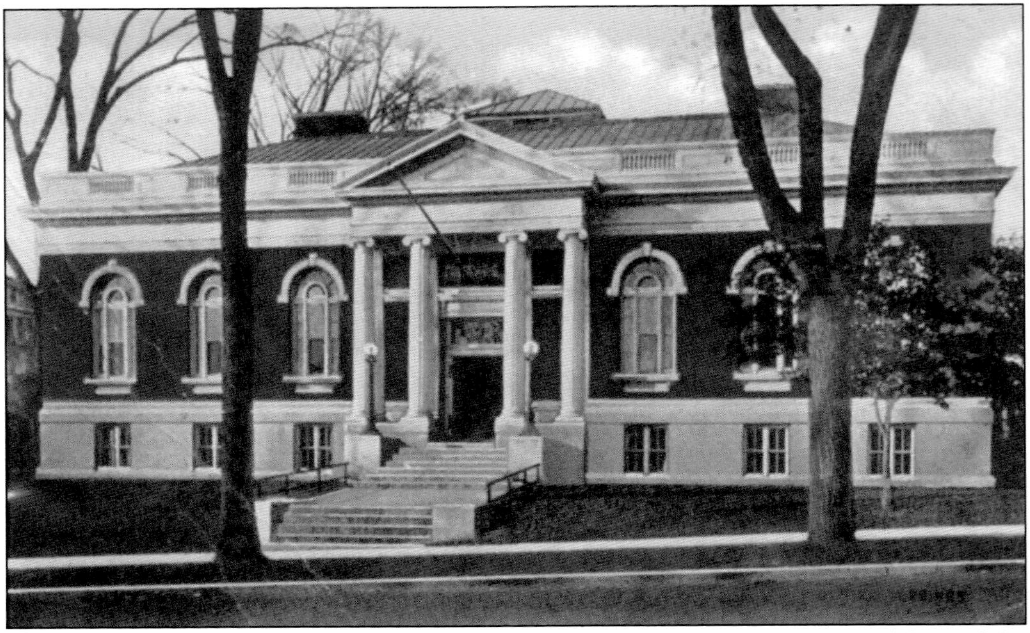

The first Bristol Public Library opened on January 1, 1892, located on the second floor of the Eber's building on North Main Street. In 1896, at 5 High Street, a home on the corner of Main and High Streets became the new library. By 1905, the library had outgrown the home. Through the generosity of private donors, the library replaced the home with this building designed by Wilson Potter. The new building opened in 1907.

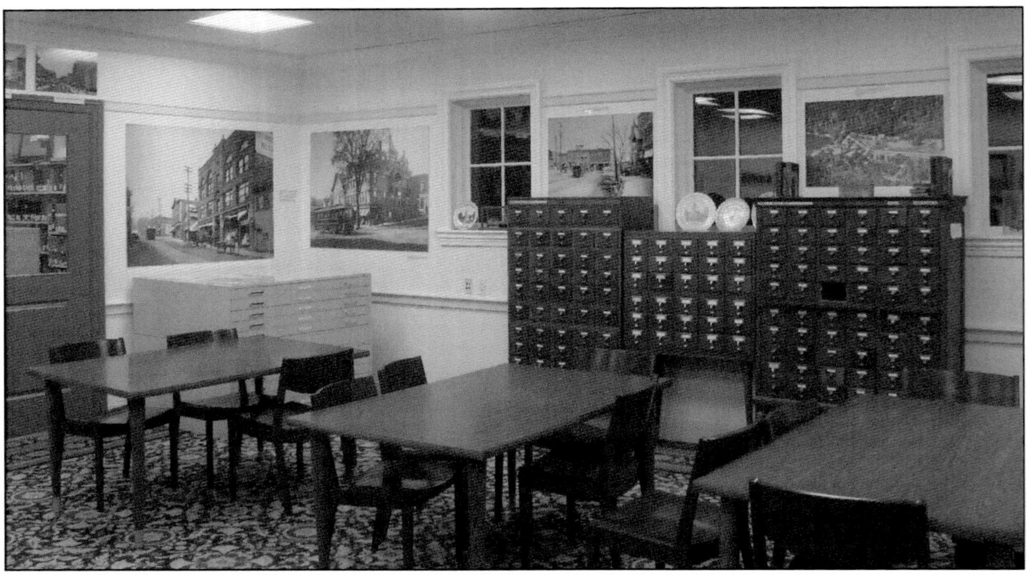

The Bristol History Room is part of the Bristol Library and was created in 1985 during Bristol's centennial. Prior to 1985, photographs, historic books, historic records, military history, cemetery records, and archival materials were kept in the library's vault. Before the expansion of the library in 2006, the first Bristol History Room was located in the original building on the second floor with limited space for items the public could see and research. In this picture of the new Bristol History Room, now the public can come in and research local history from the library's expanded collection, which is kept in a climate-controlled room.

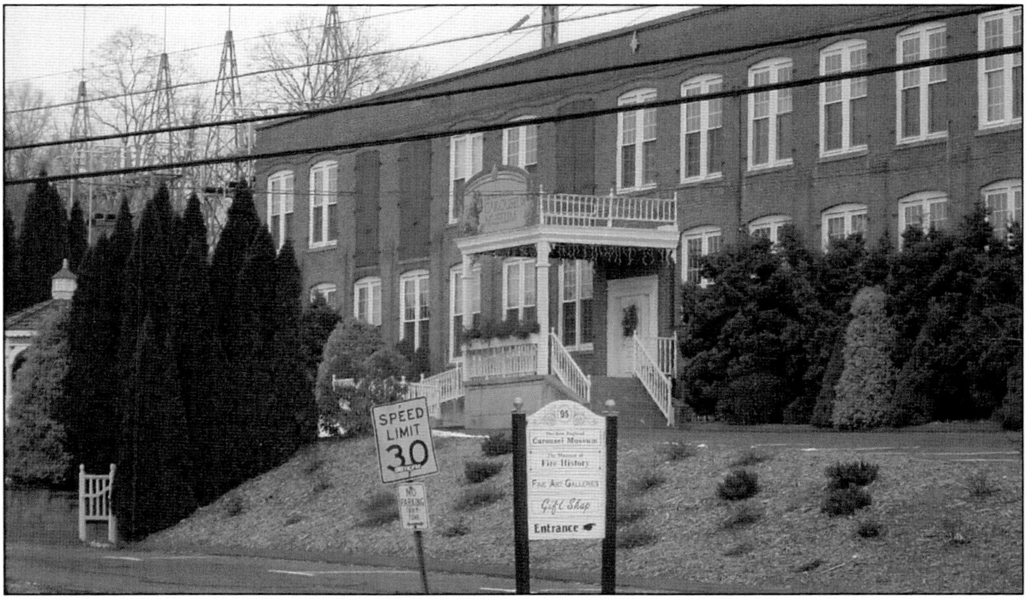

The former Bristol Manufacturing Company is the New England Carousel Museum located at 95 Riverside Avenue. It is the one remaining building left that did the carding, seaming, looping, and spinning of knitting materials. In 1989, R and F Designs owned by Bill Finkenstein moved his carousel restoration company into the building. In 1990, the New England Carousel Museum started renting the first floor of the building. Part of the second floor was used for the restoration of carousel figures that was done by artisans, carvers, and painters. In December 1998, the state of Connecticut gave a grant to the New England Carousel Museum to provide a permanent home for the museum and for the creation of the Cultural Center for Central Connecticut. (Courtesy of New England Carousel Museum.)

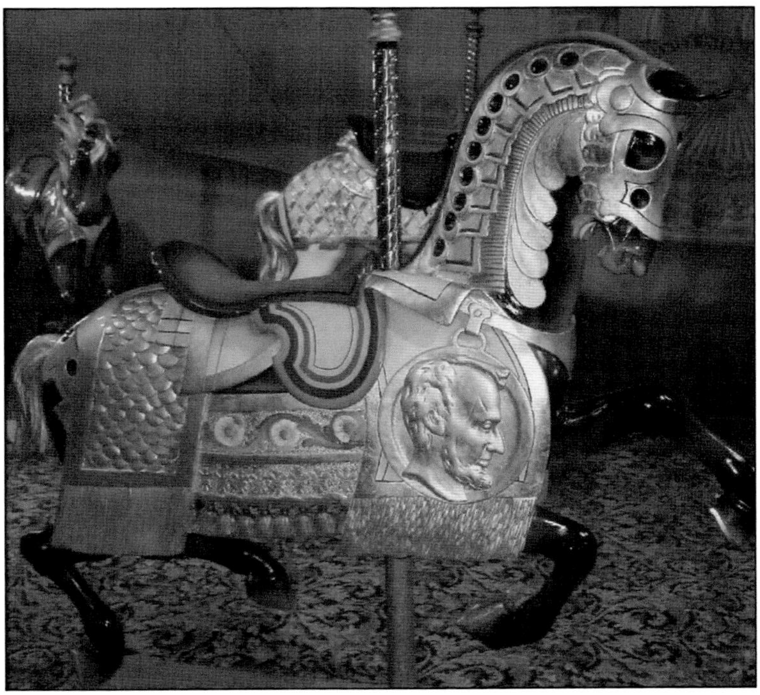

At the New England Carousel Museum, this historical carousel horse with the Lincoln Head Penny is one of the many carousel figures on display. On the second floor, there is a studio for master carver Juan Andreu, who works on the restoration of carousel pieces that come into the museum. Visitors can see the work being done or see the finished displays on the first floor. (Courtesy of New England Carousel Museum.)

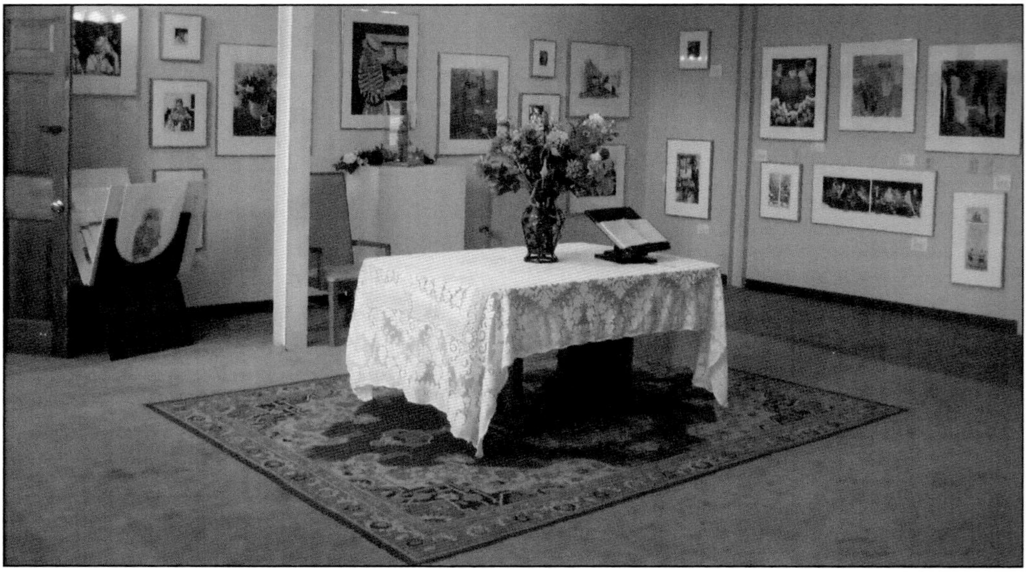

In November 2000, the Bristol Center of Arts and Culture located in the New England Carousel Museum added a fine arts gallery along with a temporary exhibition gallery on the first floor. In this picture is the permanent Glo Sessions Gallery. Glo Sessions was married to the late James McCall Sessions whose family owned the J. H. Sessions Company on Riverside Avenue. Glo, a dedicated artist, has created art of local pictures of Bristol as well as work for corporate offices and other museums around the country. (Courtesy of New England Carousel Museum.)

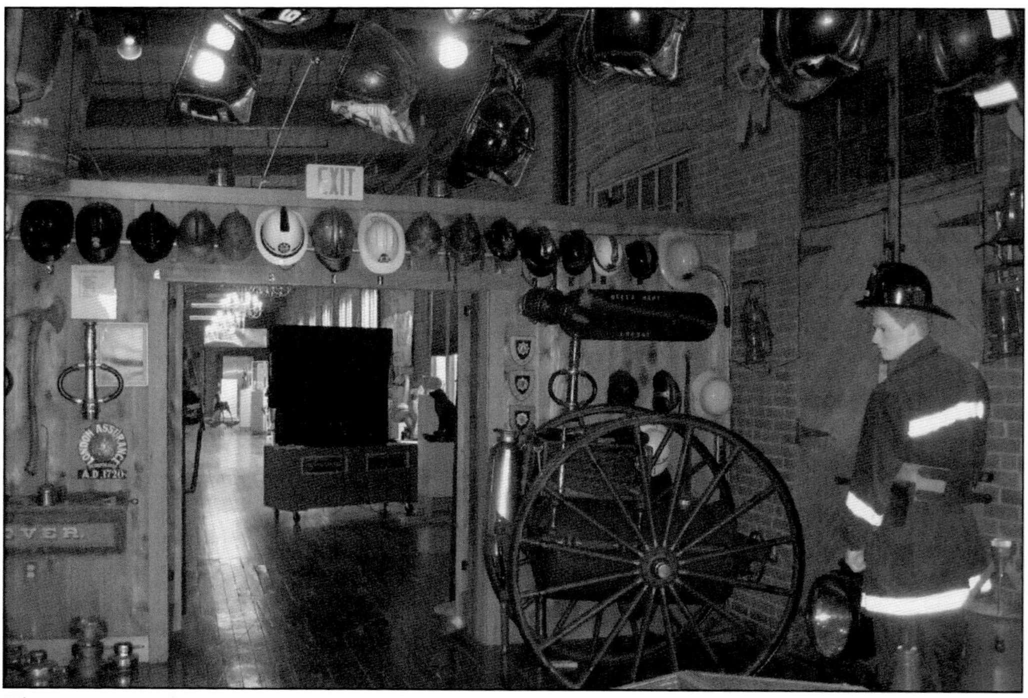

The Museum of Fire History located on the second floor of the New England Carousel Museum opened in June 2002. This collection came from Carlyle "Hap" Barnes. Hap is the 10th generation of the Barnes family that owns the Barnes Group, Inc., and Associated Spring Corporation. Hap started his collection in the 1960s. (Courtesy of New England Carousel Museum.)

Eight

Bristol Redevelops

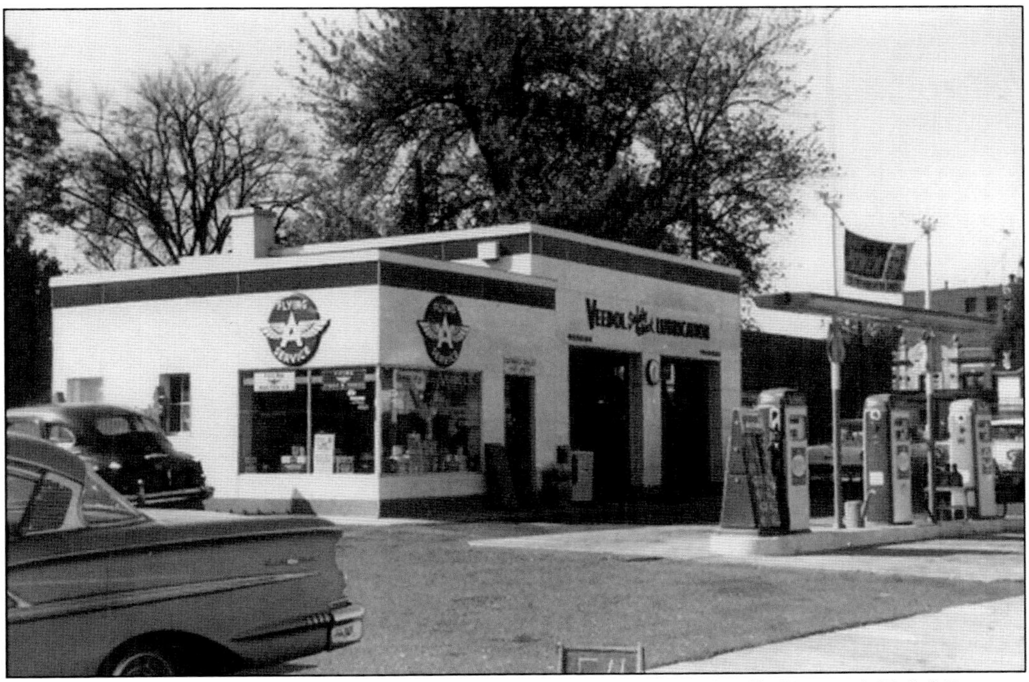

Julie R. Larese of Bristol opened his Flying A gasoline station in 1945 called Larese's Tydol Station. It was located on Memorial Boulevard and Fenn Street. The Tidewater Gasoline Company, under the name Tydol Gasoline and Veedol Motor Oil, was the brand of gasoline and motor oil used by Flying A gasoline stations. This building was torn down as part of the downtown redevelopment in the 1960s. The Wallace Barnes division of the Associated Spring Corporation built their 221,000-square-foot factory in 1970 on this site. (Courtesy of Bristol Town Clerk Office.)

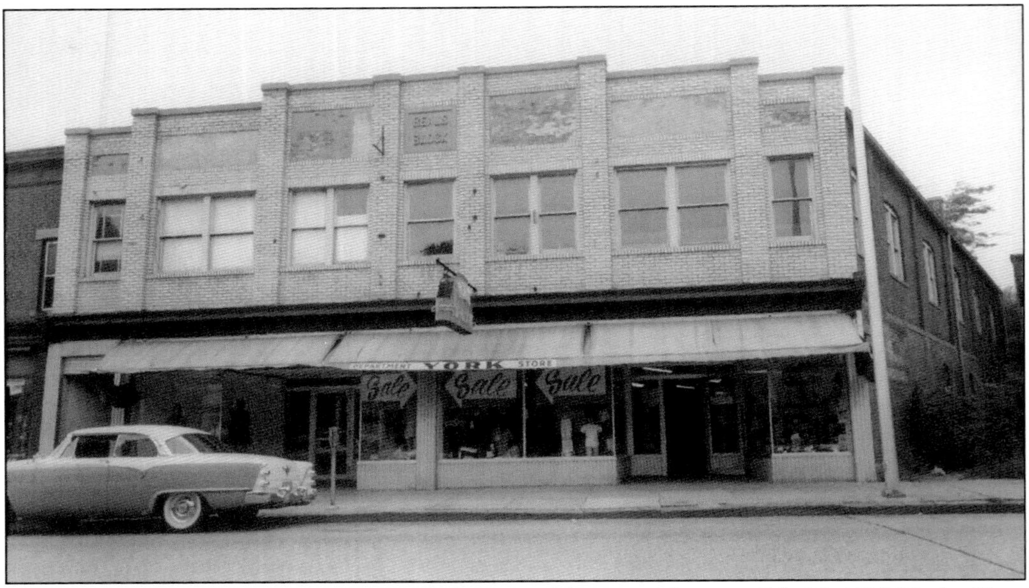

Morris Rosenblatt started his business called New York Bargain House on July 29, 1926. His building was located on 141–145 North Main Street. He sold dry goods and clothing. In 1948, the name was changed to New York Department Store. In 1951, the business name was changed to York Department Store. Upstairs over his store, there was a bowling alley. This is a picture of the outside of York Department Store as it looked in 1962. (Courtesy of Bristol Town Clerk Office.)

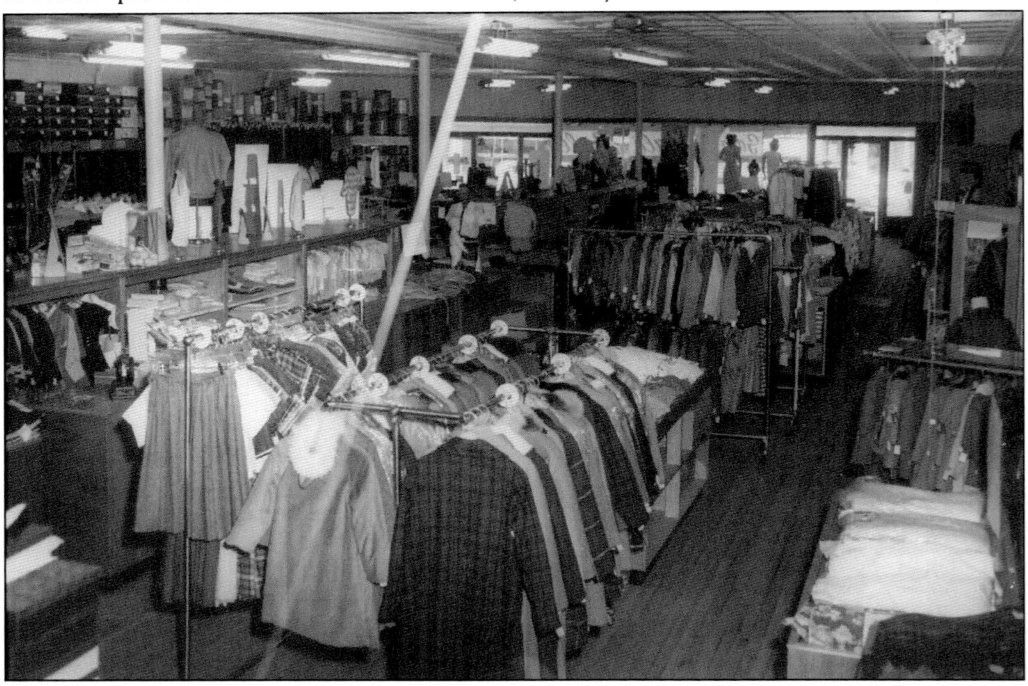

This interior view taken in 1962 of York Department Store shows the variety of clothes that the business was selling. This building was torn down as part of the downtown redevelopment in the 1960s. When Bristol Centre Mall opened in 1969, their business moved into the mall in 1970 under the new name York's with Sidney Rosenblatt running the business. (Courtesy of Bristol Town Clerk Office.)

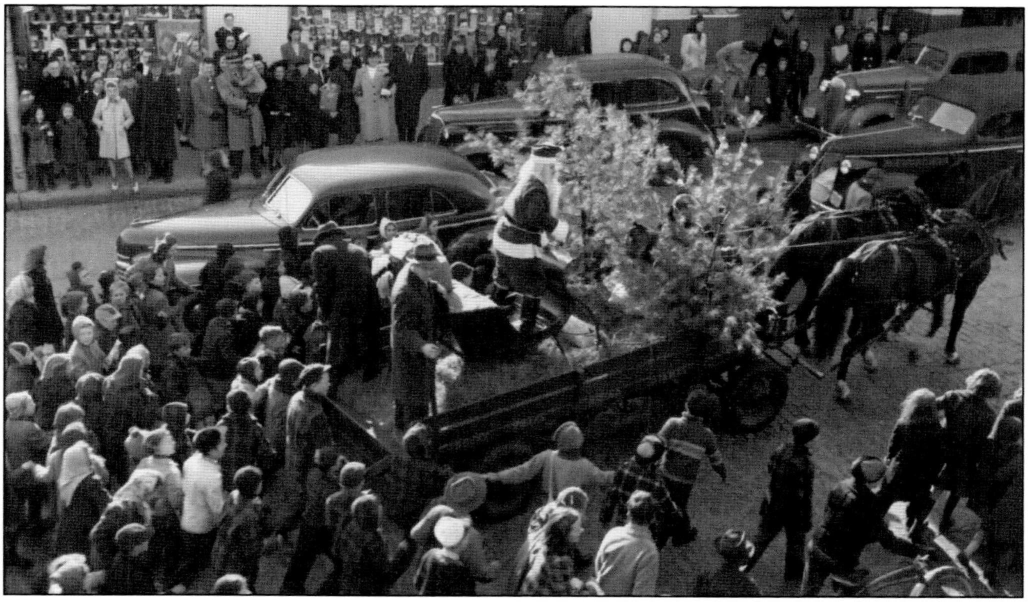

Michael and Elizabeth Rafaniello's first store was the Nursery Shop located on Prospect Street in 1940. In 1944, they opened the Toy Chest on North Main Street. In 1946, they bought a building on 86 North Main Street and combined the two businesses together and called it Tot n' Toddler. In 1951, a photography studio was added with photographer Bernard A. Gilman taking pictures of children in the store. From Thanksgiving each year until Christmas Eve, Tot n' Toddler would have a parade that picked up Santa at the train station and brought him back to the store where children would be waiting for his arrival. In 1963, the business closed. (Courtesy of Jerry Rafaniello.)

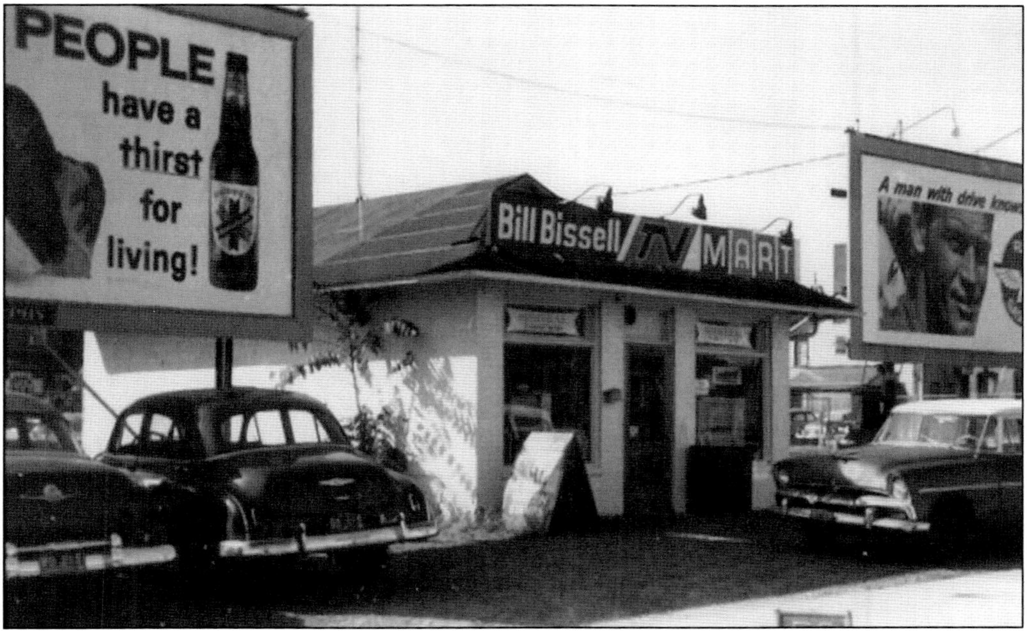

Pictured is Bill Bissell T. V. Mart, owned by John W. Bissell and located on Memorial Boulevard. The building was torn down for redevelopment. The Wallace Barnes division of the Associated Spring Corporation factory is on this property. John Bissell moved his business to 29 Prospect Street. (Courtesy of Bristol Town Clerk Office.)

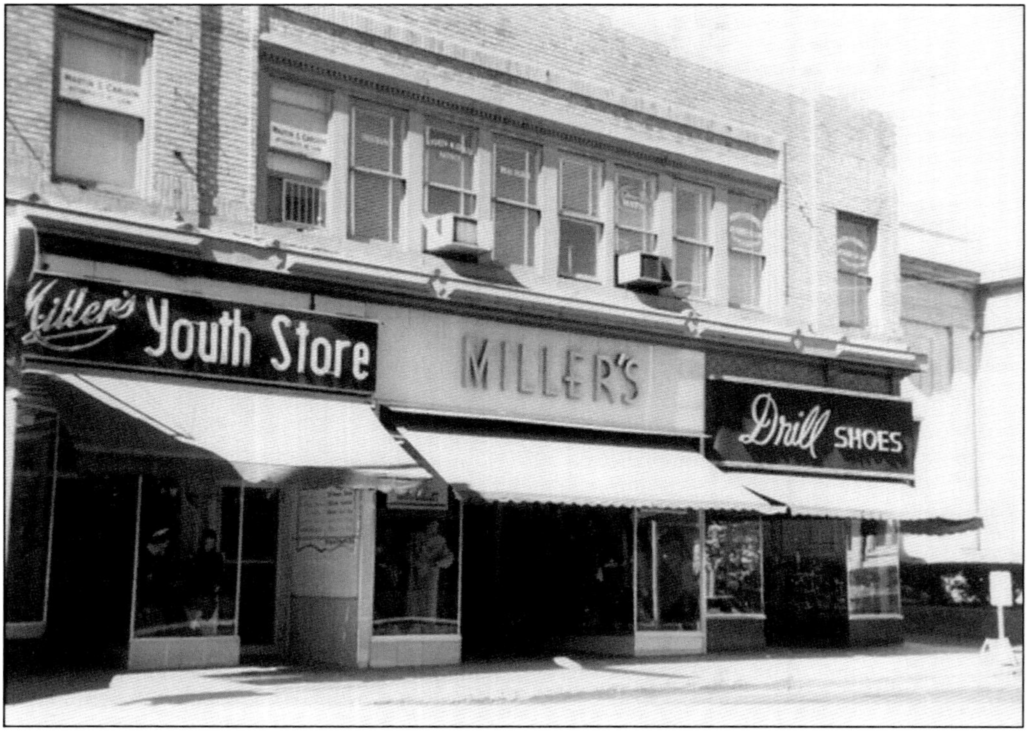

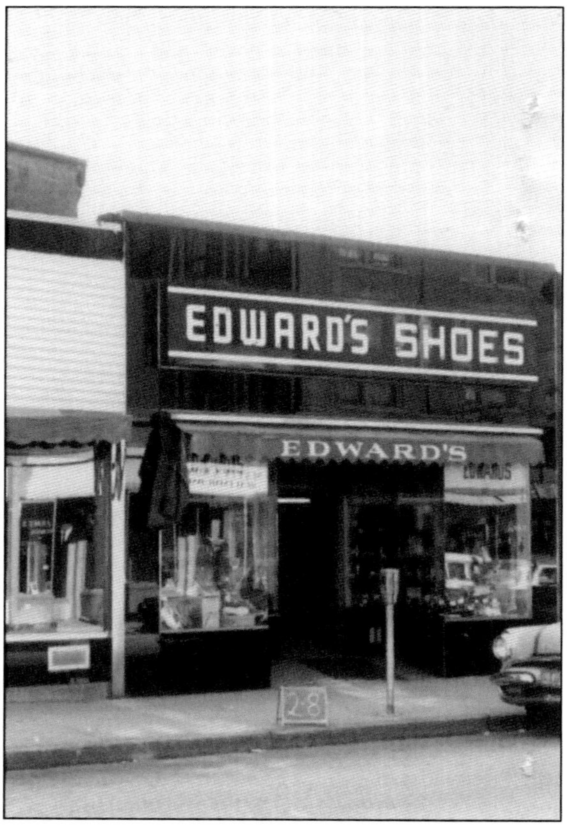

George Miller established a specialty store located on North Main Street in 1923. In 1945, Miller bought this building located on 131–137 Main Street and had three of the stores: Miller's Youth Store, Miller's Woman Apparel, and Miller's Bridal Shop. Drill Shoes, owned by David Drill, started his business in 1945 and was next door to Miller's stores. Miller's building was torn down in the 1960s. After the Centre Mall was opened, George Miller Jr. consolidated his father's three stores and opened Miller's Store in 1970 in the mall. (Courtesy of Bristol Town Clerk Office.)

In 1946, Joseph Riccio opened Edward's Shoes at 101 North Main Street. The business stayed until the 1960s when the building was torn down to make way for the Bristol Centre Mall. (Courtesy of Bristol Town Clerk Office.)

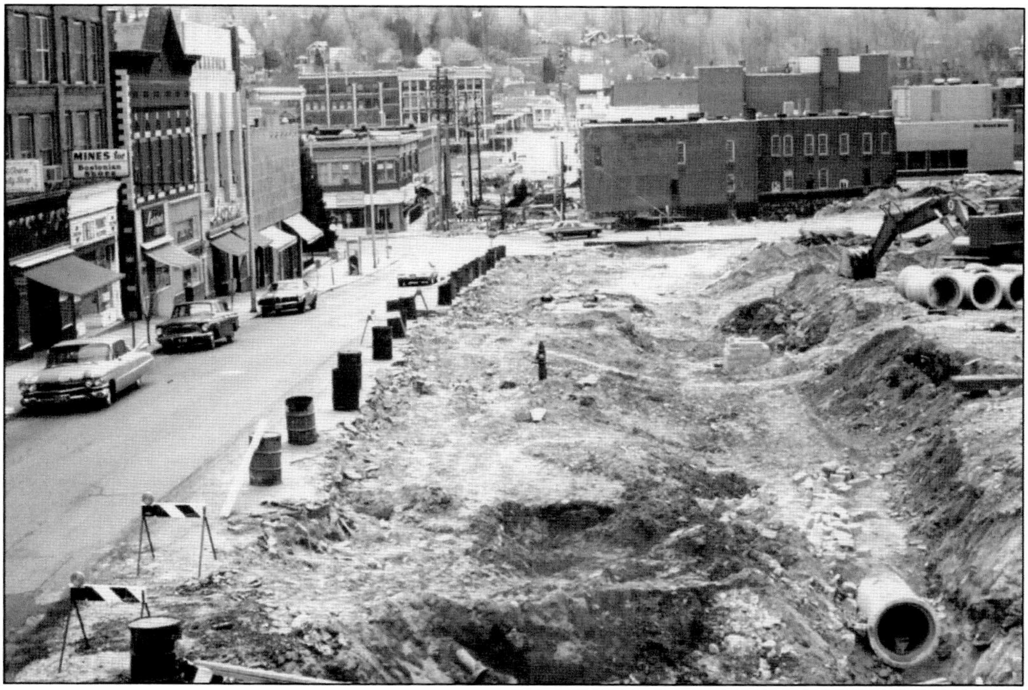

As part of the redevelopment of the 1960s, the buildings that stood on the right side in this Main Street picture were torn down to prepare for the new Bristol Centre Mall. The businesses that were here included Nanett's clothing store, Doshon's Curtain Shop, Rainbow Millinery, Ed Cercone smoke shop, the Fashion Store, Allen's Cut Rate Store, Marvoureen Beauty Studio, Hinchcliff's photograph studio, Loft's candy store, Sperry Jewelers, WBIS Radio Station, Levison's men's shop, John Hancock Mutual Life Insurance Company, Edith S. Cook clothing store, McLellan Department Store, Michael's Jewelers, A. Harrison and Sons stationers, the Central Drug Company, and the Bristol Post Office. (Courtesy of Shaffer Company.)

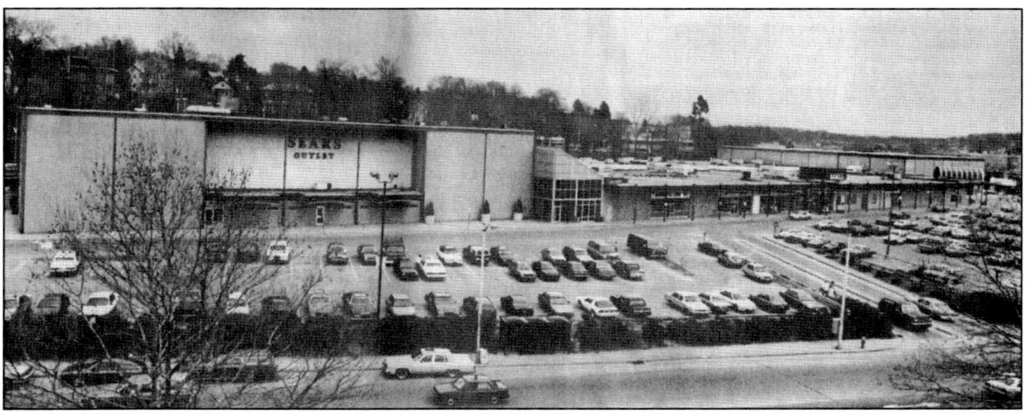

With the completion of the downtown Bristol Centre Mall in 1969, located on 17 acres on North Main Street, the two major tenants were Grandway and Raphael's. They were located on either end of the mall with room for 26 stores in between. This 1990 picture shows Sears Outlet on the left where the former Grandway store was. There were over 40 businesses, including a variety of retail stores, specialty shops, and restaurants. At the main entrance coming into the Centre Mall, a stage was added to host a variety of events that took place throughout the year. (Courtesy of the *Bristol Press*.)

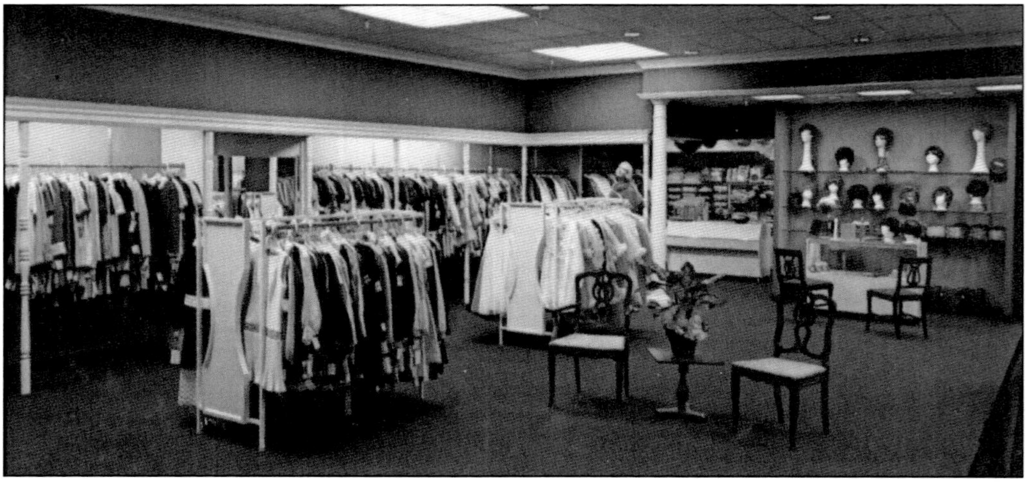

Dorothy Flieschner started Dorothy's women's furnishings in 1930 with her husband, John, as manager. The stores first location was 128 Main Street until 1946 when it moved to 194 Main Street. In 1969, Dorothy's was one of the first businesses to go into the Centre Mall, owned by Edward I. Freedman and his wife, Charlotte. They also owned Dorothy's Country Shop located in the Bristol Shopping Plaza on Farmington Avenue. In 1984, Bill Stortz and his wife, Angela, bought Dorothy's in the Centre Mall. This picture shows the interior of Dorothy's with a variety of women's clothing that the store sold. (Courtesy of Gary Potter.)

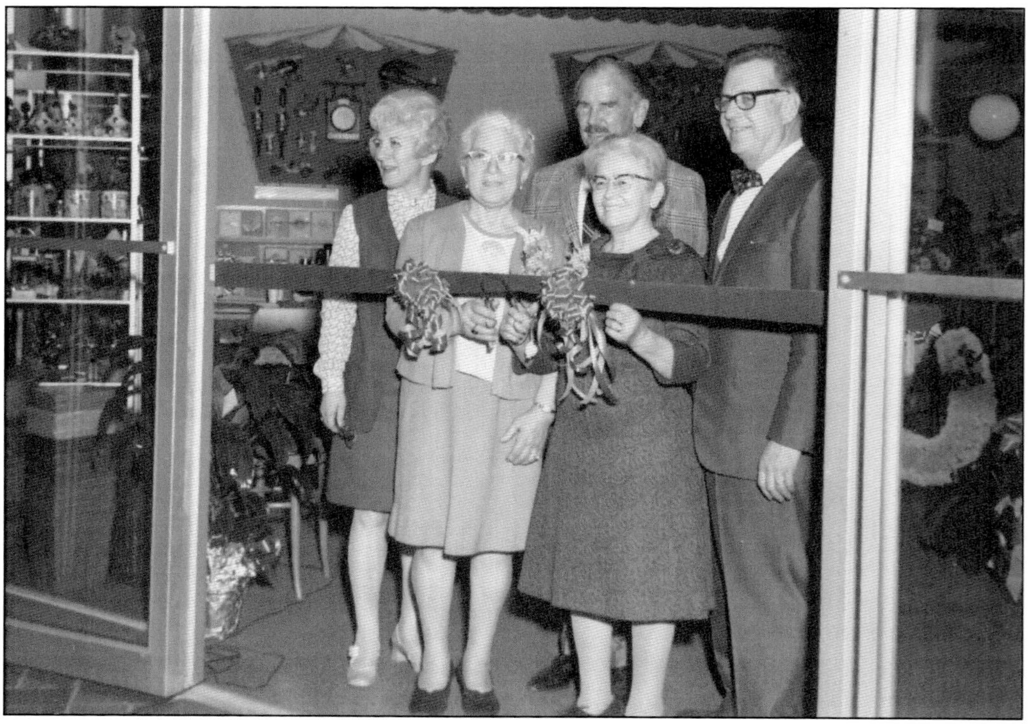

When Michael and Elizabeth Rafaniello closed their business, Tot n' Toddler, on North Main Street in 1963, they waited for the new Centre Mall to open in 1969 to start a new business. In this picture, taken on April 9, 1970, when they opened the Carrousel Gift Shop, are, from left to right, owner Elizabeth Rafaniello; Grace Nesci; Al Hoeflin, owner of the Centre Mall; Elizabeth Rafaniello (Michael's mother); and owner Michael Rafaniello. (Courtesy of Jerry Rafaniello.)

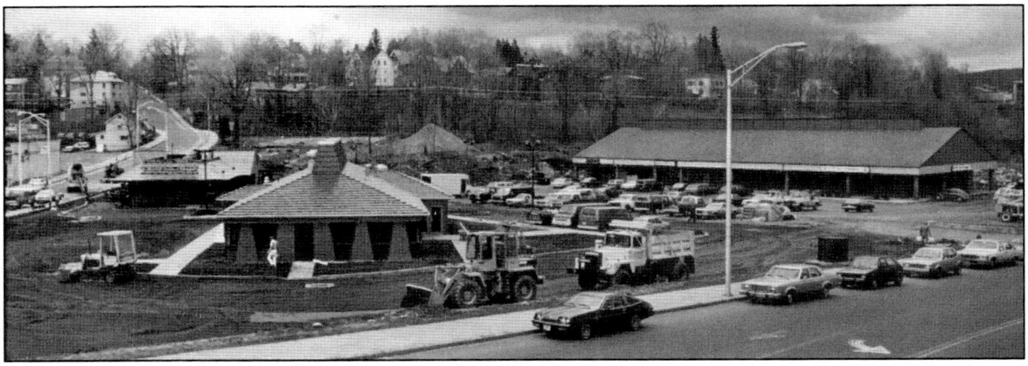

In April 1984, two businesses were ready to open at the new Northside Square, built and developed by D'Amato Construction Company, Inc. Pictured here on North Main Street in front is the new Pizza Hut and behind them is Burger King. On the right, construction was almost done on the building for Super Natural Market and Rite Aid Pharmacies to move into. The back section next to Federal Street behind Burger King would become the Bristol Career Center of Tunxis Community College.

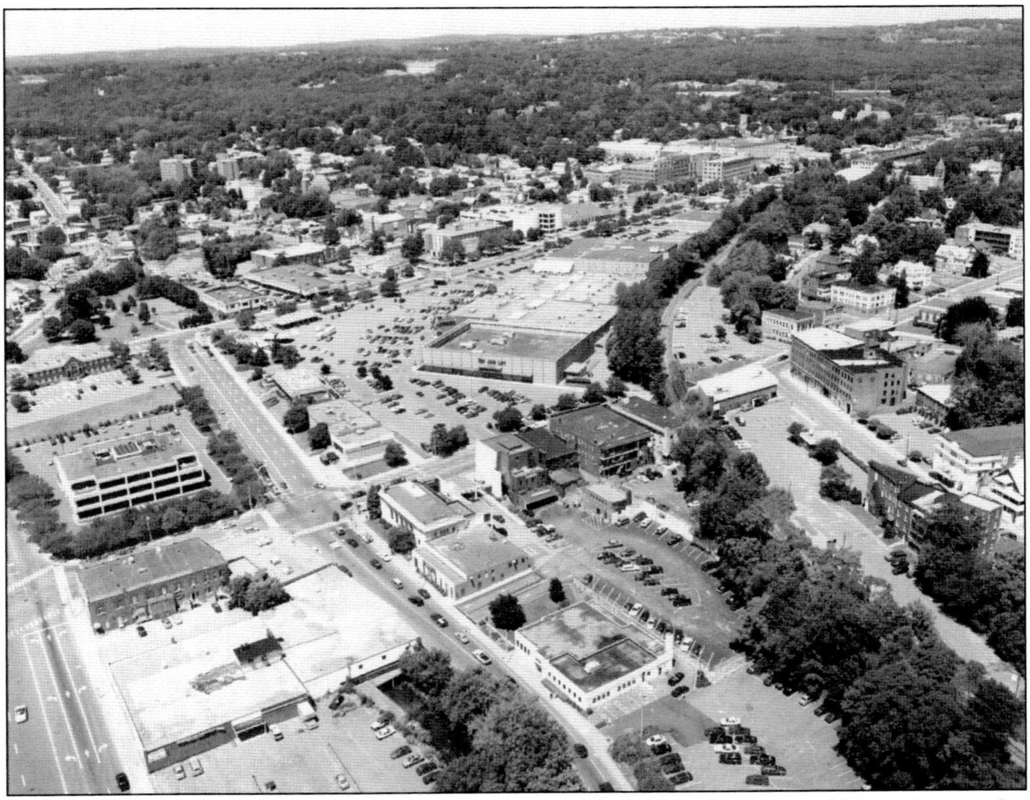

This aerial view taken of downtown on April 10, 1998, shows North Main and Main Streets. On the left is the Barnes Group International Headquarters located on Main Street. In the center is Ocean Job Lot that was in the Bristol Centre Mall. (Courtesy of Bristol Chamber of Commerce.)

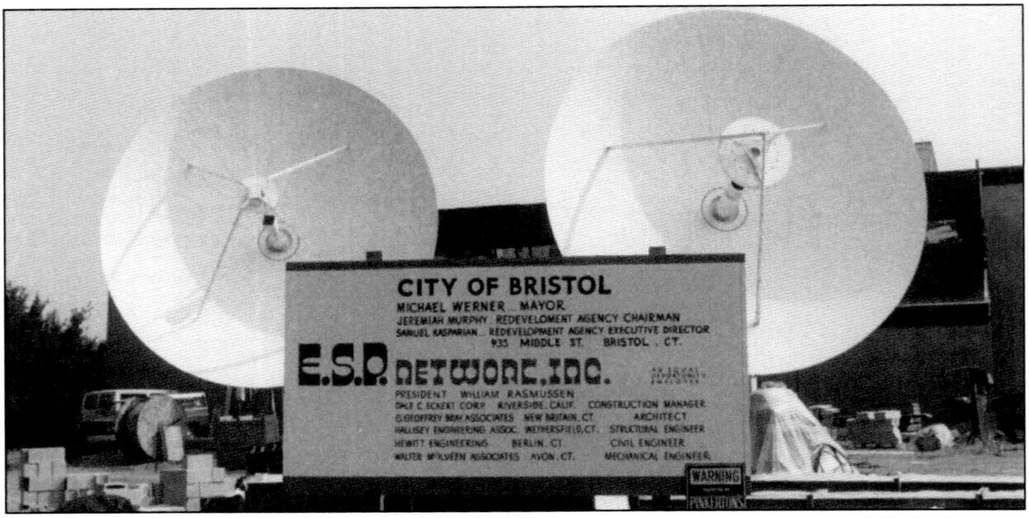

Bill Rasmussen was working in Plainville as a communication director for the World Hockey Association's New England Whalers. In May 1978, Bill was fired from his job. He had an idea to start a cable television network that focused on covering sports events in Connecticut. Bill heard of a property on Middle Street in Bristol that was for sale through the Bristol Development Agency. In September 1978, Bill bought the property and started E. S. P. Networks, Inc., with his son, Scott. When looking for a satellite, Bill discovered it was less expensive to buy a 24-hour feed than to buy a few hours at night. With the financial backing of the Getty Oil Company, ESPN launched Sports Center on September 7, 1979, hosted by Lee Leonard and George Grande. (Courtesy of ESPN, Inc.)

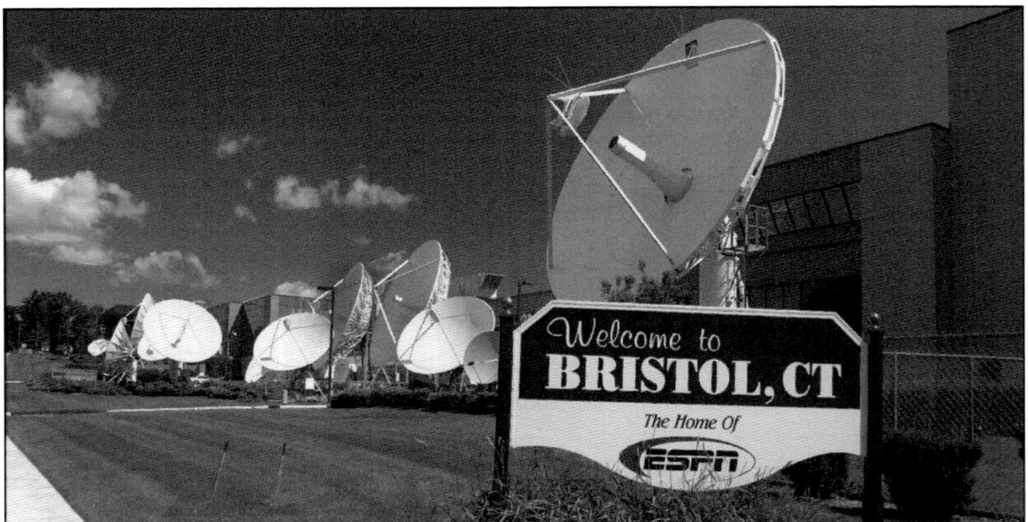

In ESPN, Inc.'s, 30-year history, a variety of sports programming was added to fill the 24 hours a day of air time. When they became part of ABC television network in 1984, it allowed more professional sports to be shown on its station. Starting in 1987, Sunday night football would last for 19 years, and Major League Baseball was added in 1990. Also in 1990, ESPN International was started, allowing sports to be seen in other countries. Today the company has grown to a 110-acre campus on Middle and Birch Streets with 3,400 employees. On June 11, 2010, they will launch ESPN 3D, the country's first 3D television channel with its first program being the 2010 World Cup. (Courtesy of ESPN, Inc.)

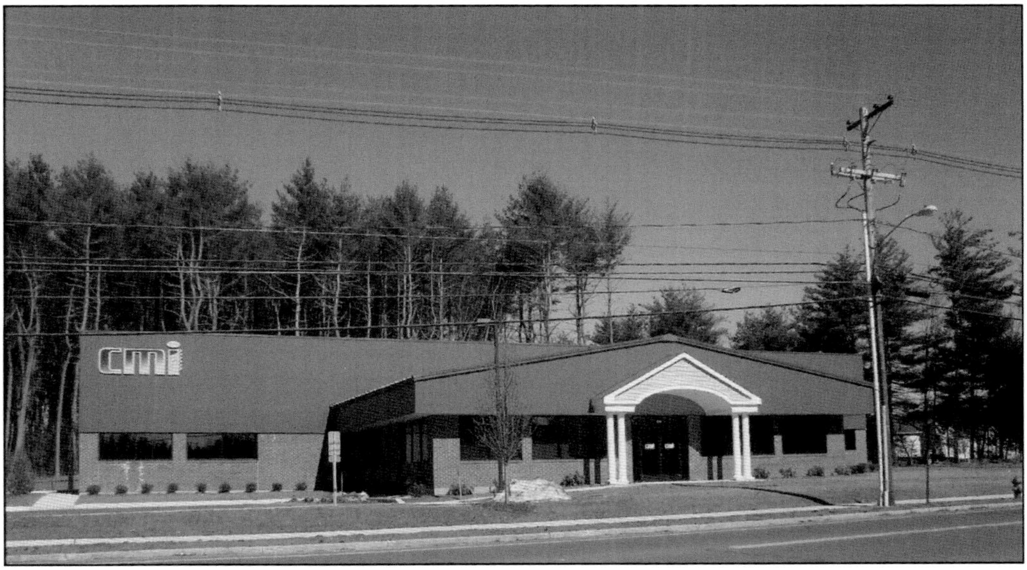

In 1980, Joseph A. Bozzuto started his company, Connecticut Metals, Inc., in Waterbury, Connecticut. The name was changed to CMI Specialty Products, Inc. In 2009, Bozzuto moved his company into the new Southeast Bristol Industrial Park located at 105 Red Stone Hill Road. CMI Specialty Products provides the electronic and related industries electro-magnetic iron products used in most automotive, aerospace, military, and industrial markets. (Courtesy of CMI Specialty Products, Inc.)

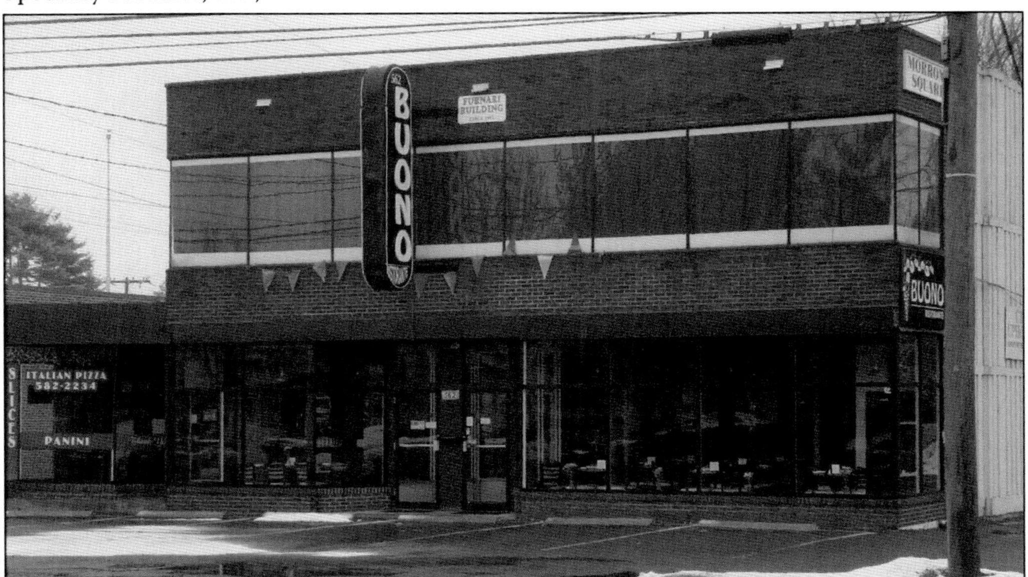

In 1955, Joseph Furnari opened Crown Wayside Furniture and Crown Upholstery at 562 Farmington Avenue. When the furniture business closed, Danny Morrone bought the building on July 17, 2002. With the front of the building empty, a new business opened called Buono Ristorante, owned by Chef Joseph Elmerath. When the restaurant closed, Danny's son, Joseph, who left Bristol at a young age, saw an opportunity to fulfill his dream to start his own business. Morrone opened Café Buono and Buono Pizza on November 18, 2009, serving authentic Italian food and his own special pizza called the Bristolese that he developed. (Courtesy of Café Buono.)